S HIRLEE SMITH MATHESON was born in Winnipeg, Manitoba, and grew up on farms in Mani-
toba and Alberta. She lived for many years in the Peace River
country of northern British Columbia, and although she now lives
in the city, she journeys north at least twice a year to "recharge her
batteries" and gather stories. She aims, through her writing, to
immortalize the adventures and philosophies of the people who
choose the bush.

Shirlee is the author of several books, including *Youngblood of
the Peace*, an authorized biography of Father E. Jungbluth, *This Was
Our Valley*, winner of the 1990 Alberta Culture Nonfiction Award
and finalist for the Roderick Haig-Brown Regional Prize, and *Flying
Ghosts*, a young adult novel based on the legends of the Alaska
Highway. She has also published in numerous magazines and
anthologies. Shirlee lives with her family in Calgary.

Other books by Shirlee Smith Matheson

Nonfiction

Youngblood of the Peace
This Was Our Valley
Flying the Frontiers, Vol. II

Juvenile/Young Adult Fiction

Prairie Pictures
City Pictures
Flying Ghosts

Flying the Frontiers

A Half-million Hours
of Aviation Adventure

SHIRLEE SMITH MATHESON

FIFTH
HOUSE
PUBLISHERS

Front cover painting, *The Big Bellanca–1937*, by Robert Bradford, reproduced courtesy Aviation Art Canada, Yellowknife, NWT
Back cover painting, *Safe on Top*, by Wally Wolfe, reproduced courtesy Wally Wolfe
Cover design by NEXT Communications Inc.

The publisher gratefully acknowledges the support received from The Canada Council and the Department of Canadian Heritage.

Printed and bound in Canada by Friesens, Altona, MB
00 01 / 6 5 4

CANADIAN CATALOGUING IN PUBLICATION DATA
Matheson, Shirlee Smith

Flying the frontiers

Includes bibliographical references.
ISBN 1-895618-46-0 (bound)
ISBN 1-895618-51-7 (pbk.)

1. Bush pilots - Canada - History. 2. Aeronautics - Canada - History. I. Title.

TL523.M37 1994   629.13'0971   C94-920093-X

Note: The people interviewed for this book used the imperial system. Rather than interrupt their narratives by adding metric conversions, we have retained imperial measurements. For similar reasons, we have not changed the word "Eskimo" to "Inuit."

FIFTH HOUSE LTD.

Contents

To George Melnyk
A trustworthy navigator and a good friend

Acknowledgements

*T*HANK YOU, first of all, to the pilots, engineers, and others whose stories are told in this book. They welcomed me into their homes, offices, and hangars, and willingly shared their stories and photographs, and general information on Canada's aviation history.

Special acknowledgement goes to three Calgarians who contributed to the book through their special knowledge: Bill Watts, who introduced me to a number of people he had come to know through his many years of flying and as past manager of the Calgary International Airport and the Calgary Aero Space Museum; Dave Scollard, for his editorial advice; and Clark Seaborn, professional engineer, pilot, and restorer of vintage aircraft, who read the stories and checked facts and fantasies to ensure authenticity.

And my thanks go also to Charlene Dobmeier, managing editor of Fifth House Publishers, who supported the project from the start.

Preface

WHEN I WAS IN MY EARLY TWENTIES, my husband and I moved to his home territory of the Peace River country. There I met people I had been waiting for all my life: characters who did not seem to give a damn about traditional achievements of wealth or power; men and women who, through hard work and positive attitudes, tackled jobs that more practical persons would never dare. I had been brought up in an environment where protocol was followed and risks seldom taken. But, after coming into contact with the flamboyant northern spirit, everything I have done since has emanated from that seminal experience.

I promised myself that someday I would write their stories; these people would become my material. And so I stored their language and their lives until the time was right to fulfil my obligation. All of the people in this book have had some experience in the North—whether flying, servicing, designing, or jumping out of airplanes. It is obvious that some of that northern spirit lives in all of them.

Pilots are generally quiet people; they fly with their eyes open and their mouths shut. "The loudmouthed type usually can't fly an airplane," one pilot stated matter-of-factly. Convincing some of them to talk about themselves was not easy. Many of their stories had been passed along from one raconteur to another, gaining in detail or suffering from inaccuracies. Here, the stories are told firsthand by those who lived them. Some of these tales were taped in the nick of time. Others are on-going stories, like chapters of a still-evolving novel.

A number of the people in this book were pioneers in every sense of the word, flying in the early 1930s in open-cockpit biplanes; some ventured by air into the unmapped mountains and inhospitable barrens of Canada's North. Others, whose stories appear here, were propelled over flaming forests to fight fires, worked to ensure safety and security for pilots and communities of the North, or picked up the pieces after tragedy struck.

My travels in search of these stories catapulted me into a world populated by characters as varied as those met by Gulliver, as modest as Gandhi—and (nearly) as eloquent as Churchill. I visited museums and hangars, as well as homes in cities and in the bush. I flew in an open-cockpit Stearman biplane, in a Cherokee, a Super Cub, a helicopter, a Twin Otter, and a Grumman

Gulfstream. I listened to stories by campfire, around kitchen tables, by tape, by letter, by telephone.

The geographic area over which these pilots flew from 1929 to 1994 includes almost every country of the world (approximately 526,600—or roughly a half-million—hours).

The people I interviewed convinced me that fliers are artists, magicians, scientists, machinists, mechanics, athletes, professors—and gamblers. Pilots must be adaptable, but also systematic, as they go over checklists with the scrutiny of tax accountants. They need strong physical constitutions—especially in the bush. Add to these requirements multi-levelled minds capable of handling numerous occurrences simultaneously, and a vivid sense of humour.

The anecdotes I heard often verged on the incredible: landing in the spires of spruce trees or on narrow boulder-strewn spits in northern British Columbia; escaping from a forest fire by jumping into a snake-infested slough; taking off from ice-islands in the Arctic; and taxiing down runways littered with elephant dung.

What defines these stories? Adventure. The sense of excitement in the teller; the love of what they do; the risks they take and the sacrifices they make to follow their dreams.

Now it is time to deliver on my promise. So let's open the throttle and let the flight begin . . .

The Call of the North

*I*N 1940, the British Commonwealth Air Training Plan was in full swing. Hundreds of training aircraft circled above Calgary's RCAF airfield (later named Lincoln Park)—up to 300 at a time, 24 hours a day. Six-year-old Michael Archibald Thomas had moved with his family from their ranch outside of Calgary to live at the air force station where his dad was an officer. He was standing at a wire fence watching the airplanes when suddenly two of them collided and spiralled down in flames to disappear behind the coulee a quarter-mile away. As he watched the ambulance attendants carry away six burned bodies, Mike was horrified. But he felt something else too—excitement. He knew then that he wanted to be a pilot.

One day when Mike was in grade 10, the students were assembled in the gymnasium. Each was expected to stand and announce what they wanted to be after graduating. "I want to be a bush pilot," Mike declared. The roar of laughter was led by the gym teacher, who shared the stage with the hapless student. Shame, embarrassment, then determination were reflected on the kid's face.

Twelve years later Mike looked up this man, who was now working at another school. The teacher was outside on the field, coaching the football team. Mike walked to the edge of the fence and stood there. Finally the teacher noticed him, and Mike beckoned to him. "Do you remember me?"

The teacher looked at the young man for a long time. "Thomas."

"That's right."

"Well. And what are you doing these days?"

"I'm a bush pilot. And I'm one of the best."

If a movie were made of Mike Thomas's life, it would be longer than *Lonesome Dove*, contain more drama than *Casablanca*, and portray more action than an early James Bond film. In the years that followed the determined youngster's announcement on the high school stage, Thomas has been a bush pilot, engineer, fur trader, business-owner, and airline captain. And finally, he's tossed it all to go back to the bush.

What follows is a striking picture of life in Canada's airways.

After graduation, Thomas worked for a seismic crew and ended up in Fort St. John, British Columbia. There he met pilot Bobby D'Easum from Vancouver, who was doing photo surveys at 22,000 feet with a Beaver for the BC government's topographic surveys department. That summer, D'Easum taught him to fly the Beaver, and soon after Thomas enroled in Vancouver's U-Fly School operated by the Michaud brothers. The school had a fleet of Cessna 140s, all with "rag" wings, except for one, which had metal wings. "When you got up to 20 hours you could fly the one with metal wings. It supposedly flew smoother. That wasn't true at all, but that was the gimmick."

Thomas's instructors were World War II pilots. "My main instructor figured you couldn't fly unless you could do loops and rolls, and he taught me things that probably saved me from killing myself in later years," Thomas says.

Once he earned his licence, Thomas was off to Whitehorse, Yukon, where he found work with the army as a lineman electrician. The shop foreman, Fred Tromans, also had a pilot's licence, and encouraged Thomas to apply for a job with a local prospecting syndicate, Triple Five Prospectors. "They've got no money," Tromans told him. "But they need a pilot and you need the experience."

Although the job enabled Thomas to build up his flying hours with the company's Aeronca Sedan, it was tough going. "I nearly starved to death," Thomas recalls. "I lived in a panel truck by the Yukon River. Although I still only had a private licence, I wasn't taking any pay, so I guess it was legal."

How he survived those two years remains a mystery to him. "I was on the edge of disaster all the time and didn't even know it. Flying around mountains— I was lost for two years. I didn't know where the hell I was half the time."

Two English girls who were working in Whitehorse as telephone and telex

Mike Thomas with Triple Five Prospector's Aeronca Sedan, Whitehorse, Yukon, 1955. *Mike Thomas Collection*

operators took pity on him and fed him, at least fairly regularly. "If it hadn't been for them, I would have starved."

After getting a 45-minute check-out on floats, he was able to land on lakes and rivers when he flew prospectors around the mountainous areas of the Yukon. "One of the old prospectors, Ira Bennett, kept me out of a lot of trouble because he knew the country. He was a big man, about 245 pounds; I flew him, his packsack, and his little bear dog all over the Yukon."

But Thomas was having a hard time managing his float plane on the unpredictable Yukon River. Strong river currents and winds, and big loading booms that stuck out all over the river to serve the sternwheelers, made taking off and landing especially treacherous. "There were willows and islands at one end, and a construction company was driving piles for a bridge up at the other end, so it was not a nice place for an inexperienced float pilot," Thomas recalls. "Most of the guys kind of laughed at me, but not Ron Connelly [a local pilot who flew for Pacific Western Airlines]. One time I came in and I had some trouble; I finally got to the dock and Ron was standing there. He grabbed the strut, jumped onto the float, and pushed me off into the river. He spent hours with me on that river, showing me how to taxi and turn downwind, how to use aileron and elevator and everything you've got going for you. I learned a lot of little tricks. Ron was a real master."

The old goldrush town of Atlin, BC, became one of Thomas's favourite places. On weekends, when the Aeronca was his to do with as he wished, he would pick up some friends in Whitehorse, throw his accordion in the back, and away they'd fly to Atlin. "I was too young to go in the bar—I didn't even drink at the time, I never had a drink until years later—but the bartender would fill beer bottles with ginger ale, cap them, and put them in the cooler for me. I'd play the accordion in the bar, and these old folks would dance."

Other local characters Thomas met were "Tail-Spin" Tommy Stromberg, a wild wartime pilot who was flying for Herman Peterson, the operator of a local air service, and a "Newfie" engineer named Jerry Mahoney. "We'd go panning gold at Ruby, Pine, or Spruce Creek. Herman Peterson would come down to the cabin and fire both these guys every Saturday night; then Monday morning he'd hire them back. Early Monday morning, five o'clock, we'd fly back to Whitehorse."

One night Thomas flew into Atlin just before dark. The wind was screeching down the bay, frothing up the whitecaps. There was a sheltered area behind the island where he should have landed, but he didn't know about it. In he came, pounding down on the big whitecaps, almost sinking the airplane. Before he could get over to the island where they parked the airplanes, Herman came out in a row boat, mad as could be. "Tomorrow morning you be here at seven! I'm going to show you a few things before you kill yourself."

He spent the entire morning showing Thomas how to side-slip down over the hospital and zip in behind the island, plus all kinds of tricks to get that airplane off the water.

"When you have an underpowered airplane you need a lot of things going for you to get any kind of a load into the air," Thomas says. "Herman used to own one just like it. He taught me that when you're doing a slow approach in gusty conditions and you drop a wing, you don't try to pick it up with aileron because all you do then is aggravate the situation. You use rudder to skid, in order to pick up that wing. Nobody'd ever showed me that. He showed me all kinds of things, especially slow flight stuff. He was a master. He flew the Telsequa-Telegraph Creek mail run with the Beaver and Fairchild 71 for 20 years, and I don't think he missed a day. He told me once, he knew every eagle by its first name, and I believe it."

"Somehow," Thomas says, "I managed to bumble through those two years."

A fellow named G.C.F. "Dal" Dalziel at Watson Lake had several Beavers and Cessna 180s. Thomas would periodically apply to work for him, but the answer was always the same: his qualifications didn't yet meet Dalziel's standards.

"Well, kid, if you had 500 hours on floats I could give you a job," Dalziel would say.

Finally, when Thomas had accumulated 499 hours and 50 minutes, he flew down to Watson Lake. "Here I am."

"Well, jeez, kid, the insurance companies have had a bad year and they've upped the ante," was Dalziel's response. "If you just had 1,000 hours on floats I could hire you!"

Back Thomas went to Whitehorse.

He never did fly for Dalziel, although he got to know him quite well. Dal had flown a Norseman on wheels for the U.S. Army when they were building the Alaska Highway. Then he had started BC Yukon Airways at Watson Lake and was there for many years until he retired. One time in 1956, Thomas was in Watson Lake on his way north to the Flat River, near the Nahanni area, when Dalziel came down to the dock.

"Where are you flying to, kid?"

"To the Flat River."

"How do you intend to make it up there and back with this thing?"

"I take two jerry cans of gas with me."

"Give me your map," Dalziel said. He put a mark on the map at Francois Lake, north of Watson Lake. "There's lots of gas there. Go ahead and use it. It's 91-98."

Well, Thomas knew that 91-98 was a thing of the past even then. They had 80-87 coloured red, they had 100-130 coloured green. But 91-98 was coloured blue—and they didn't make it any more.

"Who does it belong to?"

"Me and Uncle Sam."

It became evident to Thomas that, during construction of the Alaska Highway, every time Dalziel had hauled a load for Uncle Sam he'd hauled a load for Dalziel, and he'd cached it. Thomas ended up using lots of that gas, which was still good after being hidden for more than 12 years.

After two years at Whitehorse with Triple Five Prospectors, Thomas still couldn't land another job because he lacked experience. The only solution, he realized, was to improve his qualifications, and in 1956 he earned his commercial pilot's licence and started his own airline at Fort St. John, BC.

In partnership with the Triple Five Prospectors, he formed the North Cariboo Flying Service Limited. The total capital assets of the company at that point were the Aeronca Sedan, a half-ton truck, and a pair of pliers.

He lived at Charlie Lake and would fly back and forth with the Aeronca in the winter from the ice right in front of his cabin to the airport.

The flying service later bought two Cessna 180s, but the business was "ahead of its time," Thomas says. He again found himself working like a slave and slowly starving, so eventually he sold out to the other partners. The company is now a successful enterprise in Fort St. John.

Thomas moved on once again, and, in the spring of 1959, went to work for Mackenzie Airways "down north" at Norman Wells, Northwest Territories. "That was quite an ordeal because when I started to work for them there were two guys, Al Daines and Bob Haddie. At that time, Al was a flight engineer with Canadian Pacific Airlines on the C-46s flying the Mackenzie route, and Bob Haddie was working for Imperial Oil at the refinery in Norman Wells. Between the two of them they'd started this Mackenzie Airways. I didn't know this was just a new company.

"They introduced me to the airplane, an old Stinson 108, (CF-ICM) with a 190-horsepower Lycoming engine, which was in 400 pieces in the hangar in Edmonton. My first job was to assemble the thing. I wasn't an engineer at that time—I wasn't even a hell of a pilot then! We painted it, put it on floats in the hangar—it had never been on floats before—took it off floats and I flew it to Cooking Lake, put it back on floats, then I flew it down to Norman Wells on the Mackenzie River."

Thomas pulled up to the only dock, and had been there just 10 minutes when a 1938 Dodge came tearing down the road in a cloud of dust.

"State your business and get out of here! This is an Imperial Oil company town!" shouted the occupant of the car.

"Who the hell are you?" was Thomas's response.

"I'm J.S.L. MacMillan, and I run this town."

"I came here to fly for Mackenzie Airways."

"Not off this dock, you ain't!"

Then an Otter landed and was taxiing around the river in circles. MacMillan hollered again to Thomas, "Get the hell off Pappy's dock!"

The incoming pilot was Stu "Pappy" Hill, flying one of Canadian Pacific Airlines's Otters (CF-CZO).

Thomas had no choice. He pulled away from the dock and taxied upriver for about two miles until he found a place to get ashore. He soon discovered that his second job with Mackenzie Airways was to build an office, a dock, and a maintenance shack; the company had nothing.

Thomas flew for Mackenzie Airways all that summer. The Stinson turned out to be a good airplane. "It flew like a bird with its 900 HR engine. From May, when I first put it together and started flying it, until freeze-up, I ran that engine out. I flew 900 hours, which is quite a record year. Usually you might do 600 hours a year."

But by the time he tied it up in the fall, he still hadn't been paid a nickel. "By the end of summer they owed me $7,000, which was a hell of a lot of money in 1959." After unsuccessfully trying to get his wages, he quit. "I never did get paid for that whole summer of flying. After I left they hired a guy named Tony McCluney, an Irishman, who was a heller on airplanes, and I don't think he got paid, either. Eventually they folded."

By this point, although Thomas had accumulated about 1,400 hours, he still struggled to make ends meet. "I had a nice little truck that I'd bought and financed. I'd left it sitting at Cooking Lake. When I came back in the fall it was gone because I couldn't make any payments."

In 1960 Thomas went to Yellowknife and tried to get on with Wardair. But the chief pilot, Pappy Braun, figured "you couldn't fly unless you'd flown a Norseman," so Thomas was out of luck.

He did manage to find a job with Hay River Air Service, flying a Seabee PA-12, and a Cessna 180. Following that, pilot/operator Willy Laserich checked Thomas out on his Mark IV Norseman (CF-BTC), then hired him to haul fish. He was finally making some money.

Near the end of summer, Pappy Braun of Wardair gave Thomas a call. "I want to talk to you. I understand you've been flying a Norseman."

"Yeah, I've been flying it all summer."

"How'd you like to come flying for us?"

Thomas went back to Yellowknife with Pappy in the Bristol to begin his job with Wardair.

"We ferried freight, cars, and everything else in the Bristol, across Great Slave Lake from Hay River to Yellowknife. For a back-load we hauled empty beer bottles in cases of two dozen. Do you know how many cases of beer bottles it takes to make 12,000 pounds? Oh my God! We'd fill the airplane with beer bottles in Yellowknife, fly 45 minutes to Hay River, unload the bottles, then drive two or three vehicles into the aircraft, chain them down, and make another 45-minute trip back to Yellowknife."

Besides vehicles and beer bottles, they also hauled drilling equipment and machines. On one trip, they took a whole ball mill, a 13,000-pound load, into Taurcanus (later named Tundra), a mine by Mackay Lake about 200 miles northeast of Yellowknife.

Although Thomas didn't fly the Bristol all that much, he remembers it as "an absolute man-killer."

"The Bristol is a marvellous airplane in a lot of ways," Thomas says, "but when you had quite a bit of ice on, and conditions were bad, and you were already worried about things, one engine would invariably go into 'automatic rough.' It would just scare the hell out of you for 10 minutes, then it would smooth out again. Then the other one would do it. It was a nerve-wracking airplane because of these bloody awful sleeve-valve British engines. I don't know how many times the Bristol arrived home on one engine. Often. Very often."

Thomas left Wardair in 1961 to work for McAvoy Air Service. "Two brothers, Jim and Chuck, started that together, then they had a parting of the ways and Jim went to work for Carter's in Hay River hauling fish and doing charter work. That's when I went to work for Chuck."

Chuck McAvoy had a Fairchild 82, which Thomas calls a marvellous airplane. "It was a big box of a thing with a little tiny tail, quite long, with a 550 Pratt and Whitney on the front. The cockpit looked like an afterthought: it had little windows, the throttle was way up ahead—it was quite an odd airplane, but it would haul a fantastic load! It never went over 100 mph at any time, and it was as stable as a barn; if one wing dropped down a bit and you left it there, it would stay that way for 100 miles."

On 28 November 1962, an incident occurred that Mike Thomas—and a few other people—will never forget. The event made headlines in newspapers across Western Canada, and was featured in a film on northern bush pilots titled *By the Seat of Their Pants*, released in 1989 by Canamedia Productions Limited of Toronto.

Thomas was flying a Helio Courier with hydraulic wheel skis out of Yellowknife for McAvoy Air Service. One of his trips was to Snowdrift with passengers Ken Kerr, superintendent of the Indian Affairs Department for the Northwest Territories; Anne Pask, district health nurse; an Indian woman, Mrs. Mary Louise Nittah; and her nine-month-old baby, Mary Ann. The baby had just been released from a stay in the hospital.

The Native woman was anxious to return to her home in Snowdrift, so although the weather was poor, they decided to give it a try. There was considerable fog, and some open water on Great Slave Lake; the ice that had formed was not very stable yet. They departed from Yellowknife for Snowdrift and were near Telthielli Narrows when they started to see the open water. The fog was extremely thick and it had begun to snow heavily. At that point, Thomas decided they'd better go back to Yellowknife.

By the time he had turned around and had reached the mainland, the heavy snowfall made it dangerous to stay in the air. To make matters worse, they had also picked up some ice. In the poor visibility he choose a lake that he thought was Blatchford Lake and put the skis down, landing on ice that was covered with a mere inch of snow.

Thomas took a small axe from under the back seat, and he and Ken Kerr got out of the airplane to check the ice. After they'd chopped through nine inches of blue ice without hitting water, bad ice was the last thing on their minds. They noted, however, that the weather was deteriorating as the scant daylight receded.

"We're going to get stuck here for the night," Thomas predicted. "We'd better find a good campsite before it gets dark."

They walked toward a big stand of timber on a nearby island, and discovered an Indian foot-trail on the ice. Knowing that Indians didn't usually go very far without their dogs, Thomas assumed they were close to a camp. They started following the trail and soon they could hear open water.

"We're going the wrong way!" Thomas said. "That's the big lake [Great Slave Lake]. We're not on Blatchford Lake, we're behind Narrow Island. Now I know where we are—but the camp is the other way. That's Joe Fatt's camp."

Back they went to the airplane. There was no use everyone getting out and walking—they could just taxi the airplane along the ice and be there in minutes.

Thomas fired up the airplane and started taxiing it between the islands. He had put the skis up so he'd have brakes for better steering, and it was easy going over the clear ice. They were running along about 25 miles an hour when suddenly Ken hollered, "Black ice!"

Crash! In they went. Water bubbled up right over the engine, which abruptly stopped running. They were sinking fast.

Thomas was out the door immediately, with Kerr right behind him. By the time they got out, the wings were down almost to the ice. They ran around the other side to try to get the women out, who were still in the back. To their horror, they found that their passengers had inadvertently locked the back door.

The Helio Courier's door handle consists of a large disk with a slot on it that rotates. If you turned it the wrong way, it locked. You would then have to unlatch it with one hand while turning it with the other hand to unlock it. In an attempt to open the door, the women had turned the latch the wrong way. And they didn't know how to unlock it.

Thomas tried to kick out the window but, wearing only mukluks, was unable to break the plexiglas. He did break his foot, though he didn't realize, or care about it, at the time.

Then he saw that the women were standing up in the airplane. When it had stopped so suddenly, the freight behind the back seat had rammed the seat forward, forcing them up into a stooping position—they were neither sitting nor standing. The cargo consisted of five weeks' mail bound for Snowdrift, films in big metal boxes, and other heavy freight; it had all been propelled forward. The passengers were pinned in this awkward position, with their heads up against the ceiling, and they couldn't move.

Thomas ran to shore, found a big pole, and rammed it through the little round windows at the back to keep the airplane from sinking further through the ice. By this time, only the tail and the tops of the wings protruded out of the rubbery ice, and it looked as if they would sink at any moment.

Neither Mike Thomas nor Ken Kerr knew what on earth to do.

"I didn't even have a knife—and I usually carry one," Thomas explains. "I didn't have anything to cut the airplane open. The axe that I'd used to check the ice was in the airplane under the back seat, so it was under water and there was no way of getting it. I was just running around in a panic, watching these people drown."

Then he broke through the ice.

"I fell through right up to my armpits. It was about 20 below zero. My parka was soaked and I was wet all the way through, but I never even thought about being cold. By the time Ken pulled me out, the airplane had settled down further.

"I called to the nurse, Anne Pask. She could hear me, and she never panicked for a minute. She kept her head the whole time. But I could hear the Indian lady chanting her rosary. Then I heard Anne telling her to shut up so she could hear me."

Thomas happened to look up to the high rocky cliffs and was amazed to see an Indian man standing and watching the scene. The pilot started hollering to him in Dogrib. The man nonchalantly came down off the rocks and onto the ice and said, in perfect English, "What's the problem?"

Thomas recognized him as Joe Desjarlais, a trapper who lived in the area.

"There are people in the airplane! They're drowning!" Thomas screamed. "There's an Indian lady in there."

Desjarlais still didn't show any change of expression. "My partner's coming with the dogs and he's got an axe."

"How do you know he's coming? How do you know he's got an axe?"

"I know."

"How far is the camp?" Thomas asked, not believing that help was really on the way.

"About a mile."

Thomas took off running. His pants were freezing and his legs were becoming stiff. As he neared the cabin along came Joe Fatt, down off the island onto the ice with seven dogs, and in the carry-all—a canvas-sided box that sits on the toboggan—was an axe. That's all, just an axe! Thomas dived into the sleigh face-first and cried to the dog-team driver, "Go! As fast as you can! Go!"

The Indians seemed to know what had happened, Thomas says. They had apparently heard the plane land, heard it stop, they probably heard the men talking, and then heard them start the plane again and head toward their camp. They knew exactly what was going to happen before it happened; they knew there was bad ice there, and of course they heard the aircraft go through the ice. They knew the whole story, although they hadn't seen it.

They got back to the airplane, and Joe Desjarlais grabbed the axe. By the time Thomas had got himself out of the carry-all, Desjarlais had knocked all the antennae off and was starting to chop through the roof.

"Stop! Their heads are right there! Be careful!" Thomas cried.

They cut the airplane roof along each side, and rolled it open like a sardine can. Thomas looked down onto the heads of his passengers.

He pulled the baby out first, blue and foaming at the mouth. Thinking it was dead, Thomas tossed it aside, and it went tumbling against the shore. Then he pulled out Anne Pask and threw her on top of the wing. She was unconscious; Thomas thought she was dead. Then he pulled out Mary Louise Nittah; she was also unconscious. He turned back to assist Anne, who was wearing her duffle parka, minus the outer cover. But when he went to turn her over, he found he couldn't pry her off the wing. Her parka had frozen to the airplane! They had to take the axe and cut her free. Mary Louise regained consciousness after a few minutes.

They put the passengers into the carry-all, and threw the baby in on top of them. Thomas managed to take off his frozen parka and throw it over them. "Go!" he urged the driver. "Go, as fast as you can! Go to the cabin!"

Thomas and Kerr stayed behind to try and salvage what they could from the airplane.

One other thing the Indian men had brought in the carry-all was a gaff, a handle with a big hook on it for pulling large gill-caught trout into a boat. Thomas now used the hook to get their supplies from the airplane through the hole in the roof. His main concerns were the flare pistol and ration kit, and the mail sacks.

They finally got everything out, including the nurse's kit. Only then did Thomas realize that he was freezing. He didn't have a parka, it was 20 below, and he was soaking wet. They left the supplies on the ice and took off to the cabin.

When they arrived, the baby was romping around the floor with the other kids, playing like nothing had happened! Mary Louise was huddled in the corner with a bedroll wrapped around her—all eyes, terrified, still in shock. Thomas learned later that Anne had pushed the baby up into the upholstery where there was some air, thus saving its life.

Anne Pask said later that when Thomas had been telling her, "Anne, it's not going down any more, it's okay, we'll get you out," she could see the water coming up, measured by the upholstery stitches. Stitch by stitch it had edged up, nearer to the top, until just part of her mouth, her nose, and one ear were above water.

Anne at first was in terrible pain as the circulation returned to her legs, but within an hour she was back to normal.

So there they were in a little 12-x-16-foot cabin, a dozen people counting the Indian family and their own party. The cabin was sparsely furnished with a couple of bunks, a cookstove, a table and a chair, and that was it. And they were out of food. It was a bad time of year for travelling and they had no fish, no moose, nothing.

"I have a ration kit here. We'll open it up," Thomas said.

He'd never before had occasion to use the Department of Transport-approved ration kit everybody carried. He grabbed the big red metal box and opened it. When they saw what was in it, they all sat down and laughed: some hard candies, milkshake mix, hot biscuit mix but no oven, a fishnet that had disintegrated (there were no leads or floats for it anyway), and some rusty little fish hooks but no line.

Since all their blankets and bedrolls were wet for the first couple of nights, they slept stretched out like cordwood on the floor. They opened up the mail sacks and strung the wet pension cheques and letters on a clothesline around the cabin, and removed the films from the canisters and tried to dry them out, too.

The weather continued to deteriorate until they couldn't see more than a few yards from the cabin. It wasn't blowing, but there was heavy snow, which is unusual there. It stayed that way all day. There wasn't much chance of anybody coming out on a search. At one point they thought they heard an airplane, but it turned back.

The next day, Joe Desjarlais said, "We have an outboard and a canoe here, but no gas. If we had some gas maybe we could get to Snowdrift on the open water." So they cut a hole in the airplane wing to the fuel tank and drained the gas. They had some oil in the airplane, and mixed it with gas for the outboard motor, then dragged the canoe two miles over the ice to open water.

Within a short time, Joe Desjarlais and Joe Fatt were back—the engine kept freezing up, and they just couldn't make it. Desjarlais hooked up the dogs, Thomas wrote a note to take with him, and he started off for Yellowknife. By four o'clock in the morning, he was back. There was water on top of the ice in places, and the dogs' feet got so sore that he had no choice but to return.

They had no food at all. Antoinette Fatt, who lived in the cabin, had a little bit of flour and so made up some bannock and divided it among the 12 people. Other than that, they had nothing to eat for the first two days. On the second day, they set a net. Just before dark they pulled it in and found they'd caught a couple of whitefish, which again were shared.

The Indians often go hungry for days at a time, Thomas says, and don't appear to worry much about it. "I guess when they have food they eat, and when they don't, they don't. Simple as that. But we sure felt it."

On the third day they had nothing to eat at all, and were feeling rather sorry for themselves when Anne mentioned that it was her birthday. A short time later the kids went outside and came back in with a birthday cake made from snow. She was completely overcome.

But still no food. And unless the bad weather let up, there was little hope of any airplane coming their way. But just in case, they went down to mark out an SOS with spruce boughs on the ice near the airplane, with a big arrow pointing in the direction they had gone.

Very little of the airplane was showing now, except for the tail and the top sides of the wings; they brushed the snow off so it remained as visible as possible. But it was a silver airplane with a narrow green stripe. It would be hard to spot from the air.

Salvage crew for McAvoy Air Service's Helio Courier that went through the ice on Great Slave Lake, December 1962. *Collection of the author*

On the third night, just before dark, Thomas heard an Otter flying low, heading toward them. Using little spruce trees, they had marked out an airstrip on a channel with good ice, and had written 12 INCHES, so the rescue pilot wouldn't be afraid to land after seeing the Courier through the ice. The Otter came straight down toward the strip. Thomas ran out onto the ice, waving his arms, but the Otter flew over him, put on power and started to climb and turn, heading back for Yellowknife. The little party watched, unbelieving, as the airplane climbed into the clouds and disappeared. Thomas knew it was Joe McGillivray, because Joe was the only one around there at that time who flew instruments, but Joe had obviously not seen them. That was a heartbreaker. They piled up some brush and had some oil handy to light if they heard another airplane.

Thomas had the flare pistol, but the shells, in cardboard cases, had swelled from being in the water. He couldn't even get one into the barrel; also, they were soaked and likely wouldn't have fired anyway. That night in the cabin he dismantled one of the shells, took out the phosphorous ball, the powder and all the wadding, put this into little pie plates and stuck it into the oven to dry out.

"It's funny I didn't blow that cabin up," he says now.

When it dried, he reassembled it but the shell was still swollen. He got it all packed together and then, because it still wouldn't fit into the pistol, he tapped it into the barrel with a little hatchet. The next day he carried it everywhere. He didn't know if it was going to fire or not, but at least he felt better packing it with him.

"If it goes off, it'll be a miracle," Ken Kerr commented.

On the fourth day, they heard what Thomas thought sounded like a Cessna. They couldn't see the aircraft but could hear it flying low, going round and round, "like a bee going from flower to flower."

They got ready to fire up the brush, thinking that when the pilot got to the hills that would be as far as he could go because "the weather was too low." He would have to turn and come back.

In minutes they could hear him turning, although they still couldn't see him. They lit the brush, and soon he was headed right for them. Great black smoke billowed up into the clouds. The Cessna 180 was almost there. Not to take any chances, Thomas pulled out his flare pistol and fired it. Lo and behold, it went off! A great red flare went up, just as the Cessna came over the bush. The airplane wobbled a couple of times, and they realized the pilot had seen the fire long before the flare was fired.

He circled, then landed on the strip they'd marked out.

Pilot Bobby McLean got out of the airplane. "If you ever do that to me again, I'll leave you out here!" he snarled.

Thomas's flare had just missed the wing.

McLean decided to take the women to Yellowknife first, then come back and get Kerr and Thomas. Mary Louise Nittah said she wouldn't get into an airplane again, no matter what.

"I'll stay here until the ice is well froze, and I'll go to Snowdrift with the dogs."

McLean took Anne Pask and flew back to Yellowknife. Ken Kerr gave him a voucher to bring back some food for the Indian family, so he brought back about 800 pounds of groceries.

"I thought they were going to kiss us!" Thomas says.

When Bobby McLean was preparing to leave with Anne for Yellowknife, he had said, "As soon as I was in the air, Search and Rescue came out. Now everybody's out, the sky is full of airplanes. I'm going to have to call somebody on the radio and say I've located you and give them some coordinates. But get that SOS off the ice, get all those trees off—I don't want the air force to find you."

Thomas says there was always great rivalry between the bush pilots and the air force. So as soon as McLean took off, they removed the trees from the ice and cleaned up everything as well as they could. From the cabin they watched an air force plane approach. It started circling around a point several miles away. Then Thomas knew that McLean must have given the pilot the wrong coordinates—close enough but the wrong ones so the air force wouldn't find them.

Soon after, a white Otter (Pacific Western Airlines) arrived, and pilot Paul Hegadoren started circling. A while later, the air force DC-3 came over and flew around a few times. "After the air force had finally spotted us, they dropped a big bundle by parachute. But it missed us by about three miles. They came around again and fired out another one, and it did the same thing, drifting off to the east. We never did find what they threw out to us."

When he finally got back to Yellowknife that night in McLean's 180, Thomas had to be debriefed by the Search and Rescue officers. "The news bulletin came out that night," Thomas says. "'Air Force Search and Rescue Coordination Has Located Downed Airplane.' Which is what the air force always does—take credit for airplanes found by bush pilots."

Thomas laughs about the rivalry between the two factions. "A week before that, there were headlines in *The Edmonton Journal*: 'McAvoy says the air force has a perfect record—to date they have found no one.' And a week later I went through the ice with one of his airplanes! So Chuck was just wild. He said to the bush pilots, 'You guys find him. I don't care how you do it, but just find him!'

"Whenever a pilot goes down, whenever an airplane is overdue, everybody in the country goes looking for it: private airplanes, all the bush pilots, it's just amazing," Thomas says. "Unless they're out on something extremely important, everybody's on the search. In fact, earlier in the fall [of 1962], pilot Ken Stockall went missing with the 185 between Yellowknife and the Nahanni valley. I was out on that search with a 185, and when I got to Fort Simpson that first night, just before dark, there were so many airplanes there that I couldn't get a place to tie up. I had to land in the Liard River and pull the airplane up in the mud. There were something like 14 airplanes in Fort Simpson that night, and there must have been about 30 airplanes on that search, for quite some time. We flew for days and days, looking for Ken. He was found the following spring, by a helicopter. He'd flown right into a sheer cliff and burned, and it was very difficult to see. He was right on track, but we hadn't seen him."

In the far North, when a group of pilots are flying out of any particular base, although it's a vast country, you know every pilot, Thomas says. "From Churchill to Cambridge, to Inuvik, it's a very close fraternity, with some rare exceptions. In a situation where a pilot is missing or overdue, the other pilots know his habits, they know how he flies, they know what kind of weather he would push and what he would do in certain situations. Some have idiosyncrasies, they won't leave the river even though it might be an extra 30 miles, and we know this. Some we know are very mechanically inclined; they may be down for a day or two and then show up again because they fixed the problem. We know that some of them will stretch and fly on their last gallon of gas.

"Of course, we have our differences," he continues. "Sometimes a little fight will break out in the bar between pilots, but if you try to break it up you're liable to get yourself killed, because it's like a family feud. They stand by each other."

Generally, in the winter, temperatures around Yellowknife stick around 30 or 35 below, occasionally falling to 45 below. "You're always dressed for it, and you make sure your passengers are, or you shouldn't let them on the airplane," Thomas says. "We all carry good bedrolls, big eiderdown robes, and we always had, except when I went down with the Courier, a ration kit. After that I built my own ration kit. I used a small airtight heater as a container for my food and supplies and emergency rations. I had some pipes, an asbestos collar for the stovepipe, and a little silk tent. With that I could keep half a dozen people very comfortable even in 40 below zero, provided we weren't in the barren lands where there's no wood. About the only thing you could do then would be to run the blowpot that we used for warming the engine, and try and keep the tent warm that way. But you could survive without much of a problem."

Anne Pask is now in a retirement home in Victoria, Thomas says. "My wife and the kids went to see her about three or four years ago, had a nice visit with her. In conversation with the kids, it was obvious that she remembered every moment of the adventure–including the birthday cake."

By now, Thomas had his commercial licence, and ended up working for two companies at the same time, Ptarmigan Airways Limited, and McAvoy Air Service. That's when he noticed that every fall the pilots would all get the boot but the engineers never did. "Ptarmigan had three company houses, and Wardair had company houses; if they had a vacant house they might let a couple of pilots live in it, but when they hired an engineer they'd throw the pilot out on the street, his suitcase would hit him on the head, and the engineer had the house. I thought, 'I've got to do something different here!'"

He started putting in time in the hangar as an apprentice engineer–starvation wages again. The Department of Transport (DOT) gave him credit for the time he'd spent doing his own maintenance work over the years, but he still had to slog out two winters in the hangar, then "do a whole lot of practical things, such as gluing wood joints, making metal patches, welding, all kinds of things."

Thomas would finally get his engineer's licence in 1969. "Then I had the world by the tail. I figured I'd get the nice jobs, and I wouldn't get the boot in the fall."

Thomas flew for Chuck McAvoy until Chuck went missing without a trace in a Fairchild 82 in June 1964, on a flight north of Yellowknife. Neither he nor the airplane have been seen to this day.

"When Chuck went missing things fell apart. Gateway Aviation bought that charter licence and moved in to Yellowknife. At that point the whole picture changed, in attitudes, in camaraderie among pilots. Gateway's pilots were told not to associate with Ptarmigan pilots because 'Gateway pilots are different, we're better.' You wouldn't want to get caught in the bar at night with a Gateway pilot because you'd be in trouble. Before that, there were 36 pilots in Yellowknife, and there might be 34 of them in the bar all at the same time. When the sun went down it didn't matter who you worked for. And if anyone was overdue, every pilot in Yellowknife was out looking for him. And if you ever used fuel from a fuel cache, it didn't matter whose it was, as soon as you got back to Yellowknife you told him, 'I used 30 gallons from your cache. I'll replace it or pay for it.'

"But when Gateway came in, it was a totally different show because of their management system. Gateway went under eventually. Although they did have some good pilots, the company managers believed that a cheap pilot was a good deal. They had several fatal crashes and that was the end of them.

"And then other things started changing. I almost had to walk back from the barren lands one time because someone used my fuel and didn't tell me—way the hell and gone at Muskox Lake. The fuel should have been there, and it wasn't. I found out where it went—it isn't hard to find out who took your fuel, you know where everyone's been—and this started to happen again and again."

Thomas had taken a chance and flown up to the next lake, hoping to find fuel there. Fortunately, there was some. He knew whose it was and as soon as he got back to base he told them so nobody would be depending on it.

The camaraderie and way of life Thomas, and pilots like him, had taken for granted in the North was fading. What was happening to the country? Thomas's next job—as his own boss—showed him the underlying causes and effects of the changes.

In 1963 Thomas embarked on a new enterprise at Lac la Martre, 100 miles west of Yellowknife. "I built a trading post and had a little airplane, and I operated that for a year and a half before I sold it."

Lac la Martre lay nestled in a beautiful setting. The lake, 40 miles long and 12 miles wide, was crystal clear. Thomas could see right to the bottom at 40 feet, and view rocks and trout. The little village, located on the point at the east end, had been a summer residence for generations of Native people.

In his journal, Thomas recorded the pattern of life through the seasons of trapping, fishing, smoking and drying their food supplies, and just resting and playing. This had been their pattern for centuries.

Then everything changed.

"In came the white man," Thomas says, "who decided these kids had to be educated. So now the kids had to go to school, which meant the mother had to stay here. That was the beginning of the end. The old man can't go out on the trapline without his family, it was a family affair.

"I saw the whole thing evolve in 20 years," Thomas says. "I saw total destruction of the northern Indian in 20 years, from about 1960 to 1980, total destruction, in Snowdrift, Lac la Martre, Fort Rae, you name it."

Thomas lived at Lac la Martre for almost two years, and later lived in Snowdrift for nearly five years.

"Now you've got the schools, and these kids go to about grade six," Thomas continues. "Then they say, 'Okay, now we've educated you, go back to your people.' Some of them even made it as far as Yellowknife to the residential schools, then they sent them back. And their own people called them 'goddamned whitemen.' 'We don't want you back here, you don't know how to trap, you don't know how to fish, you don't know nothing. You can't drive dogs. You're no good to us.'

"Our society didn't want them. Who would hire a grade-nine Indian? So they would migrate to the cities, they'd end up on the back streets doing whatever they could to survive; the loneliest people you'll ever meet in your life.

Nobody wanted them. And there's nothing worse than being someone who no one wants, eh?"

After leaving Lac la Martre in 1964, Thomas's flying career took him briefly to BC's coast flying Beavers for BC Airlines, then to Winnipeg, Manitoba. He qualified, while there, for an Airline Transport licence, and flew DC-3s for Transair on the Brandon–Prince Albert run; then he was based in Churchill.

One night, they were coming down their "sked" (scheduled) run in the DC-3 from Hall Beach (which is the main DEW line site in the Fox basin geological area, located in the northwest corner of Hudson's Bay in the Boothia Peninsula) heading back to Churchill. They fuelled up "to the hilt" at Chesterfield Inlet, so were over gross weight by about a ton. By the time they reached Baker Lake, it was snowing heavily, in a black night. They dumped off some cargo and took off, fortunately with lots of fuel, for Churchill.

Mike Thomas, airline captain, 1964. Mike had planned to travel to Australia, but found himself taking a job flying Beavers to Port Hardy for BC Airlines. Then he got lonesome for the North. He never did go to Australia. *Mike Thomas Collection*

"At 4,000 feet we were picking up ice like hell, so we went to 6,000. Still picking up ice. We went to 8,000 feet. We were just on top of the cloud layer [in the clear] when we blew an oil cooler. That meant an immediate engine shut-down. All the oil was gone in seconds. We had to shut one engine down and feather it, turn the prop blades into the slipstream so there was no drag and the engine wouldn't windmill [it would stop rotating]. When you lose an engine your speed alone will make it turn as if it were a windmill, which would cause considerable drag. When you're a ton over gross and in that situation, the last thing you want is drag!

"So we cruised along on one engine at 8,000 feet. We still had eight-and-one-half hours of fuel—with two engines; now with one engine we had more than that.

"We were almost at Churchill when we were informed that the DC-4, on the DEW line-Cape Dyer run, had tried to come in and had overshot. We knew we'd never get in on one engine, so we went on to Lynn Lake.

"Lynn Lake went zero-zero [zero ceiling and zero visibility]. Right out. Okay, we'll go to Thompson. We're grinding along at 115 knots on one engine, still at 8,000 feet and we've got rid of most of the ice. Then Thompson went zero-zero. Holy smoke, now what? Maybe we can land at Brandon. Brandon went zero-zero! Well, to hell with it. Winnipeg.

"And that's what we did. It took half the night. When we landed in Winnipeg we still had enough fuel left to go to Kenora or Minneapolis, our next choices. That long range of the DC-3 saved our bacon. It was a marvellous airplane."

Thomas's next employer was Air Canada—a company that aimed to separate the wheat from the chaff. ("The only time I was ever asked by an employer to see my licence was Air Canada, in 40-some years as a pilot.")

"For years, I'd had these 15-minute medicals and everything was okay," Thomas says. "You think you're indestructible. You have a four-day medical and you find out you're half dead!

"Air Canada sent me to every specialist in Winnipeg, including psychiatrists. Somehow I got through it and got on course. And that was even tougher."

Thomas's course started in May 1966. He and his wife, Joyce, moved to Montreal, where Thomas began his training.

"Air Canada had a seven-week ground school course, hot and heavy," Thomas explains. "If you couldn't keep up, you were out the door. I had been out of school a long time. In that class were a dozen ex-air force guys, all in their 20s, professional students, university degrees, some with masters' degrees, who'd never worked a day in their lives. There were seven or eight guys from the navy, from Shearwater; and there were just three of us from the bush. The air force guys dumped on us unmercifully. They used to call me 'Bushrabbit,' 'Trapper,' everything else, and I had a hell of a time, I don't mind admitting.

"These guys were partying every night, they wrote exams every Monday morning, and they'd ace the exams, 95 percent. I was studying and working, just going nuts and barely keeping up, but I finally made it through the course.

"After we'd finished the exams, there was a big sigh of relief. We'd all passed, and Bushrabbit was number 24 out of a class of 24—with an average of 86.8 percent. We had a big bust at the Skyline Hotel and these air force guys were unmerciful; they were just on my case. Finally a couple of navy guys came by and they said, 'Don't worry, Bushrabbit. Next week we'll find out.' I said, 'Find out what?' 'We'll find out if these assholes can fly.' And we found out!

"The navy guys could fly anything; they could fly the box it came in. They were fantastic pilots. But the air force people had no experience. They had commercial licences, they'd done a little time on Chipmunks, but they'd spent their whole lives in university at the taxpayers' expense. Acing the books is one thing, but flying the airplane is quite another."

So Mike Thomas was now with Air Canada, and his career was set. He should have been happy.

Thomas says that as long as he was in the air, it was great—the air crews were fine people. But on the ground, the company, being a crown corporation, "had empire-builders everywhere."

"I was very lucky that I got in on the tail end of all the senior captains who were beginning to retire, guys who'd come from the bush in 1937. They had been on the airline all these years, gone overseas and flown bombers, come back to the airline, and were all starting to retire as I was coming into the system. I learned a lot from them. They in turn respected me because I'd come from the bush, and they gave me a lot of help to make my way up the line."

After three years, he knew he wasn't–and never would be–a "system" pilot.

But before he'd officially handed in his resignation, one of the check pilots told several of them that, "Within the next six months, you guys are going left seat. You're going captain's seat, that quick."

"Holy smoke! That meant Viscount! And we were on DC-8s," Thomas says. "We'd never flown a turbine in our lives, any of us. The DC-8s were a totally different world; now we were going to have to very quickly do the conversion and perform from the left seat as captain on a Viscount!"

The Viscount was a four-engine turbine, and the DC-8 was a big four-engine jet, Thomas explains. The Viscount was a British continental airplane powered by four Rolls Royce Darts–the most beautiful airplane he would ever fly. It travelled at 325 knots–"That's fast!"–and carried 60 passengers. Thomas hung on just long enough to get his Viscount endorsement, then left the company.

It was back to the bush.

"I wanted to go back North, but there was no way I was going without an

Mike Thomas with an oil company Beaver at Lac la Biche, Alberta, 1983. After leaving Snowdrift in 1974, the Thomases bought a three-quarter section farm near Westlock, north of Edmonton, and Mike began "free-lance" flying and engineering work. *Mike Thomas Collection*

airplane," Thomas says. "I said to my wife, 'I can't promise you anything more than a roof over your head and three squares a day, and that'll be it.' She said, 'That's fine, let's go.' And she was a city girl!"

Mike Thomas did "a number of things" while in Snowdrift. He set up a trading post and some tourist camps, and he hauled every kind of cargo he could to make a buck with his 1938 Stinson Reliant (which is now a classic). He even ended up buying the Hudson's Bay Company trading post, a highly unusual situation, because "the Bay doesn't sell to anybody."

They left Snowdrift in 1974 and never went back. They'd lived there nearly five years.

The time was right for the family to move south. "We had kids starting school, and the school was a disaster there [in Snowdrift]. We had these people from Toronto who had been reading *Hiawatha* for ten years in university and had great ideas on all the things they were going to do for the poor downtrodden Indians. They were going to organize a ball team and a hockey team—and by Easter they'd be taken out in straitjackets. It was just unbelievable."

They bought a three-quarter section farm near Westlock, north of Edmonton, and Thomas began his "free-lance" flying and engineering work. They have retained the home quarter to this day.

The children grew up, and Thomas's wife, Joyce, went back to university, eventually becoming qualified as a doctor of clinical psychology, with a practice in Edmonton.

Thomas arrived in La Ronge, Saskatchewan, which he has called home since 1987, via a circuitous route. His seasonal flying had taken him to Telegraph Creek, BC, for a summer, and to Ontario for another summer. Then he was asked to come to La Ronge as chief engineer for Dawn Air. From there, Thomas went to work for La Ronge Aviation for a couple of years, to Prince Albert for a year, and back to La Ronge. By this time, he says, he was getting very tired of aviation, so he started working in La Ronge at the radio branch as a relief operator, just for something to do.

SaskTel operates the Northern Radio Telephone Service, a system of HF (high frequency) radio communications for customers who live in remote northern Saskatchewan locations. Thomas describes it as probably the only system of its kind anywhere in the world, except perhaps in Australia, much like that used by the Flying Doctor. (The Flying Doctor of Australia was featured in a television series. He flew his own airplane, and operated on call by short-wave radio).

The 400 or so radio-telephone subscribers pay $31 dollars a month and are supplied with free batteries—nine batteries in each radio that last for weeks. Not only can they talk to the station and make calls, but they can visit with each other from camp to camp, which they do, all night long. Thomas, now an old hand at this business, knows almost everyone in northern Saskatchewan.

Meanwhile, Thomas has made La Ronge his home, aside from going back to the farm whenever he can make the break.

Throughout his career, Thomas has flown all the Cessna family, and all the Piper family, Beechcraft 18s, and Douglas DC-3s and -4s and -8s. His engineering work taught him to become more cautious about the type of aircraft he flew. "Before that I would fly anything—if it would make a noise and fly, I'd fly it."

In his 15,000 hours of flying, Thomas has never wrecked an airplane. "I had a few bad moments, but nothing very serious happened."

There were countless forced landings because of weather, plus a few engine failures that he says were caused by such things as a faulty fuel system. "I have spent

Mike Thomas, La Ronge, SK, 1993. "It's a haven for bush pilots." *Mike Thomas Collection*

thousands of hours behind Pratt and Whitneys in the Norseman, the Beavers, the Beech 18s, the Otters, and I've never had one engine let me down. The support systems maybe, but never the engine."

Thomas's flying career has spanned a time and place that might be considered the pioneer era.

"In the early years when flying in the North, our maps would show an area marked off in yellow, rather than green: 'relief data unreliable.' A few little things would be sketched in, but most of it was pretty blank. As we were crossing these areas we'd sketch in what we saw and add a few notes."

Mike Thomas has never stepped aside to avoid controversy, and even though he depended for many years on flying contracts to make a living, and could say very little about what he saw going on around him, it didn't stop him from staging personal protests.

"When one works as a charter pilot, the general rule is to keep your eyes open and your mouth shut. When you're flying people around, you mind your own business," Thomas says. "You don't get involved, or you won't get any more flying from them. You don't see anything, you don't hear anything. You fly the airplane from A to B, safely, and they pay the bills."

He is articulate, and also became a proficient writer, sending columns and articles to northern papers expressing his outrage over government mishandling of monies, Native affairs, or what he saw as the collusion of church and state.

At one point, Thomas wrote an article titled "Kidnapping Kids Down the Mackenzie" and gave it to his editor brother-in-law, who published it in *News of the North* in Yellowknife. It detailed Thomas's experiences in 1960-61, which are collaborated by his log book records.

"I was flying the Oblate Father Leising's old Norseman (CF-GTM), and Buzz Gresl also was there with a Norseman, flying for Aurora," Thomas recalls. "Anyway, the Anglicans chartered me in the fall, and the Catholics chartered Buzz, and away we went, racing down the river. Buzz and I were on the radio the whole time.

"We'd fly into a settlement, park the airplane, and when everybody came down to see the airplane, the Anglican hostel manager would start grabbing kids to take them off to school. Their parents didn't know what was going on.

"I'll never forget at Fort Wrigley, we were both there at the same time, Buzz and I. The priest and a nun were there, grabbing kids, and the Anglican guy was grabbing kids. We got the airplanes full, we flew back to Fort Simpson, and we went back down the river again, kidnapping kids. We finally half-filled both those hostels.

I was back in Fort Wrigley at Christmas. I landed on the ice and this lady came trudging down on little snowshoes. She said, 'Where did you take my kids?' She didn't know where her kids were, from the fall to Christmas of 1961! So we actually kidnapped kids.

"Then I started having a better look at this. You see, the church-run schools were getting paid so much a head from the federal government for each kid they had in the hostel. It was a very competitive business."

Thomas's article brought an immediate response. "I got a visitor from Ottawa. He came right to Fort Simpson, and he told me to mind my own business," Thomas says. "I told him, 'Look, I'm not afraid of you. I don't work for the government. I'm not a Catholic, and I'm not an Anglican.' But I never got another hour of flying from Northern Health; I never got another hour of flying from Forestry. They completely grounded me. And that was the way they operated in those days."

Thomas had broken the code of silence by speaking out, and writing, about the situations he encountered through his work. It was a brave—and in retrospect perhaps a foolhardy—move, for it cost him dearly.

Thomas's knowledge has made some people nervous. But he has fully enjoyed his career and has no more axes to grind.

"I just play games," Thomas says, with a smile. "Like playing a fish on a hook." The boldness Mike Thomas displayed in high school when he defended his desire to become a bush pilot has become the hallmark of his career.

He's back in the North now, in the bush that he's always loved.

Why La Ronge? "It's a haven for bush pilots!" he says, and breaks into a wide grin.

Whiskey Whiskey Papa

O NE OF WELDY PHIPPS'S first flying jobs was out of Dawson City, Yukon, mapping the Arctic coast. "We were flying at 35,000 feet," Phipps recalls. "It was a tough go with no pressurization."

It was then that Phipps saw the image that would forever attract him to this unique part of the world.

"Once we'd reach the north end of our lines we'd look up and in perfectly clear weather we could see the Arctic islands. When I saw that, I knew I had to get North."

Weldy Phipps became a pilot in an unusual way. He used the back-pay he had "saved" as a POW to pay for flying lessons after he had escaped and come home to Ottawa.

"I was five years in the air force in World War II. I wasn't a pilot, I was a flight engineer," Phipps explains. "But my ambition in life, always, from the time I can remember, was flying. I didn't have the education to get into a pilots' course in the air force when I started out. I could have later on because they lowered the standards and the requirements, but I didn't actually start flying as a pilot until after the war. I obtained a number of flying-related licences as fast as I could, and that's all I did for a living the rest of my life. Fly airplanes. Fly and fix."

Welland (Weldy) W. Phipps was born in Ottawa, Ontario, on 23 July 1922. He joined the Royal Canadian Air Force in July 1940, taking his flight engineer training at Brandon, Manitoba; St. Thomas, Ontario; and Fort Macleod, Alberta. In 1941 he was sent to England and posted to No. 409 Squadron, RCAF.

He was then posted, as sergeant, to night bomber operations with No. 405 Squadron. By 3 April 1943, Phipps had completed 28 bombing raids when his Halifax bomber was shot down over Essen, Germany.

He parachuted safely but was captured. He spent two years as a prisoner of war in Germany before he and another POW, Flying Officer Hugh Clee of Vancouver, escaped during a forced march and made their way to the Allied lines in April 1945.

Phipps's first civilian aviation job was with a charter company, Atlas Aviation Limited of Ottawa, in 1946. During this time he took flying instruction and eventually became one of the most highly qualified pilots in Canada, gaining his pilot's licence, air engineer's licence classes A and B, airline transport licence, and a restricted radio telephone operator's certificate.

He married Frances Coolin in 1947, and, while still in Ottawa, he acquired his first airplane, a Fleet Finch biplane.

In 1948 Phipps began work for Rimouski Airlines (later called Quebecair). In 1949 he moved over to Spartan Air Services Limited, first as chief pilot, then operations manager and assistant manager. One of his jobs with Spartan Air involved northern high-altitude photography work, flying a Lockheed Lightning P-38. Phipps tells the story:

"The air force had already covered much of the North with trimetrogon photography,[1] but at that time there were no detailed topographic maps north of Dawson City. We shot with a fan camera and two oblique cameras, which gave us tremendous coverage.

"I used a solar navigator, a device that sited the sun, to fly straight lines. I'd fly a line with cameras facing each side and vertical, then I'd move over two miles and fly down, overlapping."

Preliminary maps were then made from the photographs of the unmapped area from Dawson City up to the mainline coast.

Phipps's first design credit occurred as a result of this job. He modified the nose of the P-38 to accommodate camera equipment and an operator.

"The P-38 was strictly a fighter airplane and was also meant to carry guns and ammunition. We modified it so we could put a camera and navigator in the nose. I just had an idea in mind of the configuration we'd want. I contacted a friend at Spartan, Bill Law, a graduate in mechanical engineering, and between the two of us we manufactured a nose."

With this system in place, they did many thousands of square miles of aerial photography over northern Canada, setting up work stations at Gary Lake (200 miles northwest of Baker Lake) and Esker Lake in the Ungava District. The result was a 16-fold increase in mapping coverage of the Arctic in preparation for the building of the DEW (Distant Early Warning) line.

In 1953, George Jacobsen, a Montreal businessman who later helped finance many of Phipps's business activities, chartered a Canso—"a PBY, a big amphibious flying pig-boat"—to fly a party up to the Arctic. It was a private operation, and Phipps was hired as the pilot.

"When I got up to those northern islands I found there was no place to land a sea plane because there's just too much ice. So I finally found a spot on the central east coast of Axel Heiberg Island where I could get in on a large lake."

But there was a problem: "If you saw a stretch of water where you could land a sea plane, an hour later that could be chock-full of ice; you could be trapped, the airplane could be crushed and sunk. The thing that impressed me," Phipps recalls, "was there were literally countless places you could land if you had an aircraft with special gear on it for landing on unprepared terrain. So when I got back down south I mentioned to George Jacobsen that if I had a Super Cub I could do a little experimenting with, I could try out a theory. He actually bought the Super Cub and I experimented with undercarriages.

"I had one tractor gear, tandem wheels with the belt around—that didn't work too good; it would have been ideal for support, but too much drag. And then we tried straight tandem wheels—a pair of small wheels on either side of the undercarriage.

"When I was preparing to take an airplane North in 1956 to try out the modified undercarriage equipped with tandem wheels, I got talking to Dalton Muir, a biologist who was going up to make a film on Arctic wildlife for the National Film Board. The air force was going to drop him at the weather station at Eureka while it was early enough in the spring for the strip to still be frozen, and therefore usable—during the summer the airstrip was too muddy for landing big aircraft. I decided then to take the Cub and try out my idea.

"I took enough gas drums to get up to Resolute Bay but I had to carry extra fuel and land on the way to put it in. I went to Resolute, from there to Eureka, and then Muir wanted to go on up to Alert. Just below Alert there's a place called Fort Conger, the 1881 to 1884 wintering quarters of the Greely Expedition.[2] I had to land there on a little river outwash.

"I got the Cub in there all right and everything was going fine when I tore a brake line and I couldn't keep the damned airplane straight. I veered off into the ditch and broke the port undercarriage, fell down on the wing, chewed the prop up.

"I'd been getting a hell of a lot of static from the air force. They wanted to stop me from flying up there in case I went missing, like the aircraft that went missing out of Frobisher Bay; they said the meals alone on that search were $45,000, and that was a long time ago. They didn't want another occurrence, but they couldn't stop me because I was a civil aircraft.

"So I didn't want to call anybody on the radio and say I had trouble. I just called Alert, which was only 30 miles away, and said I had landed at Fort Conger and we were going to hang around there for three or four hours, taking pictures. Then I had to think, 'What the hell was I going to do to get us out of here?'

"The one thing—call it a premonition—before I left Mould Bay I'd put about eight feet of steel cable on board; if I had trouble with the undercarriage and had to cinch it up, I'd have a piece of cable to do it.

"We managed to prop the left wing up and get the undercarriage back in the direction it should have been, and with the cable we laced the thing so it would still support. But the wing was dragging on the ground. Not too serious. We off-loaded every conceivable thing we could, even our emergency gear, to lighten it as much as possible, just retaining barely enough fuel.

"We managed to fly to Alert. A Lancaster had crashed at Alert a few years back: they were air-dropping supplies when the parachute caught around the tail and they went down. The wreckage was still there, and we managed to scrape some tubing and stuff from that wreck. I borrowed a welding torch from the weather station and I welded up our undercarriage.

First landing made by Phipps with Dr. Thorsteinsson, in Piper Super Cub equipped with tandem gear, mired in soft ground on Black Top Ridge east of Eureka weather station, 1956. *Dr. R. Thorsteinsson Collection, Geological Survey of Canada*

"The only thing was the propeller. Both tips were kind of rolled up; we banged them out with an old pickaxe on a rock as much as we could, but finally we just sawed the tips off to straighten it up. The engine ran good enough, so then we continued north right up to Cape Columbia, which is the most northern point of land in North America, and visited a cairn left there by Peary when he made his dash to the Pole."

During this trip to try out the Cub in 1956, Phipps met Dr. R. Thorsteinsson and Dr. E.T. (Tim) Tozer, with the Geological Survey of Canada, who were working out of Eureka. They had been travelling by means of dog team early in the season, and later by canoe and back-packing. It was admittedly a very slow process, and only the geology of the coastlines could be covered very well.

Phipps took Thorsteinsson for a ride in the Cub and landed in a couple of places. "Gosh, he was impressed," Phipps says. "He told me, 'The distance we covered in an hour would have ordinarily taken several days.'"

In the fall of 1957, Phipps paid a visit to Thorsteinsson and Tozer in Ottawa to ask for a contract to fly them around in the North using a Piper Cub—this time equipped with balloon tires. This assignment marked the beginning of a new era in northern geological survey and exploration.

The following spring Thorsteinsson and Tozer pooled the monies they had been allotted by the Geological Survey of Canada for more dog sledge and canoe work, and hired Phipps with a Super Cub. That summer of 1958 they covered approximately 24,000 square miles of geological mapping. It took 300 hours of flying time to complete the survey, at a contract cost of around $12,000.

Dr. Thorsteinsson recalls that Phipps had not been entirely satisfied with the performance of the Piper Super Cub with tandem wheels, and therefore equipped the aircraft with large tires, 25" x 11" x 4", and bearing five pounds pressure. "These tires," recalls Dr. Thorsteinsson, "were standard equipment for a Stinson SR5 aircraft, and with slight modifications the hubs of the Super Cub's wheels were adapted to fit them. The increased drag of the large tires reduced the normal cruising speed from about 115 mph to about 95 mph." Approximately 450 landings were made, of which about 400 were on unprepared landing surfaces on Melville, Mackenzie King, Prince Patrick, Borden, Eglington, Brock, Cameron, and Emerald islands. This trip was later described by Thorsteinsson as "highly successful."

"Weldy was a bit of a genius, no question about it," Dr. Thorsteinsson says. "He proceeded through life with the firm belief that what anybody else could do, he could do. He would tackle any job from taking apart and reassembling a camera—and making special little screwdrivers to do the job—to fixing televisions, radios, or motors. You could almost see his mind

Weldy Phipps standing at cairn on Dealy Island, a small island off the south coast of Melville Island. The cairn was built by Captain Henry Kellett's men in 1853. Kellett was captain of one of the expeditions sent out in search of Sir John Franklin's missing ships. Barrels and staves protruding from the cairn were meant to render it more obvious to passing ships. *Dr. R. Thorsteinsson Collection, Geological Survey of Canada*

working as he observed how a machine operated. Then he'd take it apart."

Thorsteinsson recalls pilot Dick deBlicquy saying that once something went wrong with one of their aircraft, and Weldy spent 10 days fixing it, methodically going over every part and making the necessary repairs. Dick said that it would have been cheaper to bring someone in, considering the billable hours that the aircraft sat while Weldy figured out and worked on the problem. But it was his nature to know.

By this time, Phipps had become addicted to the North. He was now part owner, with Russell Bradley, of Bradley Air Services of Carp, Ontario. Following the experiment undertaken in 1958 with the Stinson SR5 tires, he returned to Ottawa and, with Bill Law and others, began experimenting with improvements on the basic idea, which involved the design of bigger tires and

Photo taken in 1958 by Weldy Phipps of Dr. E.T. Tozer with Phipps's Piper Super Cub equipped with Stinson SR5 tires, on Melville Island. Note the depth of the overburden in which they landed. "If he had been alone, he'd have been in deep trouble in this wet mud," Dr. Thorsteinsson commented, "but with two of them, they managed to get out all right." *Dr. R. Thorsteinsson Collection, Geological Survey of Canada*

special wheels. Phipps looked after the hubs, and Goodyear made the tires to his specifications.

"I picked a tire Goodyear used to make in the early days, what they called the 'air wheel,' a kind of large balloon-type tire," Phipps explains. "They had made them for planes up to the size of DC-3s, 45 inches high. I had them make a modified version, much lighter, because the DC-3 tires were 10-ply, far too heavy to fit the Piper PA-18 Super Cub. So they did a run of lightweight tires for me. I could run them as low as four pounds pressure, but usually six to eight pounds."

The "Phipps Special" tires gave much better flotation on soft ground, and superior shock absorbency on rough ground. Predicting the type of unprepared ground suitable for landing an airplane is vital, and can be difficult if not impossible without a knowledge of geology. "You have to be able to look at a geological formation and say, 'Well, that's the Christopher shale, there's no damn way I'm landing on that because I'll just go out of sight.' Then there are sandstone formations—they're okay if it's dry. The way you can tell if it's dry or not is by its colour; the wet soil will be darker than the dry soil. You get so you can go all over in a fixed-wing airplane, pick your landing spots."

But with the development of the fat "tundra" tires, Phipps was able to land just about anywhere. He won the Trans-Canada Trophy for this achievement.

But the tires were only the beginning: the equipment had been developed and stress-tested, now he awaited the opportunity to make full use of it.

In 1959, Phipps returned to the Arctic with five Bradley Air Services Super

Cub airplanes, equipped with new and improved "Phipps Special" tundra tires. The size had been increased from 25 to 35 inches, the width was 24 inches, and pressure reduced from seven to four pounds. During the season, two Super Cubs covered 110,000 square miles of geological survey work on Banks and Victoria islands, two more took geologists to Bathurst and Prince of Wales islands, and a fifth served both expeditions. The five airplanes landed a total of 3,000 times on the oversize tundra tires, without a mishap.

Phipps began to spend more and more of his time in the North, outfitting eight Super Cubs and a Beaver with the large tires to service the geology, resource exploration, and survey industries. The Beaver itself logged 600 hours in three-and-one-half months in 1960, and repeated this performance the following year. In 1961, he equipped a Single Otter with oversize tires, which flew 800 hours that year, piloted by Dick deBlicquy.

Between 1957 and 1962, the company's Arctic fleet was expanded to 10 aircraft, including Super Cubs, Beaver and Single Otters.

Phipps also became a vital link for residents of the Far North when they required medical help. In 1960, for instance, when a whooping cough epidemic broke out in the Eskimo settlement of Grise Fiord on Ellesmere Island, other planes were unable to get in due to blizzards and other problems. With four hours' notice from the Department of Health and Welfare in Ottawa, Weldy Phipps and Erwin Keller, another Arctic pilot, assembled a Super Cub that had been stored at Resolute, and flew Doctor A.H. Stevens the 260 miles to Grise Fiord, with an RCAF DC-3 providing navigation information.

"I flew from Resolute Bay to northern Devon Island, landing on the ice. I was afraid to just fly around looking for Grise Fiord because I was too low on fuel. The air force DC-3 was circling; we asked them to verify our position, which they did, then I flew to Grise."

The weather was reportedly minus 30 degrees Fahrenheit (Phipps guesses it more likely 40 below) and the Super Cub had a malfunctioning heater. "It was so damned cold! The windshield was all frosted over except in one little spot. But the worst thing was that my gyros froze up and, really, with no gyros it's hard to steer a course."

A flare path, made from small cans with rolls of toilet tissue soaked in gasoline and set on fire, had been set out by the RCMP and local Eskimos to guide them to a landing strip on the sea ice. Upon landing, the doctor took off on a six-mile dog team ride to look after the patients while Phipps worked on the frozen Super Cub. When the doctor's work was done, Phipps contacted the DC-3 to provide navigation back to Resolute through the extreme cold and ice-fog.

In 1962 Phipps formed Atlas Aviation, became its president, and moved its operational base to Resolute, NWT, on Cornwallis Island about 80 miles from the North Magnetic Pole. Using the RCAF's 6,000-foot landing strip, he thus became the owner-operator of the most northerly charter airline in Canada, if not the world. Phipps also became the first non-air force operator to stay in over the winter months and therefore the first pilot to fly scheduled flights throughout the three-month period of Arctic darkness from early November to the end of January.

Phipps felt he had to provide such a service—there seemed to be no choice in the matter.

"The settlements got one airplane, two at the outside, in the whole year, because they'd either have to have open water to land something, like the Canso, or they'd have to get in during the early spring when there was still solid ice.

"So they were essentially without an air service, which created a hell of a problem because to try to get administrative people such as nurses to stay over the winter—they just wouldn't do it. They'd be locked in for the whole winter. What if one of their kids got sick? Personal risks. After I started putting the year-round service in, there was no problem."

The establishment of Atlas Aviation started a chain of events. "At Pond Inlet, for instance, they'd been getting one trip in there a year, and we got up to 50 trips. We were flying scientists around, moving cargo, we took the mail from Resolute Bay to the settlements, to Arctic Bay, Pond Inlet, Grise Fiord, Clyde River, and to the Arctic weather stations at Mould Bay, Isachsen, Eureka, and so on."

Night flying in the Arctic required a unique set of skills. "During wintertime it's total darkness, so you have to fly at night if you're going to fly," Phipps says simply. "To start with, there's no navigational aids. Also, you have no magnetic [or directional] compass, being so close to the North Magnetic Pole, so you have to use celestial. That's fine if you don't have an overcast, and you can see something in your astro-compass."

Phipps had an astro-compass fitted to the windshield and took bearings on the sun, moon, and stars—when visible—as he flew. There were no weather-reporting stations, and usually no radio contact.

Another hazard was range. "Everything's so far apart," Phipps explains. "Bush airplanes don't have much fuel range. So when you're taking off to go some place, if you didn't get in there you were just out of luck, because where are you going to go? You have no fuel. A lot of close ones came from that."

He describes reasons for some of the "close ones":

"Frobisher Bay was a bad place. We made hundreds of medical evacuations. I don't know how many. That was part of the business— taking people from the settlements and getting them out to the hospital.

"In these cases you were under tremendous pressure to go. You're sitting in the settlement; somebody's got to go to the hospital or they'll die. The people, if you try to tell them, 'Look, the ceiling's only 50 feet at Frobisher Bay,' they can't understand that. They think, 'Hell, the airplane's only 15 feet high!' Well, you're standing there and after a while you just break down and say, 'Okay, let's go,' and you go, take a chance on it.

"One time I flew seven medicals to Frobisher Bay when I should never have taken off in the first place. From the north of Frobisher Bay the beacon was terrible. I had been bucking a head wind, apparently, but I didn't know it, and I had trouble picking the beacon up. Finally I did get the beacon but before I was over Frobisher Bay both my low-level fuel lights were on. I couldn't see Frobisher Bay but I could see the lights of the strip through the fog. I had enough fuel for one pass; I had to make it in that pass. I made my approach based only on the lights I could see through the fog, going down through dense fog till I hit the runway."

He was "flying blind," just on instruments. He felt the runway underneath and was amazed to note that both engines were still running. Through sheer good luck he eventually found the strip to taxi off the runway. When they went to refuel the airplane, the tanks—which were supposed to hold 315 gallons—took in 320 gallons! To coin a phrase, he had been running on fumes.

"I had a lot of times like that, getting in very very low on fuel," Phipps says. "You get down, you're drenched with sweat, and you say, 'Jesus, I'm never going to fly again!' and the next morning you're up and going."

Some pilots seem to have an uncanny sense of where the ground is, and others don't. When asked how you can tell, in a white-out, where the ground is, Phipps replies stoically, "You can't.

"If you know that the landing surface is good, if you've landed there before, then it's no problem, you just do a low sink sort of a landing, keep letting down until you touch. But if you aren't absolutely sure there's a good surface, it's just suicide because there could be a great big snowdrift and you just wouldn't see it."

While most people equate a long life and flying with taking as few risks as possible, every northern pilot has taken chances that could have been disastrous. Phipps agrees that "you have to take risks, but they have to be calculated risks. You can't just barrel off and say, 'Well, I hope I get through.' Although I did that on some medical flights."

Phipps has found himself with low fuel far from a gas cache, caught in blizzards, and has suffered through the perennial problem of icing conditions. "That's where this business comes in of having to get up on top [of clouds and weather] – you can't argue with icing conditions and clouds, stratus; low stratus and cloud are very severe. Even with de-icing equipment you don't want to stay in it."

Some pilots have stated that the design of airplanes is all wrong, with the pilot sitting in front and the cargo in the back—if you crash you're wearing it. Phipps doesn't think a plane could be designed to hold the cargo in front. "I don't think it would be very practical. A pilot has to be up there where he can see everything; you don't want a bunch of stuff in front of you that obstructs your visibility."

But, like many other pilots, he has experienced the discomfort of "wearing" his cargo when his plane went down. "Oh yes, it's going to come forward. Just tie it down properly. But you get lax after a while. Nothing happens so you relax, then an accident happens. You smarten up.

"On one particular flight I landed at this exploration camp with a Single Otter. I put on a good load, more than the legal weight by a long shot. You had to keep the load well forward in a Single Otter. Then I said, 'I'm going to have a fast coffee before I take off.' While I was having coffee the local crew completely filled the back end of the airplane with more gear and equipment. When I took off the tail was slow coming up. It didn't feel right. I tried to bring the flaps up but I couldn't because the airplane was going into a stall, so I had to fly with part-flap because it was so tail-heavy." In effect, these people had unknowingly risked the pilot's life by putting in the extra cargo without his knowledge.

Although close calls are a part of every northern pilot's job, a pilot must never succumb to panic. "If you ever break, you're done. But you feel like you're close some times." Asked if he knew people who had succumbed to panic, Phipps answers, "If they lost it they probably didn't survive. So you never knew what went through their minds."

The best aircraft Phipps ever used in the North was the Twin Otter. "When I started my company in 1962 in Resolute Bay, using the name of the original Atlas Aviation Limited, I had a Beaver, a very old Beaver. Serial Number 52! And then after that summer I made enough money to put a down payment on a Single Otter. My wife, Fran, had been up to Resolute for a visit—prior to that she held the fort in Ottawa—and when she was going back south I said, 'Get me a line on a Twin Otter.'

"Now Twin Otters were so damned expensive at that time that she thought I was kidding. They were worth $345,000 then, which was a hell of a price. But, the last one I got was close to $700,000. That's only in a period of five years. They became so popular."

When Phipps bought his first Twin Otter in 1966, the registration was CF-WWP, after his initials. The call letters, Whiskey Whiskey Papa, became his instant identification in the North.

Dr. Thorsteinsson laughs when he recalls Weldy asking his opinion about buying a Twin Otter. "In the fall of 1965, Weldy talked to me about Twin Otters. At that time, Beavers and single engine Otters were being chartered for $100 an hour. Phipps said he would have to charge $400 an hour for the Twin, which could only carry the load of a single engine Otter plus half a load more. He asked me for my opinion. I expressed my firm belief that buying a Twin would be one hell of a mistake. But . . . the Twin Otters were what ultimately made him a millionaire. So much for Thorsteinsson's judgement in such matters!"

With the Twin, Weldy could fly IFR (Instrument Flight Rules), it had two engines for added safety, and it travelled at 160 mph compared to the single engine aircraft average speed of 100 mph.

Phipps's admiration for the Twin Otter is boundless. "The Twin Otter made me," he says. "The turbine engines just loved the cold, so it was wonderful. And I put the big wheels on that too. Very short take-off and landing. The Twin Otter was a great success."

The worst plane he had was "unquestionably" the Beech 18. He explains why:

"Before the Twin Otter came off the line, I had been doing a lot of flying with the Single Otter; I just had to get a Twin. The only Twin available that you could get on skis was the Beechcraft. There were no strips big enough . . . well, if you had wheels under you, you had to make sure it was a very short-landing aircraft or a ski aircraft where you could only land on the sea ice. So I ordered a Twin Beech, had skis put on it, but I never cursed an airplane so much in my life.

"We had these flex controls which were frozen solid every morning on the Beech. The only way I could get them freed up was to disconnect the ends, put a hose over and pump alcohol down. I figured that for every hour I was up in the air, I worked about 14 hours on the ground on that damned aircraft." Fran would stand on a piece of plywood to keep her feet warm while she held the light so Weldy could work on the engine.

Not only did the Twin Beech freeze more easily on the ground than other aircraft, but Weldy also had trouble with the controls freezing in flight. "I had to put my feet up on the panel and pull. That happened on one particular trip coming back from Mould Bay to Resolute. It was only about 20 below. I was in the approach to Resolute when the temperature suddenly dropped to 45 or 50 below. I was all set for the approach and when I went to let the throttles off I couldn't budge them! I tried to open them up to overshoot, but couldn't. I had to use brute force on those throttles. Finally I cut the switches, cut the mixture control valves . . . "

He was forced to set down with two dead engines.

"I only had approach power on. Well, I'd have just gone, gone, gone past the strip and everything, so I turned the power off so I could come in on my approach, and when I got to that point I just chopped the engines."

Not exactly a pilot's favourite way to land. But, in defence of the Beechcraft, Phipps admits that he was operating in a very hostile climate and was probably setting a precedent working the airplanes in those conditions.

Fran and the seven Phipps children moved up to live year-round in Resolute in 1968. An eighth child, Terry, was born after the move. They were comfortably housed in ATCO trailer units that had all the amenities of home: electric power and running water. The children attended a local Eskimo school that taught up to grade six, then had to be sent out either to Yellowknife or back to Ontario.

Phipps laughs as he recalls that "during the dark period the kids would say, 'Mom, is it nighttime or daytime?' You couldn't tell."

The routine involved getting up at four in the morning. In the dark period, when there was less business, Fran and Weldy were the only adults who were not government employees in winter residence at Resolute. There were no hangars for their aircraft and mechanical work had to be done regularly in weather well below zero, usually around -30 or colder. Weldy's sister in Ottawa made large heavy canvas engine-covers that offered some protection from the cold and the wind, but that didn't alleviate the problems associated with doing precision work in bitter cold, illuminated by artificial lights.

One problem Phipps did manage to escape that adventurous pilots farther south did not, was trouble with the Feds.

"I was in a strange position because I was so far north that the inspectors didn't want to go up there, so I was left alone. In fact they told me, 'We're not bothering you. We know you have to break the rules or you'd have to shut down, but you've got an excellent record and as long as it stays that way we'll leave you alone. But if you start having accidents we'll be down on you like a ton of bricks.' So fortunately I had a good record and they didn't bother me."

Areas that the federal inspectors were quite sensitive to were flying altitudes, loading restrictions, and major aircraft repairs. Phipps explains the first category:

"With a VFR [Visual Flight Rules] operator's certificate, you had to maintain contact with the ground for navigation. But there was so much fog and stratus in the ocean expanses that you had to climb and fly on top, because if you tried to fly in it you iced up so bad that you wouldn't stay in the sky very long. You couldn't fly under it—you'd be too low and there are some pretty high mountains and stuff around. So, when I had a single engine airplane with a VFR operator's certificate I'd fly over top to stay in the clear, on top of the stratus and cloud, which was illegal. I couldn't see the ground.

"You had to break the rule or you wouldn't be doing very much flying."

Pilots also had to abide by government rules about overloading, made for structural and performance reasons. On this subject, Phipps says, "Well, that's something I was never caught at." He goes on to explain why some rules, however, can be broken without dire consequences. "In the Arctic, in that cold air, it's amazing just what an airplane will carry. Also you get very little turbulence, it's smooth. So an overload's not really a dangerous thing."

Repairs—item number three on the list of inspectors' concerns. Phipps held a "B" licence, "a very scarce licence," which allowed him to certify an aircraft after major repairs or overhauls were done.

"If I'd been sitting up in Resolute without a "B" licence—well, I'd have just gone ahead and done the repairs and said nothing about it, but this way I was legal—for a change. Well, you've got to use some common sense."

In close to 20,000 hours flying time, Weldy Phipps has only crashed once. "That's how I got my strange eye," he says, although the scar is not really noticeable. The mishap occurred on Little Cornwallis Island. Phipps had flown a Super Cub over to the island with a pilot, Steve Standish. He'd informed another pilot, Dick deBlicquy, that he would be back in a week.

"The first day we were over there I picked a landing spot but it was a dirty, windy day, with light rain. So I turned into this thing and I got caught in a wind-shear or some damned thing; the airplane just suddenly flipped and I found myself upside-down. I had full control, but couldn't rectify it, so we went into a side-slip on the one wing.

"I went through the instrument panel and this fellow in the back seat, Steve Standish, he was in bad shape. I managed to get him out onto the ground because we were soaked with gas, afraid we might catch fire. I covered him up with a sleeping bag.

"Then I started wondering, 'How the hell am I going to get in touch with anyone on the radio?' The force of the crash had thrown the radio out of its mounts; it now lay strewn across the ground, along with the batteries. I started gathering all this stuff up, plugging things back in. I didn't have power—the power wire had been pulled—so I had to jerry-rig a power line. I finally got the radio running. I could hear on the receiver but I didn't know if I had a transmitter. I called a couple of times, no answer."

After making his injured passenger as comfortable as possible, Phipps tried calling again and got the weather station advisor. When they answered he told them what had happened and gave them his location, on the northwest coast of Little Cornwallis Island, right next door to Resolute Bay. Dick deBlicquy, at that moment, was on his way to Isachsen with a Beaver full of gas. They contacted him, and he asked if he could deliver the load first and then go back to Resolute. There happened to be a doctor visiting at Resolute, so Dick got the doctor to accompany him on the rescue mission.

"I broke my cheekbone," Phipps says, "and there was a pie-shaped piece of flesh hanging down and the eyeball sitting there. I thought I'd lost the eye."

Back at Resolute the nurse did the best she could, giving Standish shots of morphine. A C-119 Fairchild Packet had taken off from Resolute just a few minutes before; they recalled it to take the two injured men to Churchill.

"I was back flying in about a week's time, but Steve was in the hospital a long time," Phipps says.

He figures the cause of the crash was just "severe turbulence," something no pilot can avoid.

And that is Weldy Phipps's one and only crash, an amazing record considering that by 1971 he had chalked up over 17,000 flying hours, most of it in the Arctic under austere conditions.

Atlas Aviation grew into a good, stable business that could pick and choose its work. "I stayed away from contracts, except for the mail," Phipps says. "I took certain contracts for oil companies, but pretty well stayed away from government contracts that guaranteed, say, 80 hours a month. I was getting 250 hours a month free-lancing, so I could more than double my production, and my revenue, by staying away from contracts that would tie up the airplane."

By the time the Phipps's sold Atlas Aviation in 1972, they had nine pilots working for them and 13 airplanes on the company's inventory.

When asked how aviation has changed the North, Weldy and Fran answer that it "certainly opened it up."

Exploration of the North continues, from expeditions organized by large corporations to small individual "adventures."

"I did a lot of supporting, flying them out," Phipps says. "Every year another expedition came up to do something, walk to the Pole, or ski to the Pole. The Plaisted Expedition was the first one to make it, with snowmobiles. But there were all kinds of harebrained ideas. One guy was going to leave Winnipeg and go up there with a motorcycle by himself. How the hell he was going to even get to Resolute Bay, I don't know."

Most of these explorers were, in Phipps's opinion, grossly unprepared for the conditions. "They had no idea. But the amazing thing was they raised money and everything else for these expeditions."

Aviation has changed the habitat, not only of the people, but of the wildlife that lived in relative isolation before man developed wings. "Well, of course they have a strict limit on the polar bears. Only the Eskimos can hunt them," Phipps says cautiously. But he agrees that the practice of taking a Native along to "use" his licence to hunt occurs frequently. "What they do is they pay the Eskimo a fairly good sum to take them out hunting. So it's under his name then . . . But we were so far north, we didn't have that many people getting up there."

Phipps got to know quite a few Eskimos, and feels that their culture has been nearly destroyed. "I think the government made a big mistake when they thought they were going to educate them and they'd be getting university degrees in one generation or something. They built hostels in the settlements for the kids to live in while they were going to school. I was chartered to go out with the RCMP and land at the Eskimo hunt camps—they lived in groups and went from hunt camp to hunt camp, when one got too filthy they'd move to another one. We'd fly the RCMP out and land in one of these hunt camps, pick up all the kids, load them in the airplane. Older people would be standing there with their mouths open wondering what was going on; they didn't know anything about education. And we'd fly the kids to the settlement.

"Then the older people—they were pretty close-knit families—hitched up their dogs and within a short time came into the settlements themselves! So we had them in the settlement and there was nothing for them.

"They couldn't support themselves because there was no hunting, but they wanted to be with their kids, so the [government] had to provide accommodation for them. Well, a bathtub to an Eskimo is just a damned good place to cut up a seal.

"It caused a horrendous problem, all these people hanging around the settlement with nothing to do, just on welfare. Exploration certainly affected the Eskimo settlements."

Nobody wants to revert back to the old harsh lifestyle. Everyone has an oil furnace, so they need cash for fuel. "Now it's come to the stage that I don't know if they'll ever go back."

Alcohol is a problem—"very much so"—and there are a lot of suicides.

The education the children received did not, in most cases, prove beneficial. "Once they get down south, they don't seem to cope. A lot of them fall by the wayside. It will take time to educate the older generations. First of all to try to get the old people, the parents, anxious for their children to get an education. They could send teachers out to their hunt camps, just do things gradually. I think it could be done, but not the way they did it."

The idea of children and parents being forced apart seems preposterous. "It wouldn't do them any good to object," Phipps says. "The kids would still go. We'd take them back by plane, and the parents would follow by dogs."

There is very little that Weldy Phipps hasn't hauled by airplane in the North, from geologists, to explorers with their dogs, sleighs, and provisions. He has even flown live caribou when the government devised a program to move the animals from Coats Island to Coral Harbour, a settlement on Southampton Island.

"They had been hunted completely out of Southampton, until there wasn't a caribou left, but this other island [Coats Island] had lots of caribou," Phipps explains. "So what they wanted to do was transfer caribou over to Southampton Island and, hopefully, convince the Eskimos not to shoot them all."

The program moved about 100 animals, but it was a difficult procedure for both the animals and the men who did the job.

"A zoologist was in charge of the operation," Phipps recalls. "They had a helicopter and guns that shot darts, drugs that affect the muscles, so they can't run, they can't walk. They'd dart the animals from the helicopter and they'd collapse; the men would haul them to the helicopter and set them on canvas pads, use ropes and ties to secure them, then put them in a net and sling them under the helicopter to a base camp. When they had eight or ten, I'd fly over and pick them up."

Phipps hauled some with a Single Otter, then more with a Twin, getting an average of six animals into the plane at one time. Sometimes, "counting the small ones," they'd load 10.

"But the trouble was, when they slung them over they left them tied, so a lot of hours passed between the time they accumulated them and when I'd pick them up to fly them to Coral Harbour. They'd cramp so bad that they'd injure their legs trying to get up.

"They finally made a corral, and when they got the animals into camp they'd put them in the corral so they could walk around. Then they had to catch and hog-tie them again, and tranquillize them to take them into the aircraft.

"When we'd put them in the airplane they'd break the stubs of their little antlers and bleed like stuck pigs. That was something awful. Blood and crap all over, Jesus. Even on my charts. You've got a caribou with a broken horn bleeding like mad, and everything's all blood. What a job."

That was Phipps's only live wild-animal-transport job. His first, and his last.

There is a saying that "the North is great for men and dogs, but it kills women and horses." But Fran Phipps says she had a great time in Resolute and wouldn't trade the experience for anything. Not only was she a partner and helpmate to her husband, keeping their business running smoothly, but she also participated in many exciting adventures.

The Phipps's were the only white family with children living in Resolute at that time. "They wouldn't allow families when Weldy first went up," Fran explains. "When it became apparent he was going to stay and work over the winter, he just said, 'Come.' When I first went up we were offered a little shack belonging to Nord-Air of Montreal, so we used that for part of a season. When we formed our own camp to provide accommodation for our crew, which swelled in the summer and diminished in the winter, we got permission to have it on the base as part of the base itself."

Fran Phipps says that she never ran into social problems in the North and felt quite safe at all times. "There's a certain chivalry. If you act properly, they act properly with you."

At first Fran looked after the books and cooked for the camp, but it became impossible to keep up with the office work, seven children, and everything else. "We had a multitude of jobs, organizing freight, loading freight, cooking when the cooks quit, just endless chores.

The bulk of their goods were brought in once a year, in August, on sea-lift. This necessitated sitting down and figuring out the number of cases of food required. Fresh supplies came in every week on the Nord-Air flight out of Montreal.

Atlas Aviation was kept busy, especially during the summer months, "ferrying around geologists and prospectors with their big grubstakes." Weldy would take them out, land them, and go back for them at the allotted time, often several months later.

Fran kept track of these appointments on a chart in the office, and ensured that no rendezvous was ever missed, for the passenger's very life depended on the reliability of the air service scheduled to pick him up.

"Between 1962 and 1978, the company's fleet had grown from one Beaver, to a Single Otter, a Super Cub, five Twin Otters, three DC-3s, one Apache and one Aztec," Weldy said. "The company's operations were confined mainly to the Queen Elizabeth Islands, North Greenland and to the True North Pole."

On 4 April 1971, Fran Phipps was the first woman to set foot on the North Pole.

Weldy explains that celestial navigation, or the global navigation system, "will put you there within nothing, very easy to do," so it is possible to ascertain when you are actually on the North Pole. "If you're three or four miles off, that doesn't mean anything," Phipps says. "The ice is drifting all the time, so if you put a marker there, tomorrow it could be 15 miles away."

Phipps had previously flown to the North Pole in 1970, and had entertained the idea of setting up tour flights to that esoteric destination in the ski-equipped Twin Otter, flying from Resolute Bay to Lake Hazen on Ellesmere Island, then to the Pole. The weather and other climactic difficulties, however, convinced him that the plan was not feasible as there were no fuel stops. "I had to carry fuel with me all the way, otherwise I couldn't get back."

Their purpose for flying to the Pole in 1971 was to set up a radio beacon to help guide pilots. Weldy, Fran, and another pilot flew up, landed as close as possible, and got out and walked around on the ice.

"We sat and made ourselves a cup of tea," Fran says, "put a flag up, and took pictures. *Time-Life* magazine did a story on it, took a picture and put it in the magazine. The sad part about this whole thing is the only picture we have is in the magazine. There was a photographer there [when we came back to Alert] who asked me for my roll of film; I gave it to him and he promised to send us back copies but we never got the copies.

"Another pilot went with us and he did the same thing; he gave away his film to this photographer and they printed all these things and never sent back copies. Weldy's sister went on our behalf to the archives in Ottawa, but there was nothing available. They have only what *Time-Life* put out in the magazine."

"When Fran came with me to the Pole, I was going to fly a party up a couple of days after that if I hadn't experienced hitches on this trip," Phipps explains. "I had a radio beacon, and I thought I could go up ahead and put a tent at the Pole. I had a landing spot all picked.

"We put the tent up, installed the beacon and a propane heater, along with a big battery pack that should have lasted for weeks—and I don't know what the hell happened! When we came back up we couldn't receive the beacon, so the tent, the beacon, and all the rest of it are still out there."

He tried to cache fuel, which would work if you could ever find the caches. "It's incredibly difficult to spot a cache on the ice. The ice drifts, breaks and shifts, and the pressure ridges build.

"I put out another beacon for the Plaisted Expedition from Minnesota,[3] and took a solar generator unit worth $35,000 to keep the beacon running. Couldn't find it."

Four hundred miles of ice. "Yeah, that's all it is," Phipps says.

His knowledge of the Arctic prompted Weldy Phipps to run for a seat on the Northwest Territories Council; his campaign got him elected in December 1970, and he found himself representing a widely dispersed population of approximately 2,500 people in the High Arctic region.

"I was the worst council member they ever had, I think. All they did at a council meeting was debate the budget," he says. "Well, the budget was compiled in Ottawa and there was no way the council could change it. So why

Weldy Phipps picking up Plaisted Expedition at True North Pole, 1968. *Weldy Phipps Collection*

spend all your time debating it when there were other things that were far far more important?"

The prevalent issues were, he felt, the social conditions of the Natives. Phipps was also concerned about the lack of local labour being hired for northern projects, and felt that to some extent the territorial government contributed to this negative situation. Health issues concerned him as well, and he noted that encroaching white civilization had brought in tuberculosis, measles, and mumps, and a variety of venereal diseases. He reported on the severity of the situation in an article published in the Toronto Telegram in 1963.

Phipps felt that southern laws did not make much sense to the Natives. "For instance, in Resolute Bay this one Eskimo was a real bad actor. He was charged with assaulting his wife, and then for raping a 13-year-old girl. Usually they couldn't find anyone who'd testify, because the Eskimo women were afraid they'd get a worse beating if they did, but his wife did testify. He got a $10 fine, his wife got a $15 witness fee, so he was up five bucks on the deal. He was released back into the community then, a minor hero."

Looking back on their career in the North, both Fran and Weldy feel it was a great adventure. "And our kids feel the same way. Something that they'd really like their children to see." Both, however, agree that there is a time to come out.

"But it's a funny thing," Fran says. "When you come out you can hardly wait to get back in again."

Fran acknowledges that the Arctic has its own beauty. "I guess you take it for granted when you're there. You come down south and see the trees and the shopping centres and the big terminals and everything down around Montreal, but once you get away from that and get back up into the Arctic it has its awesome beauty. It's hard to explain."

"We'd take the Nord-Air flight back," Phipps says, "and that's something else that had been established—a big airline running up to the North. For years we didn't have anything like that. To get a part for an aircraft, we'd try to have it flown up in the air force plane; but that system was hit or miss. But once Nord-Air started scheduled runs out of Montreal to Frobisher Bay and Resolute Bay, that helped a lot."

Although there are now "major facilities" in places like Pond Inlet and other settlements, the economy of the North has taken a sharp downturn. "Since the oil business has died, I don't know if very much is being done, if anything, in the way of development," Phipps says. "Everything seems to have slowed right down. I got out at the right time, I guess."

When the Phipps's sold Atlas Aviation in 1972, it signalled the end to their northern—and Weldy Phipps's flying—adventures.

"Strangely enough," says Phipps, "when I sold out they wrote in the contract that I couldn't do anything involving aircraft for five years. Well, airplanes had been my whole damned life! I have a top engineer's licence so I could have gone into engineering. But no, the only thing I could do connected with airplanes was buy an airline ticket. And, as time went on I just didn't get around to going back to work."

They found that there is, however, "life after the North," and adapted to the culture and climate "south of 60." The family moved to Prince Edward Island for 10 years, where they bought a sailboat and learned to scuba-dive. "Our spinnaker sail had the old colours of the airplane, dark blue and yellow and dark red," Fran says. "We'd chosen them because they would show up against the white snow in the Arctic if we were ever down. A totally practical idea. Also, the sun warms up dark surfaces first, taking off the frost. If you've got a white airplane, the frost will stay on it for hours."

After some deliberation they decided to name the boat "Whiskey Papa" after the good-luck call-letters of their first Twin Otter, WWP. "We thought if anyone heard the name of our boat they'd associate it with Whiskey Whiskey Papa of the North, but no one ever said anything about it."

Life in Prince Edward Island was a complete turnaround from the pace they'd experienced in the Arctic. "They're really laid back in PEI. They want things to continue in the old traditional way," Fran says. "But when you think of it, the reason you went there is because you were attracted to what it is, not because you wanted to go in and change it. After we'd lived there for a while, I thought, 'how can we go in . . . it's like people trying to change the Eskimo ways, asking, 'don't you want something better? Don't you want to be upgraded?'"

The Phipps's learned firsthand that one can become a northerner easier than one can become a maritimer. "You have to be born there. Otherwise, you're always 'from away.'"

Weldy and Fran now live on a boat and in a tent. "We dock at West Palm Beach, Riviera Beach, wherever we happen to be," Fran says. "In the summer when it's too hot in Florida we camp in the North, and in the fall we go back and move onto the boat and put our tent away."

Fran and Weldy went back North a few years ago, as far as Pond Inlet. "We got an offer to go up when we happened to be in Ottawa visiting. We got in late at night and everything was closed; we couldn't go to the Co-op or to the Hudson's Bay store and talk to anybody," Fran recalls. "We walked around, and there was only one Eskimo woman who, when I mentioned Weldy's name, had heard of us. She recognized the name and said, 'Oh yes, you flew my daughter,' but we didn't know her—you don't remember the passengers unless it's someone you know.

Weldy and Fran Phipps, taken at the campground where they were staying in Calgary, August, 1992. *Collection of the author*

"So we just went to our hotel and had dinner, strolled around, and talked to some people in the terminal before we flew out the next morning."

Weldy was astounded at the number of changes, especially to the airport. "They'd changed it all since I'd gone in. They'd put in real facilities in these places. I was operating from strips I'd prepared myself, with the help of the local mechanic, picking off stones, levelling things up. The strip I'd used for years in Pond Inlet, I couldn't even find! Everything had changed so much. They've got major strips up there now."

Although Phipps flew right up to the time they sold the airline in 1972, he has flown only once since then.

"My friend, Dick deBlicquy, flew down for a visit in a Cessna 172, and I flew that, but that's all."

Weldy Phipps would be considered one of Canada's top "bush" pilots, even though much of the territory he flew over was as barren as the surface of the moon. "You could call me just a northern flyer, I guess," Phipps says. "But they still referred to us as bush pilots because we had to rely on our own navigational skills for the most part—find landing spots, get in, get out. And I did some of what you'd call bush flying when I started out many years ago, in Ontario and Quebec."

The man who humbly calls himself "just a northern flyer," in addition to winning the McKee Trans-Canada Trophy in 1961 for his contribution to the advancement of Canadian aviation, was named a member of Canada's Aviation Hall of Fame in 1973 and a Companion of the Order of Flight (City of Edmonton). In 1976 he was appointed a Member of the Order of Canada.

Not a bad record, for a man who turned the experience of being a prisoner-of-war into a multi-million-dollar flying enterprise. He's made money, sure, but he and his family have also enjoyed the unique opportunity of seeing the world from its highest to lowest altitudes, from the extremes of High Arctic ice and snow, to the shoals and reefs of the warm Florida waters.

Who could ask for anything more?

Weldy Phipps following his induction into the Canadian Aviation Hall of Fame in 1973. *Canadian Aviation Hall of Fame*

Notes

1. An assembly of three or more fan cameras set at fixed angles for wide lateral coverage with overlapping images.
2. Lieutenant Adolphus W. Greely, an American, was commissioned to head one of 14 international circumpolar scientific stations that resulted from the second international Polar Conference held in Berne, Switzerland, in 1880. The following summer, Greely and his party sailed north in the *Proteus*. The men and supplies were off-loaded at Lady Franklin Bay in northeastern Ellesmere Island where Greely established a base camp, which he named Fort Conger.

   Plans called for the party to remain there for two years. A relief ship was due to resupply the party in the summer of 1882, but this failed to materialize because of adverse ice conditions in the region. By the fall of 1883, Greely was greatly concerned over the possibility of another failure of the relief vessel to reach his party and decided to move his men to a more southern latitude. Fort Conger was abandoned in August 1883, and the party, using small boats, reached Cape Sabine some 220 miles to the south, on the east coast of Ellesmere Island. There the Greely Expedition spent the following winter under appalling circumstances. Out of 25 men, Greely and six others were finally rescued by the *Thetis* in June of 1884, the remainder having died mainly from starvation.
3. Ralph Plaisted, a Minnesotan, was the head of a United States–Canadian expedition that travelled from Ward Hunt Island (north Ellesmere Island) to the North Pole in the spring of 1968. Plaisted reached the Pole on 19 April using motorized speed sleds (snowmobiles) and air-dropped supplies by Weldy Phipps. He followed more or less along the same route as Robert E. Peary in 1909. However, Peary's claim to have reached the Pole is now largely discredited, and Plaisted is now credited with having made the first surface travel from land to the Pole.

The Jackpine Savage

*F*EW *PILOTS HAVE SURVIVED 16* "uncontrolled landings" in
one of the most unforgiving terrains in the world—Canada's
North. Jimmy Anderson has, but he's "never left a plane in the bush, or injured
a passenger" in over 20,000 hours of flying time.

Anderson's physical appearance is as interesting as his stories, and has
inspired journalists to stretch their word-power to portray a visual description
of the man:

> In the late afternoon light, the veteran's face is as heavily creased and travelled
> as a topographic map and his nose is battered from taking a compass on the
> beak. His voice is as coarse as a cement mixer and his upper gums are
> distinguished by a solitary front tooth, rotten and teetering like an old
> wooden picket . . .
>
> Anderson's right hand is gnarled and missing its pinkie finger—the
> result of arm-wrestling a chainsaw 20 years ago—and his left hand is badly
> scabbed from a recent welding torch burn. And, oh, yeah, he smokes and
> drinks too much, too.[1]

What does it take to be a bush pilot? A late friend of Anderson's used to
say, "If you find some stupid s.o.b. who's not good for anything, make a bush
pilot out of him!" Anderson might agree. But he's specific about what being a
bush pilot really entails.

"A lot of guys call themselves bush pilots just because they fly over it," he
says, disparagingly, "but they often have an airstrip to go to." His own standard
of professionalism is considerably different: a bush pilot's a guy who can take
a trapper or a prospector out to his territory, make arrangements to pick him
up at a certain date, perhaps land him in another camp or bring him in at the
end of the season, and *be there*. In plain language, a bush pilot can land where
nobody else would dare: pick spots, understand them, get in and out, and come
back.

Lyle James Anderson, a.k.a. Midnight, a.k.a. Jackpine Savage, a.k.a. just
Jimmy, was born in Milden, Saskatchewan, on 13 March 1926. "I always say
I'm 26, 'cause I was born in '26," Jimmy grins from beneath his trademark
oil-spotted, flat-crowned Stetson. So how did this prairie boy learn the rugged

Jimmy "Midnight" Anderson. *Jimmy Anderson Collection.*

rock piles of British Columbia so intimately that he could land his Super Cub on mountain tops, gravel bars, in the lofty spires of spruce trees—hence the name given both him and his plane: "Jackpine Savage"—and even in nightmare spots like a river in a box canyon—at midnight—winning him his other nickname of "Midnight"?

Anderson credits an unforgettable experience as spurring his interest in airplanes. He was three years old when he was taken for his first airplane ride, in an open-cockpit aircraft flown by an early barnstormer visiting rural communities to take local people for rides. "I know it didn't happen, but I saw the airplane fly across town toward where we were standing in the schoolyard, shoot high into the air, then fly *backwards* down the flag pole. Then it took off again. I can see that right now. It didn't happen, of course, but that's the concept I got as a kid."

That incident determined Anderson's whole course. "Three years old, and since then I always wanted to fly," he says. A tattered—and treasured—old photograph shows Jimmy "hardly out of rompers," standing proudly with his father and uncle beside the open-cockpit airplane.

Anderson's father operated a livery stable in Milden. When the family moved to Fort St. John, BC, in 1930, they occupied one of the most northerly homesteads in the Cecil Lake area.

"We had horses, and the old man always had his mules. I had my own horse, a buckskin, when I was five years old."

After horses came trucking. He learned by driving a neighbour's truck around the yard until he knew the gears, then hauled gravel at Taylor Flats for construction of the Peace River bridge. Truckdriving contracts for construction of the Alaska Highway followed. When he turned 16 someone discovered he didn't have a driver's licence. Anderson didn't know he needed one—"You could have the best driver's licence in the world and you wouldn't drive on the Alaska Highway if you didn't have a U.S. Army permit. When I went to get my licence I showed them that permit and they wrote the licence out, just like that."

His parents opened a lodge at Mile 147 on the new Alaska Highway, and the family operation continued for many years until the lodge burned down.

In 1944 Anderson joined the army. When they sent him to the Canadian Infantry Basic Training Centre, he was livid. "A foot slogger!" he says disgustedly. He immediately asked for, and got, a transfer to the airborne paratroopers, but in Shiloh, Manitoba, he broke his foot on the assault course. Next he joined the 6th Division for duty in the Pacific, but before his training was completed, the war was over. Early in 1946 he got a farm leave and returned to the North. He was in the services not quite two years.

In 1949 he got his own trucks with "Jimmy Anderson" stencilled on the doors. He went trucking up the Alaska Highway, hauling oil equipment and horses. "That's when my cowboying came in," he says. "We used to break horses on the way to Alaska for pack horses and saddle horses—every night we had a rodeo."

He began taking flying lessons in Dawson Creek in 1957, but completed the course in Fort St. John. "I think I had only 30 hours flight training, all that was required. It's not much."

Was he a natural flyer right from the beginning? "Nobody is," he says emphatically, "but it all depends on how interested you are. I'd rent a plane from the Fort St. John flying club to start out, and away I'd go. I was on a student permit yet. Well, Jesus, I was doing more on that student permit than a lot of guys who had pilots' licences! I would want to go out some place so I'd tell them where I was heading, and fly across country. I was behaving with the airplane—I wasn't going jam-ramming or anything—and they trusted me."

He tells of his first flying excursion:

"Norm Hill, an instructor with the flying club in Fort St. John, bought a plane in Peace River, and he wanted me to drive down with him and fly it back. I was a pilot then, but damned green. We landed in a field at Grimshaw where they were constructing the Mackenzie Highway, so Norm could meet a friend.

"Norm's plane was a J-3—a forerunner of a Super Cub, you might say—and it could get in and out of good tight places."

Anderson went back to Peace River to gas up the airplane, and when he landed he was told the Mounties were looking for him. The Grimshaw farmer had phoned the police to say that an airplane had landed in his field and had knocked his crop down.

He knew the crop hadn't been damaged, because he'd landed in a little scrubby patch of the field where growth was light. "You can't land in a standing crop without upsetting the airplane—it would have got tangled up in the wheels."

So they phoned the farmer, who by that time had checked things out and discovered that his crop wasn't ruined at all. "But," he'd added, "I don't want guys thinking they can use my field for an airport!"

It was the first example of Anderson's knack for landing in tight places, and for gaining the attention of the law, an aspect of his career he is sensitive about.

But that wasn't the end of Anderson's adventure on this flight. The magneto started acting up. "It wasn't working good anyway," Anderson rationalizes. "Also, we had the other magneto. Very seldom will the second magneto quit. It's something like being out in a car, which, after all, only has one distributor and one coil, and it runs good. So why won't an airplane run good with one magneto?

"Old Norman had just bought the airplane and he didn't want it crunched yet. He wanted to ground the plane, but I said, 'I ain't riding back in the car with you.' So I jumped into the airplane and flew it back on one magneto to Fort St. John. But I followed the road pretty well all the way back; I was in good country and there was no reason to worry. I could have landed in lots of places—on the road, any place. You don't take no chances."

Anderson has since had magneto problems a number of times, mostly with other people's airplanes. "It usually occurs when you're out in the bush; you take it off, take it apart, clean it up a little and think it will be all right, but you're not even supposed to do that."

The first airplane Anderson owned was a Piper Super Cub; he's since had "a whole bunch" of Super Cubs. After he'd crunch one, he'd trade it in. He paid for his planes through his guiding and outfitting business, Anderson's Mile 147 Lodge, which he and his brother Ben took over from their parents. Flying, plus some rig work, brought in extra money.

In his lifetime Anderson has owned five Piper Super Cubs; a Waco, which he bought as a wreck; and his present airplane, a Piper Cherokee 6-300, which he calls "bad medicine for a bush pilot, with nowhere near the versatility of the Super Cub—you can get them in there but can't get them out—low wing, too big, too fast." Anderson swears by Super Cubs, and was one of the first pilots in the area to fly them with big rubber tires. That he's still here to tell the tales attests to the aircraft's—and his—versatility.

There were limits to the flying jobs he'd do, but the definitions become hazy. "I never did haul grub to a rig. Well, I won't say that, I did. Jobs would come along and I'd just go, but I never was commercial.

"I've flown from one side of a river to another on gravel bars, moving stuff across so the pack horses could swim and then the cowboys could repack them. *That ain't a very long flight.* A lot of guys would never do that."

He refused to take jobs he considered boring or scheduled—"just turning around and going and flying people some place."

When he began flying, Anderson spent a year working for Don Peck, who ran the Trutch Lodge at Mile 200. Flying Peck's Super Cub through the Tuchodi Lake area along the Rocky Mountain Continental Divide taught Anderson about working in the mountains. "I like the mountains," Jimmy says, "You've got side-walls to hold you in."

He recalls landing on lake ice so slippery that the airplane skidded right off the lake and into the buckbrush lining the shore, then straightening out bent props by removing the chinking from between logs in abandoned cabins, and sticking the propeller blade between the logs.

Peck himself wasn't a pilot, although he owned the airplanes as part of the operation of his lodge. In fact, he considered flying "a necessary evil." When Anderson eventually got busy with other flying jobs, Peck hired another pilot—and another one. Anderson was then brought back on occasion to bring Peck's wrecks out of the bush, patch them up, and get them down to Edmonton for repairs. "Things like that happen," Anderson says, referring to the number of planes wrecked in the bush. Then he adds, defensively, "I'm not the only one that had them problems up there!"

"When you start off flying you're Fair," is Anderson's analysis. "After a while you get Pretty Good, then you get Extra Good, then you get Excellent, and then you get Immaculate. Then you scare the shit out of yourself and you're Fair again. Right now I'm a little below Fair."

Anderson has an interesting and diverse family, and they have weathered some difficult times, wondering when—or if—they'd again hear Jimmy's Super Cub buzz over the home lodge at Mile 147. None of them have chosen to follow Jimmy's flying career and acquire wings.

His family may or may not agree with journalists' hyperbolic descriptions of Anderson's physical appearance, but they don't deny many of the reports of his aeronautical experiences, some of which have recently been chronicled by his son, Jamie, in a book titled *Outlaw Pilot*.

"Anderson's reputation as a bush pilot is larger than life," agrees *San Jose Mercury-News* journalist Tom Harris in an article published 27 July 1975. "Certainly [his reputation] dwarfs the man's stature, a slight five-foot-eight-inch frame perched under a weather-beaten Stetson. He has taken on jobs and dares that do not sit well with that careful image pilots in such a dangerous land are working hard to mould. Anderson, to them, is reckless and dangerous and conveys that image to a public that might be more interested in less excitement than he offers. The chain-smoking Anderson seems unruffled by this lack of acceptance by his peers. 'Let them fly their way, and I'll fly mine,' he says."

The stories told, and substantiated, about Anderson's experiences are "mind-boggling," states the reporter: "He has landed upside down in a raging mountain river, parked his Super Cub in the spires of a nest of scrub pine 40 feet off the ground, and yawns at recollections of landing and taking off from virtual mountain tops with no more room than a large city backyard. What gets him in trouble with his peers is accepting dares to do things like land his airplane on a flatbed truck rolling down the Alaska Highway at 40 miles an hour.

"'What I do with my life is my business,' responds Anderson. 'But I never take chances with my customers, and I've never had anyone injured by my flying.'

"When one watches him rescue a stranded rafter shivering to death on a tiny river sandbar and complete a take-off into the face of a nearby sheer cliff, it is hard to argue the point."

When asked to relate some close calls he's had, times that scared him, Anderson becomes stoical. "Well, you haven't got time to be scared," he says. "You do a little shaking after you get to the ground. But when I was down on the Akie River that time with Jim Radley [a prospecting partner], I knew we were having one of those—what do you call them? close calls—when we were trying to flip the plane over in the river, to get it back on its feet, and I was doing the backstroke under water . . . "

Anderson sketches out the basic details, like a journal summary: "September 1966—down for seven days in the Akie River, across the Continental Divide, about 50 miles east of Fort Ware. Plane upside-down in middle of river."

When asked what seems like a silly question, "How did you end up that way?" Anderson's answer is frank and honest: "By a mistake."

With some persuasion, he tells the whole story.

"The Akie is about 60 air miles west of Pink Mountain. Just across the Rockies. I had formed a prospecting partnership with Jim Radley, and Bill Young, who owned the Frontier Hotel in Fort St. John. We'd been doing a bit of prospecting in there so one day Radley and I went out to look at the place, just going to fly out and back, never took anything with us. Never even had boots in the plane. We were going to land on a gravel bar, stake claims.

"If I'd have landed the first time over, or the second time, I'd have been all right. But I always check it two or three times. The third time I came on in. The reason I checked it that much was because I should have come in upriver and landed on the bar but we had unstable winds, picking up then slacking off."

Anderson landed at one end of the bar, bouncing over brush and rubbish, small poles and rocks. "I came in and landed and bunkered down and psst! If I'd have hit the brakes I'd have still been all right, but I just let it roll a little bit. We only had 200 feet, but it was plenty because the wind was pretty good; I got it touched down and the wind picked up. Wham! It took the weight off the wheels again.

"The brakes were locked and the gravel was spewing, so I dropped the flaps, hit the throttle, and was going to make a run for it. Take off into the wind. Then the wind receded."

The receding wind caused him to lose his lift. "I had no choice. I just kept boring it anyway. I picked it up and it hung on the prop, but to avoid rolling it into the rock pile, I had to make a little bit of a turn." This all occurred in a split second.

When the wheels touched the water he was over far enough—except for some big boulders right at the edge of the river. The wheels hit, hooked on a boulder, and they were upside-down.

Luckily the men were uninjured. They jumped out into water just over their heads, and started pulling on the airplane.

"When we got our feet on the ground we pulled the plane over a little way farther, and we just about got it right up to shore, then gurgle gurgle, the wings filled with water and it sunk.

"No supplies. We even had oxfords on! Damned fools."

They had nothing to eat, but, as Anderson sardonically recalls, "We had lots of water."

And then the weather turned bad. First they lit a fire. Then they built a shelter caved into a little water-wash, by taking out a root or two, laying some spruce boughs on the ground, then placing the cowling of the airplane and some branches over top for protection from the rain. They had only crude tools: a hunting knife, a pair of pliers, an eight-inch crescent wrench, and axes but no file, so very quickly the axes became dull and almost useless. "I never take my axes out of the airplane, no matter what, but somebody must have taken away the file I always pack for the axes. You can find a file in my airplane right to this very day, I never travel without one. And our firearms, they never come out either."

At that time, Anderson always flew with a .45 Colt and a .357 Magnum, short guns. Never long-barrelled guns. He cites a time when a friend went down with "the old faithful," a long-barrelled 30.30 rifle that proved useless. "His barrel got bent in the wreck, so of course they didn't get anything to eat because the damned thing would shoot around a corner. Just wouldn't work. You've really got to have a wreck before you can bend a barrel on a pistol!"

Anderson's knowledge of wilderness survival, together with the two guns and ammunition, were invaluable. When the weather went bad they knew that game wouldn't travel, so anything in the area would likely stay put. When the clouds lifted, they spotted a mountain goat on a rock bluff across the river, up 75 feet or so; they'd see the goat, then the fog would come back and they'd lose him.

"Well, that's sandwich meat," Anderson said to Radley. "I'll swim the river, go around, and come up the back-side of the bluff. I want to shoot him downhill so he'll fall off the ledge into the river, not hang on the ledge. Then you can swim out and we're set. Get him to shore and we'll eat."

That plan didn't work, but then the weather started to break, bringing the sun out early in the morning, and game along with it. When the men crawled out of their wickiup, they almost smacked head-on into two moose "coming to beat hell."

"You always try to think ahead," Anderson says. "We were on their trail, on one of their main runs. Get one person to guard the trail, the other to pull the trigger, and you get something to eat. But they were too fast. Radley was standing right beside the trail. I was going to take off to block the other trail when they came right up the bank, along the river! The moose started to prance around a little. First thing I see is Jim slipping the old .357 by my nose. I dropped back and started shooting too.

"Everything went to hell. They took off. I called out, 'Follow them!' because I thought they'd be on the other trail, so I blazed some more and by God they took to the river and they crossed. The river looped, tight turns in the mountains, and they crossed again; they got to the bank on the other side and they stayed there.

"So all day we watched them things."

The moose, in turn, were watching them, but as the following day wore on Anderson noticed there was only one moose keeping vigil. He thought they might have hit one but he couldn't be sure.

Later in the day they decided to "do an ambush job," with Radley going out on the gravel bar, keeping the moose's attention on him, and Anderson venturing up the river into "grizzly haven." "In all my career I'd never seen more grizzlies in an area than there was there," Anderson recalls. "We always slept using our pistols for pillows—we never let them get too far away—and we'd always keep a little bit of a fire going. We'd get up in the morning and there would be grizzly tracks all the way around the fire, about six feet away. Average-sized grizzly tracks, some good ones but mostly average, just kind of curious. They didn't bother us, there was plenty of food around. They had more than we did.

"If they hadn't been so tough and mean," Anderson adds, "we'd have probably tore down on one, though I'm not much for grizzly steak. But if it had been necessary we'd have sat up all night. It wasn't fear that we didn't try, but you want to get damned close before you shoot. Whereas a moose or something will take off, if you tried that with a grizzly he might decide to have you to lunch. We had enough problems without looking for more. So that's how come we waited for the moose."

There was no hope that a search and rescue party would be out looking for them. This was 1966—"there wasn't too much for search and rescue in those days. That was normal."

They weren't even sure they had logged their flight. "There was a screw-up in that because I'd mentioned to the family that we'd be back that night, but they'd been kind of sleeping so they weren't too sure what my plans had been. Also, we hadn't wanted everybody and his dog to know where we were staking claims. The family had phoned Bill Young in St. John and he'd said, 'Don't worry about it. Jim Radley said when he got Anderson into the mountains they were going to stay there till they finished the job.'

"So this is how these things go. Since that time I always—always—say what I'm going to be doing. If you say you might do this or might do that, then nobody knows. But you take one plan and stay by that, come hell or high water—which was just about what we were experiencing."

It was September, cold and raining. They had no food, poor clothing, guns and ammunition, axes but no file, and their airplane lay upside-down, the wheels in the air, the engine in the Akie River.

They first turned the fuel valve to the 'off' position to air-lock it. The next task was to drain the water from the gas. The only vent was in the wing-tank gas cap, so they raised the tail to drain the wing tanks. When they saw a little slick appear, they'd lower the tail a little, preferring to retain water rather than lose gas.

The next job was to put the airplane back on its feet. To do this, they needed to dig a hole in the river bottom, push the airplane's nose into it, and flip it over, "otherwise we couldn't do it. A horse couldn't even pull it over." They made shovels to dig with by chopping stumps, whittling the trunks into handles and using the widened stumps for the shovels. For a dredge they used a plywood freight-board out of the airplane, burning holes into the wood so they could loop ropes to it.

But how does one dig a seven-foot hole in a waist-deep running river; then, without winches, flip over a 1,000-pound airplane—with the fuel and water in the wings adding further weight?

"If you left the hole too long, the current would come along and fill it up with water. Right next to the shore the water wasn't too fast, so we packed rocks and tried to shore it up—but water still leaked in."

Then they hit on a plan to flip the airplane: they removed the prop so it wouldn't become bent more than it already was. They threw a rope on the wheel—that was Radley's end. To attempt to push the nose down into the hole—that was Anderson's end—Anderson would submerge himself in the water, grab the engine, and when he was ready to lift he'd blow bubbles. When Radley saw the signal, he'd pull on the wheel rope.

Their first try was unsuccessful. Anderson spewed out bubbles, Radley started pulling, but Anderson admits he didn't have a good hold on the engine. "First dunking, it's cold."

But down he went, under water, to give it one more shot.

"The bubbles went and, God, I could feel it coming finally! I got my head above water and Radley done everything he could, trying to jerk it down. One more try! We got it a little ways and down the nose came, into the hole, and she flipped over.

"So there we were with the plane right-side-up, but we were farther out in the river. We got the plane anchored so it wouldn't run away on us, turned it around and brought it back to shore. Once we got it up there we said, 'to hell with it, we're looking good, we don't care if anybody comes out or not!'"

It had taken three days to get the airplane upright and out of the water. Then there were repairs to make—with sore muscles and empty stomachs.

"But getting back to our grub. On the fourth day, Jim's over on the gravel bar keeping these animals looking at us and I'm back in the bush, being careful so I don't wake a sleeping bear, watching for moose to ambush. All of a sudden right in front of me I hear a hell of a noise. I'd spooked a partridge! It flew over and sat on the stump, cluck, cluck, cluck. I was ready to shoot, I was aimed already, but if I'd hit something like that I wouldn't even find a feather.

"So I made a run for it and broke out into this clearing and looked . . . and there wasn't a damned thing there. Jim signalled that they'd gone.

"But I happened to look toward an old beaver dam and bushy area, and I saw something. A moose! It was the one we'd shot at and wounded, and it had come here and died. Moose will always stay by water, or they'll go to water. And the other animal, the companion, nine times out of ten will stay with it. If you come along it will lead you away, like a chicken will; a lot of people don't know they'll do that. And that's what that other one had done, but when I came out of the bush it had spooked and got out of there immediately.

"I signalled to Jim, 'Come over—lunch will be on when you get here.' I lit a fire right away and went to work skinning it out and butchering it."

They realized that their meat would attract the grizzly bears—"everything will attract the grizzly bears, and they were stalking around it, too"—but they were ready. Anderson says it would have taken a hell of a bear to take that meat away from them.

Anderson and Radley worked feverishly getting the airplane into flying condition. They opened the two wing petcocks and drained them until just gas started to flow, shaking the airplane by the wing struts to get rid of all the water. They took the sediment bowl off and, one at a time, turned the wing tank valves until straight gas came out; they'd wiggle the airplane around until they had filled a one-quart oil can with the gas-water mixture, then pour the gas back into the tank. When they got down to the water that settled in the lower part of the can, they threw it away. They repeated the process countless times, through the inter-tanks—the little tanks that come down from the wing tanks—right down to the carburettor.

They heated the engine to dry the condensation, then heated it again, not letting any more water in, keeping it closed tight.

Their campfire smouldered steadily, cooking their meat. "Whichever way you liked your steak, you just ran over to that old fire, took your knife and cut off a chunk of meat—burnt, rare, medium, or raw, depending on how far you cut up the shank."

In the meantime, they cleared and burned debris off their strip, including logs that had come down the river and were embedded in the gravel bar. By the time they had the strip ready for take-off, the river had come up, and "things started to add up pretty good."

When Radley made a move to get into the airplane without bringing anything with him, Anderson chided him, "You're a real dude! We came in here with none of that—where's our travellin' grub?" So back he went for the meat.

Their adventures weren't over, however. Because they'd floated downriver, they had to taxi to reach the gravel bar where they had intended to land in the first place. From the cockpit, Anderson waited for Radley, who stood outside to do a final check for obstructions. Radley gave a little reef on the wing, but before he could clamber into the airplane the tail end swung around, hit him in the back end, and threw him back into the river.

They finally made it off the gravel bar and flew over to guide-outfitter Donny Beattie's "top" hunting camp just off the Continental Divide, where they landed to check things out. Anderson discovered that the sediment bowl was filled with water that hadn't completely drained out of the gas line, and they were about a quarter inch from flooding out. Too close. He drained the screened sediment bowl and put it back on, then borrowed some gas.

Then they hit a rainstorm near Beattie's "base" camp. "We couldn't out-climb it so we got beneath it to about 1,000 feet, then started climbing gently to 10,100 feet. Finally I saw some lights on the Alaska Highway and I said, 'Jim, right now I wouldn't give a damn if the engine fell right out of this thing!' I felt my seat come back two inches, and he barked into my ear, 'Don't talk so goddamned loose!'

"We came on in and buzzed the place at 12 midnight—that's where the 'midnight' stuff comes in again, see. The plane was shaking like crazy as we landed. But I taxied back down, spun it around, and said, 'To hell with it. We're here.'"

They grabbed their gear—"which didn't amount to a hell of a lot, some nice moose steaks"—and went up to the lodge. They were a very welcome sight.

The next morning an examination of the airplane, to see what had caused it to "go haywire" just before landing, revealed that they'd lost a cylinder. The primer plug had fallen out of the block, and a spark plug was loose—"two things in the one jug."

"We must have missed checking one spark plug and the primer plug on the same jug. That's all that could have happened. It was very unusual that we'd miss checking these two things, side by side. They were snug, I guess, but not tight."

Disaster could have resulted if they'd been in the air when it went. "You either go down again, or shake the engine out of the plane. We probably would have been able to fly farther, but when we went into descent, as we cut the power off to come down, the hot engine cooled down and contracted; when we climbed it heated up and expanded again, increasing compression. Every time it fired and compression occurred, it had a tendency to blow things out, like the primer plug or spark plug."

The Akie River was just one of Anderson's famed 16 crashes. And that wasn't even a crash in Anderson's books. It was, well, another "uncontrolled landing."

He can't remember the 16 crashes in order—"No, God, no!" But most were due to bad weather and then picking the wrong landing spot. "You either do that, or 'fly and die,'" he says. "You don't decide the weather's the pits, it's decided that for you already. No, you're down."

Author Shirlee Matheson and pilot Jimmy Anderson with his present aircraft, a Piper Cherokee 6-300, which he calls "bad medicine for a bush pilot," at his home at Mile 147, June 1992. *Bill Matheson Collection*

Asked what kind of navigation knowledge a good pilot needs, Anderson replies: "Know exactly where you're at, at all given times. If you do get into a weather situation, put that airplane down while you can still see the ground and never leave that spot. If the weather breaks a little bit, go to another spot, try to work your way out, but don't think you're just going to up and fly through it, back to your cabin. You won't make it. You'll die. Damn, you'll die."

Anderson has seen a lot of pilots go. "You pay attention to these things. Plus, I've been on that doorstep myself, and it's not a good feeling."

"And on the way down," he adds, "you better not hit the old panic button. That little office that you're in right there is the busiest one in the world, from the time that you have the problem until you hit the *terra firma*."

Anderson's story-telling ability is of the same calibre as his flying ability; listeners are fascinated as "Midnight" Anderson reels off scenarios of his escapades, such as the time the airplane iced up and he found himself locked in a box canyon about 15 miles up the Halfway River—at midnight.

"Ice in the carburettor, the oldest thing in the book," Anderson recalls. "I'd just brought the airplane back from Edmonton. Had George Ross with me. He and I travelled a lot together. He'll swim any river with you, and he's worthwhile swimming them with, too. He's been my friend for life.

"What happened that time was the linkage on the throttle cable to the carb was off-centre and once in a while it would stick.

"So anyway we got carb ice. Carb icing you can get even on a warm sunny day, just due to atmospheric conditions. I was on let-down, getting down below the weather, and I just went too long and my carb iced up.

"I wasn't in any trouble yet but when I went to warm up the carburettor again—the heat-exchanger on the exhaust system takes hot air into the carburettor, which melts the ice; you hear a gurgle and a chomp-chomp and it swallows the ice and you're gone again—I didn't have enough heat in my engine. I kept playing with it, but nothing happened. I kept floating down.

"Christ, it's the middle of the night again. I was over the river so all I was working on was water-glaze. I was following the river, and I had to come down, down, down. I didn't have much farther to go, so I just watched and I could tell that engine sure as hell wasn't going to run again. So I paid a little attention to getting a place to land.

"Finally there came a spot and I knew there was water running—you get a kind of outline of the water as dark as it is—well anything at this point would work. So I swung into that box canyon, where it's a little flat and you get a little bit of outwash from the river. So I squeezed into that, not knowing what was coming. I had to save my lights because they were on one breaker—landing lights should really be on separate breakers. If I had a short or something, once in a while it would blow the breaker.

"So just when I was coming on in I figured I need the lights. They don't do any good when you're high 'cause they just throw a big ball of white in front of you. So all I gotta do is get to that outwash. I knew the wash was around there and I did get to it, but there was a tree right there. I grabbed the switch and the lights came on and there's that damned tree coming on! I side-slipped around it and just got by it when the lights went out.

"I'd grabbed one toggle switch but I got the wrong one—the one with the short in it that I hadn't found time to fix, and when I pulled on the landing lights the breaker blew. Now you've got lots of things going through your mind when you're about ready to scratch your ass on a rockpile.

"But I did correct it enough that I thought I'd be going straight and could touch down and just walk on the brakes, 'cause I'd lost 'er all right there. I'd lost it before, but I lost it worse now.

"By God, I got straightened out some, missed the tree, but still I came in a little bit sideways. Well, down we came. That airplane give a jerk. We weren't going fast but she spun up into some bush, ripped the gear out from under her. Never even bent the prop but we were sitting right on the ground."

The impact threw Anderson against the Pioneer compass mounted on the windshield. The compass was driven right into the bridge of his nose, leaving a lifelong scar. "I blew my nose and blood just squirted out of the top, between my eyes," he says. "That compass came out of there right after that!"

"So anyway I got out of the plane and oh! I'm peed right off. What a heart-breaker. I'd just got the machine back, redone and everything, so what the hell, I kicked a hole through the side of it, and George and I walked away. So I had to fix that when we came back, too."

They walked over 10 miles down the trail to an outfitter's place, and got him up. He took them the extra 20 miles to Mile 147. "In the meantime, of course, he had a little supply of ginger ale out there so we got into it. You know,

Adam's Ale, fire-screech, Smirnoff Express. So we weren't feeling no pain then."

At that time Short Tompkins was working east of Anderson's Mile 147 Lodge. When he found out about the accident his response was prompt: "Take my airplane out and see what you need to get 'er out."

Anderson refused. "I'm not even interested in flying again, Short," he said. "Ah, get in there and fly," Tompkins said.

Anderson must have looked like a guy who'd learned his lesson well, and had decided to stay out of the air. His eyes were black and swollen, his nose spurted blood at the slightest provocation, and he told anybody who'd listen that he "didn't give a damn about that thing out there."

He and George Ross discussed the situation, however, and agreed that Short showed pretty good faith in handing his airplane over to a guy who'd just walked out of a wreck, so they jumped into Short's airplane to go take a look. "Ah hell, it ain't too bad," they said, and began the process of getting stuff together to get it out.

"I will not just patch something up and think that's good enough," Anderson says. "It's got to be good or to hell with it, I'll go get another one."

It wasn't necessary to cut back the brush for a runway—they'd trimmed it up real nice going in. They pulled the airplane back a bit and got the prop clear. "By God, we fired her up and everything was working good."

The machine ran like a jewel, "but that is how little things can create some of your worst escapades."

Another close call occurred when he was forced to land his airplane halfway to heaven—an escapade that reconfirmed the name "Jackpine Savage" for both Anderson and his airplane.

"We ran out of gas, but I'd put two new magnetos on the airplane and I thought the problem was the magnetos. If I'd just have switched over to the other tank . . . but I was coming over a hill and the wind was blowing like hell. When it sputtered out, I thought, 'Jesus, what! two new mags!'"

Anderson knew there were only two things that could have caused the engine to quit: gas and spark. If the problem had been mechanical there would have been a clunk. This time there was no clunk.

"I'd had quite a few hours flying by then, but I had too many things on my mind. Never go into tight flying if you've got too many things on your mind—if you're worrying about something, forget flying."

As he swung the airplane around, another good lesson flashed into his mind: never pull your airplane back up unless you've got power, or you'll fall over frontwards and drive it straight into the ground.

"I'd made a 90-degree turn so I wouldn't land downhill—if I'd come over the hill and landed going downhill I would have dumped right over on my back. If I'm going to land any place I'm going to land uphill so I've got everything going ahead of me and the nose will stay up. So I made the turn

Jimmy Anderson refuelling "the Jackpine Savage" (Super Cub). *Jamie Anderson Collection*

lengthways with the ridge and had her set up to put her into the tops of the trees."

On a sudden inspiration, he thought of the gas, and switched to the other tank. And then he realized his problem hadn't been magnetos; it had been an empty tank. He had just enough time; he might have been able to pull it out—he thinks now he could have—but the airplane suddenly jumped to life when it took gas because of the wide-open throttle.

"I thought—and this goes through your mind so fast—if I pull 'er up and the thing quits again, I could be a dead man. So I cut the power and put it right into the tops of the trees. Six feet up, into little poplars and big willow. And there she sat, rocked over, kind of on a tilt."

The perch proved sturdy. The airplane didn't hit the ground—not yet. Anderson climbed out, took an axe and chopped away a couple of trees that were leaning against the airplane so the wind couldn't rub them against the fabric and wear a hole in it, then he left the scene. Two months later, after the frost came and he could drive in close to the airplane, he removed the wings and hauled it out.

That was crash number three. Only 13 to go.

Anderson's mind flicks back like an insurance adjuster's computer. "One time I pulled in on a gravel bar on the Sikanni Chief River, bad weather again. Evening. I was alone this time. I wanted to get to the place I usually landed, so I came on in and I couldn't land. I was right in the canyon. I didn't dare go any farther. No way. The fog and crap was right to the deck, right to the water. Bad deal. There was one little wee spot and I damned well had to get in. I mean, that's all there was to it. And I'd have to stay overnight, come out in the morning.

"But when I came in, it was too short. Well, I overshot is what happened. I sprung my own trap, not enough precaution. When I touched down I knew I was going too fast, I'd have drove right into some rocks and a bunch of stuff. So I gave 'er a whirl and spun the plane around on the gravel bar, but I hit some snags and rocks. Bent the tail section a bit, broke the tail wheel mount, and ripped a chunk out of the fabric on the tail end about four feet long and two feet deep.

"Well, if I hadn't got in there I could have died.

"So I lit my little campfire, swung the airplane around by hand, and tried to move rocks and stuff in the light from the campfire. In the morning I wired up the tail bracket, tucked the chunk of fabric up, and secured it with some stuff I call hundred-mile-an-hour tape."

When he tried to leave the next day, Anderson discovered that the river curved just ahead of where he'd landed. He could easily have ploughed right into a bank, thinking he was past that particular bend, but the Sikanni has a lot of bends and their sequence becomes confusing.

"There are times when I think that the good Lord and I are on a first-name basis, all right," Anderson says.

Stories about Anderson are favourite topics at some northern gatherings. Few who've met him are indifferent to the man. On the positive side, his scrapbook is filled with letters from people whose lives he's saved, such as the Reverend Bill Hickinbotham of Grants Pass, Oregon. Hickinbotham and his fellow passengers had gone down in bad weather in Kluchesi Creek, 40 miles west of Trutch. Anderson managed to find them wandering 10 miles from the crash site.

"Indeed, you will never be forgotten," Hickinbotham wrote on 7 January 1970 in his annual letter to "his saviour."

"He wasn't a preacher then," Anderson notes. "But he is now."

Another letter of gratitude is from P.D. Crofton, director of travel promotion, British Columbia House, London, England: "I do want to thank you for rescuing me from the bank of the Prophet River. How you were able to bring the plane down and take off again from that narrow, bending, rock-strewn strip is beyond my powers of comprehension."

Crofton had been a member of the disastrous International Press Tour, arranged by the BC Department of Travel Industry to acquaint international visitors with the beauties of northern BC. A further reference to the event appeared in an article published in the 4 July 1975 issue of the English language *Asahi Evening News* of Tokyo. "The raft carrying Yano and J. Oishi, cameraman for Junon, as well as Bill Dyer and prospectors John and Al, also overturned twice. Marooned on a rocky section with their clothes soaking wet and their raft no longer usable, they had to wait until Jimmy Anderson spotted them from his Super Cub and then landed on the rocky beach, where no other pilot would have dared land, to take them off one by one."

And businessman Al Meyers, in a letter from Anchorage, Alaska: "Jim, you showed me more about handling the Super Cub in the few times we flew than a whole batch of instructors I've had. I'm sure that some of the instructors I've flown with don't really know what a Cub will do; they are used to tricycle multi-engine crates and seldom, if ever, slow fly an airplane."[2]

Anderson took part in a mission in May 1978 involving the air search for a Cherokee carrying four Canadian cowboys on a flight from Salem, Oregon, to San Francisco. The pilot was Saskatchewan cowboy Brian Claypool, with passengers Gary Logan from Sundre, Alberta, Calvin Bunney of Duchess, Alberta, and Lee Coleman of Pierceland, Saskatchewan. Although the U.S. Civil Air Patrol decided to close the search after 21 days, the Canadian Rodeo Cowboys Association raised $150,000 to finance a private search. Anderson, a friend of the missing men, was quoted in the Red Deer *Advocate* as reporting that the search effort would continue, using about six aircraft, until searchers were satisfied the airplane could not be found. The search coordinator, Canadian rodeo cowboy Don Johansen of Strathmore, Alberta, in a further *Advocate* article by Robert Lee, described Jimmy Anderson of Fort Nelson, BC, as "a legend in that country with a Super Cub."

Alberta rodeo promoter and recording artist Ivan Daines, who later wrote a song about the crash, referred in the *Advocate* to Anderson as a good bush pilot with "a reputation for smelling out wrecks."

"I went down for one week, and stayed for seven," Anderson recalled. The search, unfortunately, was not successful. The airplane, with all passengers aboard, was discovered that fall, some four months later, by hunters, where it had crashed and burned in the mountains.

Another rescue mission that Anderson was involved in still remains a mystery. On 29 April 1982, a Cessna 185 (CG-JLJ) went missing in the rugged Monkman Pass between Fox Creek, Alberta, and Prince George, BC. The airplane carried five men: Rick Gascon, George Maurer, Larry Anderson, and Darryl and Brian Trottier. The Trottier boys were brothers of Dale "Trapper" Trottier, seven-time Canadian bareback champion. The search inspired help from a "brotherhood of cowboys who came to look for two of their own," forming the Rocky Mountain Air Search Association. Assistance came also from military and civilian flyers, and personal friends such as Jimmy Anderson.

The official search was conducted over a 21,000 square mile terrain between Grande Prairie and Prince George, 85 percent of which was mountainous country, at three altitude levels. "I believe we had 57 civilian planes registered, not counting the armed forces," Anderson says. "I stayed right to the end, 90 days, logging more than 400 flying hours in the search operation."

It bothers Anderson a great deal that the case has never been solved. "We don't know what happened, but they're in that given area. We just failed to find them, and it frustrates me. Very much so."

As Anderson optimistically says, "They haven't phoned in yet."

On the debit side of Jimmy Anderson's personal ledger are incidents such as that reported in the *Alaska Highway News* on 1 May 1974:

LAW THROWS BOOK AT PINK MOUNTAIN GUIDE

A veteran big game guide from the Pink Mountain area has lost his guiding licence for at least five years, been prohibited from being issued any hunting licences for the same period of time, and will not be allowed to carry firearms until November 1978.

Jimmy Anderson [is] well known locally as one of the best bush pilots in northern BC, but those stiff penalties [were] imposed against him after having pleaded guilty to two charges in connection with illegal hunting practices. [On] November 16, officers from Fish & Wildlife laid charges that Anderson had been hunting from an aircraft and guiding outside of his allotted guiding territory.

According to the article, Anderson was seen herding caribou by flying low overhead into an area where nonresident hunters were waiting. The spokesperson for the Fish and Wildlife branch in Fort St. John said they had "also learned that Anderson had been spotting moose for hunters, and incredibly enough had also been directing hunters on the ground by cutting his motor and yelling directions to those on the ground."

On the charge of hunting from an aircraft, Anderson was fined $300 or in default 30 days; on the second charge, he was fined $200 or 30 days.

Anderson's response to that incident: "I paid the $500 fine and got the hell out. It was a trumped-up deal."

Anderson's views on the wildlife situation in the North are based on years of first-hand observation. "I always used to have a seat in my plane for our 'Fish and Worm' branch, but God, then they go overboard! Like, I showed them one place where I used to hunt. Now if I'd have hunted from the airplane I'd have really been abusing game. In a two-by-eight-mile area—something like that, damn small anyway—I counted 179 moose at one time. That was in the 1960s. There were lots of moose around.

"I told them of the 179 moose in that little area, so they were up right after that. 'That's bullshit,' they said. 'That's not bullshit! Jump in the airplane,' I said. So we went back out and counted them again, and I think we counted 181 or something. Same area.

"And before we got out of the place, by God they opened up a two-moose season, that's where she started to go downhill. Two moose per person instead of one moose per person because they thought there were so many. Now there's hardly any in that same valley right to this very day."

Anderson, with the bird's eye view of a bush pilot, has seen evidence of many outrageous practices in the North, among them signs where people have killed bears for their gallbladders and claws. The only way such activities can be controlled, or stopped, he says, would be to "put a heavy enough fine on it if they're just shooting them for the gall." But, considering his own experiences with the Fish and Wildlife branch, he doesn't know what his role should be in monitoring such violations.

"Well, if the Fish and Worm branch would say 'we're going to be men about it,' they wouldn't have to do it all themselves. But, Jesus, if they'll turn around and pinch you for turning the page wrong in the book, are you going to tell them anything? It's the next thing to dictatorship."

Anderson's opinion of how aviation has changed the North leans to the positive. He admits, however, that "a lot have taken advantage of it." Although aviation has opened up formerly inaccessible areas, Anderson does not feel this is necessarily detrimental *if* there is respect for the country. "Wherever I've landed or made camp I've always left it better than it was when I got there."

Anderson hastens to add that it's not necessarily outfitters—it's local people who've brought about the damage to fish, forests, and wildlife. "I've seen the time when I've flown 20 miles and seen 17 animals down that were never brought out. If they've got a pack horse they usually get them out. But they just walk in and shoot, and their endurance is not there to get them out. Then they walk on out, and if something happens to be closer they'll shoot it, take it, and leave the other. I know situations where out of five animals somebody's hit, only one of them's come out. The rest are walking around wounded.

"And I find them, I see them when I'm flying, 'cause wherever there's a bunch of ravens come up, I circle and look. There aren't that many natural kills in hunting season. Come on! Especially when you don't see it in the rest of the year. Anybody with a half of an eye and a quarter of an asshole can tell that, you know. God!"

What to do about it is another question. "Our laws got teeth but they don't put them in the proper perspective. Jesus, I've done more for game; the only thing I've ever shot from an airplane is timber wolves. And I was accused of hunting from the air and everything. Well, they can go to hell.

"Why would I need—if I go put halters on caribou [captured without injury for the Alberta Game Farm], and put them in a rock house that we built on top of a mountain, and live with sheep in a cabin at Tuchodi, through sleet and storm and cold and all the elements, put them in an airplane and fly them out, and have them in good shape—why in hell would I want an airplane and a .300 Magnum to go out and hunt with? Jesus! Where's our brains?"

Anderson's reputation has two sometimes-conflicting sides: his maverick outgoing attitude, versus his professed concern for attention to detail and his resolve not to take chances—to live to fly again.

Howard Phillips, a pilot from Burns Lake, BC, tells a story that illustrates the maverick side. "Someone asked Jimmy Anderson how he flew in rough weather. 'I have a wing leveller,' Jim replied. 'When there's turbulence and I can't see my artificial horizon any more, it gets too bumpy and starts to blur, I take a bottle of whiskey, drink half, and set the bottle on the dash. If I can't keep that level, I drink the rest and enjoy the ride!'"

He laughs when he hears the story. "It's a little slogan we pilots always use, yeah. Drink the rest of it and enjoy the ride. Well, you know, you've got to get those little jokes in there."

Anderson goes on to relate another of his mythic "advice to pilots" stories to describe what he calls a bush pilot's instrument panel. "You use a black cat and a wild duck for bad weather flying if you lose sight of the ground. We don't have instruments in some of these bush planes because you can't use them in the mountains anyway—you've got to be able to see the ground at all times, or the side of a mountain or something, to fly by, otherwise you just ain't gonna make it—so I always say I carry a black cat and a wild duck. Got them in the back for when the weather gets bad, when you can't see if you're on one side or on the other, going up or going down.

"So what you do, you grab hold of your cat and you set him on the seat beside you. Have you ever taken a cat and dropped him? He lands on his feet. Well, if he's standing on the roof, you're upside-down. If he's in the back, you're going straight up. If he's on the dash, you're going down. On one side, you're going too far that way. If he's sitting right beside you, you're going straight and level.

"So now you don't know where you're going. You might run into a hill, eh? So the cat's sitting beside you, and you grab your duck, open the window and throw him out, then follow him. You never seen a duck run into a mountain, have you?

"That's a bush pilot's instrument panel."

The "high risk" stories abound, always told with a sense of tragicomedy:

"Another time I was piloting an airplane that had gone down a couple of times before—they'd put pieces on that thing from hell to breakfast and back. There is a little deal in the front of the machine that the mag grounds go through for the 'on' and 'off' switches, and it was shorting out. It would cut the mags and then bingo! So any time I wanted to run good I just went out and tore them wires off and then away I'd go.

"So anyway they were supposed to have been fixed, and I borrowed the airplane. I had a big plane, and I'd take hunters and their gear in as far as I could with the big one, then land at a strip and reload the stuff into the small plane to go the rest of the way. So I got in and had just nicely picked it up when I realized suddenly that I had too much altitude above me and too much strip behind me. The creek came around and there was a bunch of rocks in it at the end of the strip. That's why they couldn't make any more strip, nothing you could do with them rocks, right up in the high country. So I'm fighting this thing—I had to pick up more to get over the hill there.

"She started to shake and quit and I couldn't get it to pick up; I couldn't get it to do a damned thing. It was loaded too. And I had a big guy with me, a hunter from the southern United States. God, he was a big man. And there's the rest of the hunting group standing at the end of the strip watching this happen.

"So I started into the wind a little bit and I knew something was going to happen. I was maintaining altitude but I couldn't climb. I would have stuck her in the mountain if I'd have kept going. And to make a turn downwind and come in and land would be suicidal. I was at the mercy of everything.

"But there was a nice big patch of tall willows, thick as hair on a dog's back. I turned for the willows and then the ground came on up. Only one thing to do: cut the power. Then, when she started in, just rock back on her, drop power.

"Well, she rocked in.

"The guys on the ground were going to run back to camp and radio for the meat wagon, 'cause they make a terrible noise when they go in, you know. And it had actually quit, lost power. Can't idle up there. You don't stay in the air.

"We shocked the hell out of everybody. They thought we were goners. But we got out of the airplane and walked out to the end of the strip. Some of the guys were standing down there and others had gone to radio to holler for help, nobody even came down to see us! They didn't know what to think.

"There was this big old boy—he had to weigh 250 pounds—and he and I just came walking down the strip. Finally he said, 'You know, Jim, I got a boy about your age.' He stopped and I said, 'Yeah?' 'He is a crazy sonofabitch and he's just worried me all my life, all his life. But I'm *sure* that he's never done nothing like this!' Then he just turned around and started walking.

"But anyway, we left this old airplane just hanging in the willows, and we didn't even unload the sonofabitch. One side of the undercarriage was ripped, two little holes in it, not big. I didn't even bend the prop on that one.

"I flew the rest of their stuff in with my big bird. Little did I know but there were two doctors and two lawyers there. Afterwards, when they all got together, they got full of whiskey and started to say things about whiplash, and about money. I thought we were going to have quite a lawsuit over this. I'd borrowed the airplane, no papers on it. I was just doing the guy a favour. They went on and on.

"He should have been damned thankful he was alive! There had been many airplanes run off there and just totally wrecked."

Anderson eventually brought the wrecked airplane out.

About a month after the accident, Anderson was moving in some more hunting supplies when he was approached by a fellow wearing a big hat, who stuck his hand out and said, "Hello there!" in a familiar manner. Anderson thought he might know him, but the man had a deep southern accent—he later said he was from Louisiana—and Anderson figured he looked too clean to be a guide.

"How've you been doing, Jim?" the fellow said.

"Not too bad," Anderson said. He shook the man's hand, still trying to place him.

"I got talking to a buddy of yours," he said. "He sends his best regards. Yeah, and he gave me some good advice."

The men began to unload the airplane. "What was that?" Anderson said.

"Never fly with Jimmy Anderson! Never get in an airplane with you."

Anderson looked at the man. "Well, that's nice. And he says he's a buddy of mine?"

The man grinned. "But he also said, 'If the chips are down and there's problems ahead, or the weather's bad, don't fly with anybody else *but* Jimmy Anderson.'"

At that point, the advisor's identity became clear: the big old boy who'd been in the airplane with Anderson when he'd hung it in the willows.

Anderson gets a kick out of recalling the variety of passengers he's carried, from dogs to caribou, and priests to grizzled mountain men. Prospector Art Pollon was one of his more colourful passengers, a good friend, and "tougher than a tramp's ass," according to Anderson.

"I'd leave him in the bush back of the Tuchodis for six weeks with a jug of rye and a gallon of wine and some grub—salt, dry stuff like macaroni, beans—then I could never find him again!"

One time Anderson flew Pollon out to his mining territory, having pre-warned him to arrange with another pilot for pick-up as Anderson had to get some work done on the airplane engine and then was taking a holiday. When Anderson returned six weeks later, he discovered that no one had picked up Pollon.

"I slapped the engine into the plane, test-flew it, and headed for the Tuchodis, and then for the Gataga River, looking for him. Couldn't find him. Nobody'd seen him. I asked up and down the Highway in case he'd come out and got in a snap-up around Mile 422 near the Racing River, or the Toad River Lodge, or in Fort Nelson. But to no avail. No Art.

"So I go hunting for him in the mountains. All I can find are cold camps. Well, I'd been gone for six weeks and then it was six weeks again. Pretty near three months."

Pollon finally showed up, walking over the mountains from the Gataga River via Don Peck's old trail to a hunting camp. From there he sent a message to Anderson at Mile 147 that said tersely, "Are you coming to get me?" Anderson felt like sending one back saying, "No!" and letting Art stew for a while.

But Anderson flew up again, and this time he found Pollon's warm camp. He buzzed over and prepared to land on the little airstrip on the west end of the Tuchodis.

"Art always said that he'd never fly with me after dark, because he knew those mountains. 'Goddamnit,' he said, 'anybody who flies in them after dark is crazy. Isn't ever going to make 'er.' And he wasn't going to be along when it happened.

"I had to come in along the mountain, but the strip was on a slope and damned small. I had to come in fast, in the dark, and land downhill. I didn't want to do that. Plus there was a little log bridge over a wash that the airplane had to cross. I had to turn and come in with the lights pointed down so I could see the ground—but then I'd be going like hell. When I'd find the strip, there wouldn't be enough room left to land so I'd have to take off again. I didn't want to get too low until I could get pointed down and find the strip.

"I hollered at Art from out the plane window to get over there and light a fire at each end to mark out the strip, so he did that. I flashed on my landing lights and came in for a landing.

"I got out and I shook hands with him. Finally."

Pollon had taken his dog, Lucky, in with him. But when Anderson went in, Pollon had no dog. "You ate your dog!" Anderson accused.

"No," Pollon said, "Lucky just didn't make it. Played out on me."

But Anderson maintained that Lucky had not met with a natural death, later questioning why Art's "shank of sheep" hanging from a tree branch had paws on it. Art had been completely out of grub for over six weeks, living only on what he could snare or shoot. "Nobody else could have lived. He was living like the mad trapper, Albert Johnson."

But Art Pollon had another surprise for "Midnight" Anderson. As soon as the men had shaken hands, Pollon said casually, "When are you coming back to get me?"

Anderson was astounded. "I'm here!" he said.

"I'm not flying with you after dark."

So Anderson shook his hand again and said, "Good, I know you're alive now. You're on your own."

"Well, let's talk about this . . . " Pollon said.

"How long would it take you to break camp?"

"Well," Pollon admitted, "It wouldn't take too long 'cause I ain't got nothing." But he was still hesitant about leaving right then and there. "Let's move up here and camp until daylight, then go."

Now Anderson was angry. "I've got another outfit to check on the way out, and I have to take off in the morning again. How am I going to get you worked in on this with your damned foolishness?" Then he turned on his heel and said, "So long."

Pollon was angry, too, but he wasn't exactly in a position to argue. "Well," he said, "looks like I'm going to have to chance it."

He went down to break camp, they threw his scanty outfit into the airplane, and took off. At midnight.

The take-off was as risky as the landing. Anderson had to run the airplane down the strip with the lights on, then lift up into the valley with the lights throwing a big ball of white in front of him. As soon as he'd left the ground he would shut the landing lights off and keep climbing. Then, in the dark, he'd gain his depth perception.

As he'd told Art, he had to check on some guys further back in the mountains. He shone the lights toward their cabin, they waved, and away the two men flew back to the lodge at 147.

Anderson discovered later that during the six weeks he'd spent looking for him, Art Pollon would quickly get a fire going whenever he heard an airplane. But by that time Anderson would be over, even though he was flying low and slow. One day, Pollon told him, Anderson had flown right by where he was camped on a mountain. "I was going to take a shot at you but you were the only s.o.b. out there looking for me so I decided not to," Art said testily.

But Anderson got his revenge: "I wouldn't even give Art any clean clothes when we got to the lodge at 147, and he looked like hell. His whiskers stuck right out and he'd just kept hacking them off with a knife, never shaved. His hair was long. He said he didn't care about that, it didn't hinder his eyesight because it was behind him. Same suit of underwear he'd gone in with. Three months. What was left of it. The only washing it'd had was when he fell in the river or swam it.

"I guess he was clean enough when he went in, but out in the hills it was hard for him to clean up, so he didn't. He'd found some tarp out there, and when he wore the front out of his jeans he just laced them up with this tarp, with some moosehide strings.

"And he'd gone through his shirt. Honest, all he had left were the cuffs, the front part and the collar. It just looked terrible. And on his feet he wore only moccasin rubbers. Socks—he always had a little bit of stuff with him so he'd make them out of anything. But he'd gone through everything.

"So we got him cleaned up. I gave him clothes anyway that night but I decided to have him for a show for a while. We'd maybe be sitting in the bar and I'd say, 'Art ate his dog out there.' Little did I know that Lorne Harrelson, a trapper who had a stopping place on Mill Creek, Mile 363, near Steamboat Mountain, had accused him of eating his dog a few years before. So nobody up there would loan him a dog. The Indians wouldn't loan him a dog. Nobody."

Pollon's reputation as a hard-drinking wild man who could survive in the mountains under any circumstances exceeded even Anderson's. But there were limits to what the two men would put up with from each other.

"Art never did fly with me when he was looped. 'Cause I just refused to take him," Anderson says. "I don't mind anybody having a drink or two, but to go out in that country drunk, you're crazy. And if I was full of whiskey going out there, I wouldn't be talking to you right now."

67

Bush pilots and booze are poor combinations. In his book *The Last of the Bush Pilots*, Alaska pilot Harmon Helmericks comments that if pilots mix flying with booze, it's the end. Anderson, despite his reputation as a drinker who can keep up to the best of them, heartily agrees.

Although he admits that he's had drinks when he flew, he states that that only occurred "on very easy flights. And I never did work with them under my belt." Not with passengers, paying or otherwise. "I never did go out and work that way! No. It's a pretty bad combination, flying and booze. One of the worst."

He probably could have made a good living from flying, if he'd played his cards right, if he had a different personality. But the cost was something Anderson would not pay. "I would have had to send everybody else out and sit at a desk. I wouldn't have known what I do about the hills."

Anderson acknowledges that he's "always been on the borderline of experimental." His critics have called his experiments—from equipping his aircraft with big tires which enabled him to land on gravel bars and mountain tops, to capturing and air-lifting untranquilized wild animals—"Anderson's folly." But he scoffs at such reproach. "I was out there doing the job while they were saying 'he's going to kill himself on that one.'"

"But, one time I should have died—when that caribou was in the back of the machine and I got on to the highway there . . ."

Rock House on Klingzut Mountain. Anderson and the other team members established a base camp on the mountain, building a "rock house" topped with canvas.
Jimmy Anderson Collection

The men and animals grew to trust one another. Here one of the men is having an afternoon nap alongside the animals in the "rock house." *Jimmy Anderson Collection*

It all started with a verbal agreement in the summer of 1963, between Jimmy and Al Oeming, owner of the famed Alberta Game Farm 14 miles east of Edmonton, Alberta, for the delivery of 20 caribou (he eventually delivered 21) and six Stone sheep (he delivered seven). The area of capture was the Tuchodi Lake region, east of Summit Lake and south of Trutch, BC (Mile 201 of the Alaska Highway). The area of delivery was the barns behind the lodge at Mile 147.

Everyone had expressed doubts about the project, including people like Leo Rutledge, a respected long-time guide and outfitter from the Peace area. It involved capturing the animals, in this case from a grassy sloping plateau near the 6,000-foot peak of Klingzut Mountain in the Tuchodi Lakes area, transporting them by air to the lodge at Mile 147, then by truck to Alberta. The program would involve an extraordinary mixture of luck, perseverance, and tenacity.

Anderson had shown Rutledge his plan for clearing off a 1,000-foot airstrip on the precarious perch, to bring the Super Cub close to the capture area. He had removed the airplane's back seat, laying two-inch foam slabs on the floor to cushion the animals, which were to be tied but not tranquillized for the 45-minute flight from the mountain top to the lodge.

The plan went according to schedule: Jimmy Anderson and the other team members first established a base camp on the mountain, building a "rock house" topped with canvas. This served to house both men and animals while awaiting the next trip out. Then the animals were tied and transported one-half mile by all-terrain vehicles and loaded into the aircraft. Animals and men got along amazingly well. Photographs show the men catching naps alongside the animals in the "rock house." The men were considerate of the animals' fears and determined to cause them no harm, either psychologically or physically.

All went well—until it didn't. The Super Cub had been loaded with a four-year-old bull caribou, not tranquillized or in any way sedated, just tied up "cowboy style." Anderson was to take off first, with the bull as his passenger, followed by Al Henderson in his Super Cub with Al Oeming as his passenger. Anderson tells the story:

"I shouldn't have left that night. It was just getting dark. I used landing lights to take off. Henderson was going to make a run behind me; he started and the fog just closed right in, psst! He shut down, aborted his take-off, and went back. But I went on over the edge, into the fog, and dropped down to the foot of the mountain. I managed to break out of it, but at a very low altitude. The fog was caused by one of them wind deals, where the weather can move in so fast it will trap you. The fog came in, moving faster than we did, until I was suddenly in the middle of it. With a caribou in the plane. Just me and a four-year-old bull. And no way could I get back to the mountain."

"I didn't know it then but if I would have flown over the hump of the Bucking Horse River, straight across for a quarter-mile, I'd have been out of the fog. The moon was out and everything, it was clear as a bell there. But I didn't dare take that chance. A lot of people die in 100 yards. So I swung around and went back down into the draw, which I had just come out of, because the weather was not so bad down there."

There was definitely no possibility of returning to the mountain, so his only hope was to rise to the relatively high elevation of the Alaska Highway that ran along a ridge and then over Trutch Mountain, and land on the road.

Back and forth he went, trying to get onto the ridge. The wind helped him.

"If the wind had stopped blowing that night I would have had to put it in, and I damned near did anyway. I would work my way up, then the fog would get so bad that I'd have to come back into the valley by the creek, where there was a nice big buckbrush flat. I was going to put the plane down in there, turn the caribou loose, and then walk out. At different times I heard that buckbrush rattling on the undercarriage! All I had to do was cut the power and put 'er in. But, Jesus, the weather would break a little, the wind would blow the fog past, and I'd hit the power again."

It took an hour to go less than 20 miles, flying very low, around and around, toward the highway and then back to the valley. Meanwhile, the caribou was not impressed.

"It was probably the first airplane ride he'd ever had, and every time I'd put one of them tight turns in, when I'd have to crank 'er around, well, you know that funny feeling you get when you make a violent turn in an airplane. He'd just groan and beller. And shake his head and snort and blow snot all over the back of my neck. I had the windows open and the door open."

Time after time Anderson attempted to guide the Super Cub through the dense fog to get in to Trutch, but he couldn't make it. He'd get halfway up the hill, a distance of a mile and a half, but it was impossible to land. He would punch through the fog, catch a tantalizing glimpse the highway, then the fog would come in again, thick, impenetrable. Back down into the valley he'd go, to try again.

The animals (note the caribou in the airplane) were tied, but not tranquillized, and transported one-half mile by all-terrain vehicles and loaded into the aircraft. *Jimmy Anderson Collection*

"I don't know how many tries I made, I lost track. I just couldn't take it any more, every move was split second. I was absolutely beat. I'd decided to turn around and put the machine in the bush down where I could see, let the caribou go, to hell with it. I was very low, when all of a sudden ssskk! there went that highway!" Finally he'd found what he was looking for—an opening in the fog.

"I cranked on that thing and set it right in the bottom of the draw where the highway dips low and then climbs again. I threw the old landing lights on over the wing and landed on the highway. Oh, was I ever happy!"

Vehicles weren't a problem. Anybody who would risk travelling on such a night would be going very slowly, or would have pulled over and parked. Even on the ground, visibility was less than two feet. As soon as he landed, Anderson followed the exit road and taxied up to a gravel pit on top of the hill. He pulled over where the road widened, parking the airplane between the highway and the gravel pit. "I left the beacon on and everything, that's how I followed the road up there, you couldn't see nothing out." His calculations showed that he was at Mile 187 on the Alaska Highway.

"Now to try to get somebody to help me," Anderson says. "That old bull caribou and I went through hell. The inside of that airplane was snot and saliva all over hell's half-acre, foam and fuzz. No crap, though. He had it puckered up so tight I don't think he could! I know I was.

"So I got out of the airplane and of course he calmed down; he was happy not to get into any more of those performances. I knew I had to get him out because he'd been there for an hour, and tied. But I needed help.

"I shut off the airplane and left the nav lights and the beacon going; it was right beside the road so somebody could see it. I got out and for the first time in my life my knees were springy—I was just bouncing. Any step I took I'd just spring. I knew then that I'd come pretty damned close."

The next item on his agenda was to flag someone down. The first vehicle to stop was a stationwagon with two men.

"Hi, there! Can I catch a ride 30 miles down the road with you?" Anderson asked. "I just got forced in here."

"Oh, sure," one of the men answered.

Anderson noticed that the back of the stationwagon had the seats down, a perfect place to lay out his caribou. That's when the trouble started.

"I have a caribou in the plane over there. We're catching some over here on the mountain."

"Oh yeah, no problem" one of the men replied. "We can put a piece of him here, and a piece over there, kind of level the vehicle out a little . . ."

"No, no!" Anderson replied. "This one's alive. We're catching them for a game farm."

The men looked toward the airplane and noticed that there was movement inside. "What did you say?"

Anderson explained. "This is a live one. But we can slide him in and I'll hold him until we get there."

The driver started to shift the car into first gear. "Oh, well, somebody else will be along who can help, I'm sure of that!" he said. He rolled the window up and started driving away. Anderson ran along beside the slow-moving vehicle, trying desperately to talk them into it, but to no avail.

"Well, they were spooked," he says. "They thought I was a nut case of some kind."

After a while, Anderson spotted another vehicle driving slowly toward him. As the vehicle crawled to a stop, Anderson jumped in and sat beside the driver, not taking the chance of him getting away.

"I got a caribou in the back of that rig!" he announced in a forceful no-nonsense tone.

"Oh, have you?" the driver replied nonchalantly. "I'll have to get a look at that." He got out of the car. Thinking he might quickly jump back in and take off, Anderson hesitated a moment but then he too got out. They walked over to the airplane. The man went around behind the wing and looked inside. The caribou was lying absolutely still, like they do when they're hiding.

"I need a hand," Anderson said, opening the door of the airplane.

The man finally focused on the scene inside. "Well, I'll be damned!"

At that moment the caribou let out a snort that blew snot and slobber all over him.

"Christ," he said reeling back from the impact. "I can't give you a hand. I couldn't even lift him."

Anderson admitted it was true. The man had a small build and was quite lame. "Well, send word back up somehow," he said.

Finally a friend, Blackie Thatcher from St. John, came along and Anderson sent word with him to get hold of Bud Armstrong or Don Peck.

Bud Armstrong was sitting in the cafe at Mile 200 having coffee when the SOS message reached him: "Jim Anderson said to get you or Don Peck, he's in trouble down the road with a caribou, Mile 187."

"Okay, I know exactly what the rest of it is," Bud said. He left his coffee and came as quickly as he could drive, bringing another fellow with him for help.

The three men started to unload the caribou. They got him onto the ground and untied him. He was wearing a halter, so the men hung onto him while Anderson massaged his legs before they let him up. "He was wobbly, about like me," Anderson says. "The caribou tugged at the halter a little bit, then stood, prouder than hell, shaking his head, and finally let go and had a long-awaited pee. And from then on, everything was good."

By this time, traffic was pulling up and stopping, so Bud and the other guy took over. Anderson needed it; he was about at the end of his endurance. They decided to throw the animal as one would a steer, "not harm him or anything, just bring him to the ground, tie him up again," when one of the spectators said, "I have a ranch down in Montana and I never did throw a caribou. Do you mind if I help?"

"No, go ahead," Anderson said.

But when the fellow went to flip the caribou, the animal out-manoeuvred him and landed squarely on top of him. The caribou struggled to its feet, looked at Anderson as if to say, "Why do you allow greenhorns to deal with this?" and pulled at the end of the rope a bit.

"They're quick little bastards, ain't they?" the Montana rancher said. "Can I try it again?"

He tried it . . . and again wound up on the underside of the 300-pound bull.

Finally, both Anderson and the caribou had had enough. "I went over, grabbed the caribou and down he went. We threw the strings on him and put him into the back of Bud's panel and away we went to Mile 147, with me holding his head and calming him down. We put him in the barn, turned him loose—had a couple more in the barn anyway—and went back up to the lodge. After that it was time to have a hot toddy or two, by God, I'll tell you. Which we did."

Not all projects to transport live animals end so positively, and other pilots can tell tales of such manoeuvres that ended tragically for animal, pilot, and airplane. Anderson prides himself on his ability to handle animals. In total, he ferried out 21 caribou and seven stone sheep for the game farm. "I never lost an animal, never even pulled any hair out of them."

Anderson has lived a life that many would envy but few would trade for. At 68, he's philosophical about his accomplishments, and he isn't done yet. He's so well-known along the entire 1,500-mile Alaska Highway that a letter addressed "Jimmy Anderson, Alaska Highway" was delivered without a problem.

A bout of throat cancer in 1992 gave him a six-month sabbatical, but the inevitable dread of the disease was tempered by his incurable optimism. "I've always been afraid of a knife at my throat or around my belt buckle," he said, trying to laugh about the whole thing.

In June 1992, at his home at Pink Mountain, BC, he talked hesitantly about the forthcoming surgery. His throat hurt, his voice was scratchy as an old 78 record left lying in a pile. It seemed unthinkable that the voice of this extraordinary storyteller could possibly be stilled.

Two months after the surgery he's on the phone, describing the procedure: "I was in the operating room at 12:30, up to my room at 1:00, into my jeans by 1:30. They drug a bunch of stuff out of my throat—cigarette butts, beer bottle caps."

As Anderson's voice recovered, so did his itchy feet. He wanted to get back to Pink Mountain, where his snow-covered Cherokee awaited him.

He'll have to have it checked over before he can put it into the air again—this time, neither he nor his airplane is licensed. But Anderson is confident that a little mechanical work on the airplane and a medical check-up for him will have them both right as rain.

He's got another idea, for a tourism plan that will knock the socks off the industry. It involves modifying a big all-terrain snowmobile where up to six people can sit inside a closed-in cabin—the weather can hit 40 below, it won't matter. From the comfort of this thing-a-ma-jig, Anderson's customers will be able to travel the hills and valleys of the vast northern country, seeing moose and caribou up close, viewing, from the ground, some of the spectacular sights that Anderson has seen so often from the air.

Meanwhile, Anderson fully expects to be up in the air again soon. Oh yeah! Clean the birds' nests out of the Cherokee, tack his flight plan to a tree, and let 'er rip down the longest airstrip in the world—known to some people as the Alaska Highway.

Notes

1. Larry Pynn, *Calgary Herald*, 19 April 1992.
2. Slow flight is the range of airspeeds between the maximum endurance speed for a particular aircraft and the point just above its stalling speed for existing flight conditions. Proper technique and precise control of the aircraft are essential in this speed range (Transport Canada *Flight Training Manual*).

Ballad of a Bush Pilot

Olden Bawld (a.k.a. Charles R. Robinson)

In days gone by I used to fly
    a Fairchild 82;
And was it fair or stormy air
    we'd always muddle through.
For hours I'd sit upon the bit
    of kapok-padded seat,
My knees tucked in beneath my chin
    in comfort, hard to beat.
The instruments, the cowling dents
    the grease spots on the glass;
I still recall them one and all,
    as through the years I pass.

"Strange things are done 'neath midnight sun,"
    'Twas said in days gone by.
This still is true in '42
    For malamutes now fly!
The Northern Lights still see queer sights—
    I've flown o'er Dawson's Trail
(Where dog teams plied and strong men died)
    a Condor full of mail.

I've carried boats and smelly goats
    in Junkers 34s.
I froze my toes in Barkley-Grows
    on Great Bear's rocky shores.
In summer heat and winter sleet
    I've flown them old and new;
With radio beams and endless streams
    I still do muddle through.

(Composed in Boeing 247D, (CF–BVT) while flying down
the Mackenzie River, 21 Sept 1942.)

On the Fringes of the Average Life

L ORNA *(BRAY) DEBLICQUY* has lived in tents in northern Manitoba, bunked down in "skid" shacks on isolated construction and drilling sites, and was even awarded her own fur-lined outhouse seat on Ellesmere Island. She has visited Arab and Bedouin camps in Saudi Arabia, has careened down "ski-jump" airstrips in New Zealand, and has delivered famine relief in Ethiopia, all in her line of work—flying airplanes.

The story of Lorna's career is anything but standard, and like any good story, contains its share of conflict. But her major problems came not from the airplanes she flew, nor the unforgiving terrain in which she flew them, nor even from the men she encountered in the bush-sites. Her nemesis was the sociopolitical field that surrounded job opportunities for women in aviation.

Designed and controlled largely by male government officials—many of whom were ex-military personnel—the wording and implications contained in the regulations made it extremely tough for females to win any of the job competitions advertised by the Department of Transport (DOT). "Air force training, then available only to men, is concentrated, thorough, and desirable. I never had that, and most of the other applicants—being male—did," Lorna explains.

When job offers didn't come, Lorna declared war. The wins are still being counted.

Lorna Bray, born in Blyth, Ontario, on 30 November 1931, was always interested in airplanes, but the chances of a young woman becoming a pilot were remote when she was growing up. Even the Air Cadets offered no hope to females wanting to become pilots: girls were not eligible for flying scholarships. Rather than being trained as pilots, they learned clerking skills, with possibly some training in Morse code thrown in.

In 1946, just after the Bray family had moved to Ottawa, Lorna had the good fortune to see a sign on the door of the new and struggling McGuire Aviation School at Uplands Airport (now Ottawa International Airport): $2.75 WILL GET YOU STARTED! Excited by her brother's stories, an RCAF pilot who later became a bush pilot, and senior captain with Pacific Western Airlines, Lorna borrowed the money from her cousin, and began her initial training on a J–3 Piper Cub. While attending Ottawa's Glebe Collegiate Institute, she continued training with Atlas Aviation in Ottawa, where she learned to fly various light aircraft including J-3s and PA-11s.

Money for her 15-minutes-per-week flying lessons—which cost $11 per hour—came through the usual child-labour efforts: babysitting for 25 cents an hour, and then as cashier at the Elgin Theatre for 42 cents an hour. During lesson time, she had to keep her parents' strict rules in mind: take a bus to the airport, take the lesson, and be home on the next available bus. No loitering around the hangar. "Girls who hang around airports are bound to be tough," her mother admonished.

"At 15 minutes a week, which is all I could afford, progress was

Lorna Bray, 1946, McGuire Aviation School, Ottawa. *Lorna deBlicquy Collection*

slow," Lorna says. "Still, we didn't have to pay for ground time. There wasn't any. If you didn't solo before eight hours, they usually told you to quit. I made it under the wire in seven hours and 40 minutes, starting in October and soloing in May.

"Ground School consisted of reading a little 40-page grey book that contained all the air regs you would ever need to know. Anyone doing a pre-flight inspection was thought to be too frightened to fly—or perhaps showing that you didn't trust the engineer. If someone had told me that following hour four the next lesson would be learning to fly backwards, it would have seemed quite logical to me."

Lorna practised for her private pilot's licence test, which was scheduled for January 1948, just one month after her 17th birthday. She describes the standard test procedure: "When the tower flashed a light, you cut the throttle and, without using any more power or even brakes during the landing, you came to a stop beside the examiner's car. You practised the approach flying high and fast—about 65 mph in a J-3 Cub—slipping like mad and then fishtailing wildly during an adventurous ground roll. Then you climbed to 6,000 feet directly over the airport, did a three-turn left spin, then a three-turn right spin, and again rolled to that power-off stop."

Previously, the DOT examiner had stayed in his car as he observed the candidate's attempts to make four spot-landings from somewhere in the circuit. But the procedure was changed just prior to Lorna's test date, and she was chosen as a guinea-pig for the new system. Now, as she watched the examiner

Lorna Bray in training at McGuire Aviation School, Ottawa, with J-3 Cub, 1946. *Lorna deBlicquy Collection*

climb into the aircraft with her, Lorna was filled with dread. She had to pass, otherwise she would face a 30-day waiting period before she could try again.

They went through the usual routines of "precautionaries"[1] and forced approaches, which she managed even though the examiner covered the instrument panel from her view. [2] But when he said, "Go back to the airport," Lorna lost it.

"He might as well have demanded a trip to Mars," Lorna says. "I was suddenly hopeless."

The examiner had to take over the landing.

"When I failed my first attempt, an exception was made and I was allowed to try the old type test before the 30 days were up." She passed, and was awarded her licence.

One of her first flying endeavours was barnstorming in northern Quebec, with pilots Weldy Phipps and Bill Law. "Barnstorming in this context," Lorna says, "was simply landing beside a fair or a ploughing match and taking people up for rides—no stunts at all. That show was seen by the people as simply an aircraft driver making money."

While attending Carleton University on a scholarship, Lorna gained her commercial pilot's licence with the Ottawa Flying Club in 1952, flying "those fast and sturdy Canadian-built Fleet Canucks with the powerful 85 hp engines."

But she had to do it on her own; there was no financial help at all for females wishing to train as pilots. "Boys at Carleton could join the ROTC (Reserve Officers' Training Corps) as officer-cadets. Girls could join the Reserve Air Force as AW2s (Air Woman, Second Class), pushing little magnets around plotting boards at an officer's command. Boys received a $100 grant towards a pilot's licence and another $100 if they went into aircrew training in the RCAF."

The following year, after graduating in 1953 with a Bachelor of Arts degree, Lorna "considered herself lucky" to be hired by Spartan Air Services in Ottawa as a navigation clerk.

"At least Weldy Phipps, a pilot employed with the company, saw that I got to come along as a passenger in some interesting and exotic aircraft they used, like the Ventura; or in the P-38 Lockheed Lightning, where I was stowed on the shelf behind the pilot with a knee dangling beside each of his ears. Gradually, too, I got a few trips here and there ferrying spare parts or even taking photographers up in Cessna 170s or Piper Clippers for the occasional contract for 'photo obliques.'"

It appeared to Lorna, however, that her chances of actually being paid to fly were about zero, as thousands of experienced wartime male pilots were still available in the early 1950s. "I was dimly aware of women like Marion Powell Orr, or Vi Milstead—

Lorna Bray Nichols, 1950 with Fleet–80 Canuck, Ottawa Flying Club. *Lorna deBlicquy Collection*

Ontario pilots who had found flying jobs in the 1940s with the Air Transport Auxiliary," Lorna says. "In fact, once on a crosscountry to Windsor, Vi had refuelled the aircraft in which I was a passenger. I was too in awe of her even to say hello."

After graduating, Lorna continued her education, taking extra courses in Philosophy, and Methods of Education from the Ontario College of Education. Because work as a pilot was so sporadic, she needed to rely on teaching to augment her income.

In 1953, Lorna married geologist Tony Nichols, and moved with him to northern Manitoba. She immediately applied for flying jobs in the North. Her licences and skills were fine. In fact, they were much in demand. There was only one problem: she was female.

"With a commercial licence, a few months' experience as a navigation clerk and occasional photo-pilot for Spartan Air Services, and seaplane endorsement—but with many letters from companies stating that I was a nice girl but they didn't hire girls—I found myself housed in a tent in northern Manitoba, after flying 1,300 miles from Ottawa in my own Aeronca Chief on floats," Lorna recalls.

"But when the local operator, Jock Hunter of Taylor Airways, found that his newly arrived male employee had no float rating, he was desperate. So he took a chance and hired me to fly a 1930s Waco Standard ZKS-6 biplane (CF-BBQ) out of Wabowden, on the Hudson's Bay rail line. He left me alone with this monster to fly fish, move Indian encampments, and pick up what charter work came available.

"My instructions were contained in a ragged and oily note on the panel listing manifold pressure and rpm settings. It became obvious that even if I had chanced to understand anything about constant speed units, these settings were in the realm of fantasy."

The Waco was the first constant speed prop airplane [3] Lorna had ever flown, and she "never did get the numbers the manual suggested. I was really an accident looking for a place to happen." [4]

After more than two years of living in a tent on skids, while flying the Aeronca Chief and "old BBQ" [5] for drilling camps in the area that is now Thompson, Lorna developed survival knowledge and flying skills to cope with the northern climate—and its inhabitants.

One night she was bunked out in a tent by herself when a horrendous storm blew in. She could hear the drillers arguing outside. She couldn't hear what the argument was about—could it be that someone wanted to bother her, and another was forbidding him to go near her? Lorna, tired from the day's work, simply pulled the sleeping bag over her head and fell asleep.

The next morning the men explained. Worried that Lorna's Aeronca Chief would slip its moorings, they had reinforced the tie-downs, then had "argued" about whether it would be better to come up to her tent to keep her company in case she was afraid of the storm, or if it would frighten her even more to find someone crawling into her quarters. Comfort her, or leave her alone? They decided to leave her alone, and that was the closest "intrusion to her privacy" she ever experienced in the bush camps.

"I certainly had no trouble living in the tent as the only woman within miles," Lorna says. "I often used the aircraft to get out to the 'metropolises' of The Pas or Flin Flon, or to fly over a few lakes to visit other women in similar conditions.

"I had no children then. I was young, and the flying was great." But she laughs when she considers the image she must have presented: "I'm five-feet-four inches tall. I was dressed like a pear, because the tent would be cold on the floor and warm above, so I wore many pairs of socks, and quite a bit of clothing from the waist down—not so much from the waist up."

The people she met in the remote settlements were "usually proud Natives," Lorna says. "I would go into houses quite happily and be accepted, I believe, and have people in my tent. They lived off the land and there were not so many of them that it was impossible then. But, at that time there were still signs on the bars in The Pas: 'Women, Dogs, and Treaty Indians Not Allowed.'

"I'm glad to see the world has improved in some respects at least."

Following two years in Manitoba, the Nichols moved to Sudbury, Ontario. Over the next five years Lorna added to her qualifications by becoming a Class II instructor (*ab initio* "from scratch, pre-solo, pre-licence" floats and skis) for Sudbury Aviation at Azilda, Ontario, flying a Fleet Canuck made for wheels, skis, and floats.

"I believe that instructing is one heck of a fine job," Lorna says, "if you disregard the long hours, low pay and low prestige! But one-on-one training can be a rewarding experience for both sides."

While in Sudbury, Lorna's full-time "day-gig" was teaching at the high school, while also instructing part-time at Sudbury Aviation. In 1962 she became an instructor for the Kingston Flight Club at KFC Air Charter, flying Cessnas, including a Cessna 195 on crosswind gear. This was also the year she knew her second husband would be pilot Dick deBlicquy. (Her first marriage had ended while she lived in Sudbury.)

The deBlicquys' flying career took them to New Zealand, where they were married in 1963.

Lorna found that the strips in New Zealand resembled ski-jumps, "but once I was there and got a checkout or two on them, with the local people or local pilots, it was not that difficult to adapt." For three consecutive winters, Lorna flew as a Category "B" pilot (similar to Canada's Class II, indicating some experience) for the Marlborough Aero Club in Blenheim, and for Sounds Scenic Flights in Picton, flying various light aircraft such as a Cessna 185, DH-82 Tiger Moth, Fletcher, and Auster.

During the New Zealand off-season in 1963, Lorna returned to Canada and qualified for her Multi-Engine and Private Glider licences. She returned to New Zealand as an instructor with the Wellington Aero Club, then came back to Canada as an instructor for the Ottawa Flying Club. In 1966 she got her endorsement to teach instrument flying.

The deBlicquys' Arctic sojourns also began in the 1960s, in opposite seasons to the New Zealand work. During the summer while Dick was employed as a pilot for Weldy Phipps's company, Atlas Aviation Limited, located at Resolute Bay on Cornwallis Island, the deBlicquys flew to the various islands of the high Arctic, taking their new baby, Elaine, with them. Lorna flew an Apache, a De Havilland Beaver with wide tundra tires, and copiloted a Twin Otter with her husband. One of their adventures was the "rescue" of five members of an RAF Mountain Rescue Team who were stranded on Ellesmere Island. Interestingly enough, Dick was their pilot. The Twin Otter had lost an engine, and left Dick and his party stranded 5,500 feet up on a glacier.

Realizing that if the story got out it would be "poor PR" for Atlas Aviation, Lorna was elected to go to the rescue in the Beaver. She admits that what happened next was "brave but stupid."[6]

She took off in cloudy IFR (Instrument Flight Rules) flying weather, believing that conditions would soon clear. After two hours the clouds broke through, but the pattern of mountains below did not match her map. She was low on fuel, on a rescue mission, and lost. To have one Atlas Aviation pilot in distress was serious, but to have two of them missing—and one a woman, and the wife of pilot #1—would be disastrous.

An hour later, Lorna had oriented herself and managed to land at Eureka. Meanwhile, Resolute Bay had assumed—correctly—that she was lost. When she arrived at Eureka, they radioed the Resolute base, and then her husband, informing them that she'd been found. "I didn't know she was lost!" Dick replied when he heard the news, after walking out to Tanquary Fiord base camp.

Most of Lorna's flying in the High North took place during the summer. "I was only working out of Resolute during the dark period for maybe three weeks at a time, once over Christmas and New Year's. You steel yourself to the cold, and it's kind of pretty. One Christmas we were flying when a Scandinavian airliner flew over us. Its crew was singing Christmas carols. We sang back to them. It was quite an inspiring moment, with the whole Arctic archipelago spread out below us."

Lorna has flown as far north on Ellesmere Island as Disraeli Fiord—where, at the Defense Research Board camp, she was given the luxurious caribou-hide lined seat—and spent some time close to the North Pole. "But Franny Phipps, the boss's (Weldy's) wife, was the first woman at the North Pole, so if you read somewhere that I was, I wasn't."

Lorna says that women were definitely "not welcome on the voyage" by companies operating at that time in the eastern Arctic. "In 1963, Fran Phipps and I were considered tourist guests of our husbands at Resolute Bay, which was then administered from Winnipeg by the DOT, and managed by the Tower Foundation Company as a staging point for the eastern Arctic. A week before we were to arrive for our northern 'holiday,' the Tower Foundation manager received a telegram from Winnipeg warning him that in no way was he to cooperate with those 'free-enterprisers' who dared to bring females to Resolute Bay. When told that we'd live off the base in tents, the poor man was at a loss to indicate just where the base property ended. Nowadays camping in the High Arctic is the 'in' thing to do. So we like to think of ourselves as pioneers!"

One experience Lorna vividly recalls during that time was the day the weather clamped down just before she arrived at Mould Bay in the Beaver.

"When flying from Resolute Bay to Mould Bay, on Prince Patrick Island, there is a fair distance between 'comfort stops,'" Lorna says. "My instrument flying was pretty awful at the time, and our instrumentation, including the astro compass, left a lot to be desired. Fortunately, a couple of fuel drums marking the strip appeared through a small hole in the fog just as I was about to attempt the let-down.

"Because the approach at Mould Bay consisted of one low frequency beacon, and the heading indicator had to be set with the astro compass, and most especially since it had been a long time since I'd seen an outhouse, fur-lined seat or not, the wiser course was a rapid descent through that small hole and a 'short short' field landing."

When spiralling down to the short landing, however, Lorna noted she had a reception committee waiting below, with faces directed upward to watch her let-down. "Most of the men in that joint U.S.-Canadian weather station had not seen a woman in months, and also they were worried about me flying in such weather. So every person and vehicle in the entire base had gathered and were waiting for my arrival. At the near end of the strip they were lined up on snowmobiles, small tractors, D-8 cats, trucks of every description, or standing along the edge of the strip.

"I taxied madly away from the mob and parked the Beaver sideways on the strip. But there wasn't even a tree in a thousand miles that I could hide behind!" Lorna says, laughing. "All I can say is those big tires have many applications for which Weldy Phipps never designed them. I barely won that race!"

The story is often told of the time Lorna's arrival at Eureka coincided with that of Pierre Elliott Trudeau. Here is Lorna's version: "Trudeau was visiting the Arctic, I think for the first time, shortly after he'd become prime minister of Canada. I was flying that day and didn't get in until fairly late, although during the summer season it was daytime all the time. They had put on a celebration for him in Resolute Bay, but he was leaving by the time I got there, supposedly to go on to Alert. So we all had a party anyway, at least those of us who'd worked late that day.

"The next morning nobody was feeling too well and my husband, Dick, and I had a scheduled trip from Resolute to Eureka on Ellesmere Island. We agreed that one of us would sleep for part of the trip, and the other for the second half. We had no load on the way up to speak of, so we put a mattress in the back of the single Otter we were flying."

The two pilots drew a line on the chart between Resolute Bay and Eureka. "You start," Dick said. "You do the flight planning to the halfway point. Then I'll take over and land at Eureka."

When the halfway point came, Lorna got him up and she, in turn, crawled onto the mattress and fell asleep. About five minutes before they were to land at Eureka, Dick woke her. She was not pleased. "I let you sleep for the first half without interruption! Why couldn't you return the favour?"

"Trudeau's aircraft can't get in to Alert and it's landing at Eureka," he said. "If he sees you, you may get a chance to talk to the new prime minister!"

When they landed, the prime minister and his entourage had already gone down to the barracks-like place where the reception was to be held. There, Trudeau noticed the American cook quickly doing up the buttons on a white shirt.

"Oh, you don't have to do anything special for me," Trudeau said to the flustered cook. "After all, I wasn't expected. Just be yourself."

The cook drew himself up to his full height. "But, it's not for you, sir!" he said. "Lorna deBlicquy is flight-planned in here!"

Lorna laughs when she recalls this story. "It was sort of indicative of how few women there were in that area at the time," she says, with a Trudeau-esque shrug. "You could have a face like a horse and a personality ten points below Idi Amin. All you had to be was female."

While Dick flew almost year-round in the North, Lorna flew North in the summer but returned to Ontario in the winter months to continue her flying career there and look after the baby. Following two seasons flying in the High

Arctic, and a winter in Florida, Lorna thought it was time to settle in one place to better accommodate her daughter's education.

From 1968 to 1977, Lorna gained a Class II IFR rating, a Class I Instructor's rating (1971), as well as a Commercial Rotary Wing licence (1972) operating a Bell 47.

Although licensed to fly helicopters, she says it is not her forte. "Flying helicopters is a whole different operation from flying normal fixed-wing aircraft, especially when I learned. The controls were not boosted and you couldn't let go of them for two seconds to scratch your nose or you'd lose total control. It's a lot easier now as far as the actual management of the helicopter goes, but I'm not up to date on it and never have used one enough to be an authority."

In September 1972, she got her Canadian Airline Transport Licence.

Even though over-regulation may be considered a nuisance by pilots, Lorna states, "It's been my experience that a lot of the regulations were, and are, badly needed. For example, I can remember searching frantically for the starter in a Cessna Golden Eagle, at night, in the cold, with four frozen passengers waiting for the 'sked' run to Sudbury out of Ottawa. On that evening both the pilot and I, the copilot, were expected to cope with an aircraft that neither of us had ever handled—we'd expected the usual Beech 18. PPCs (Pilot Proficiency Checkrides—now compulsory for work on new types of aircraft flown with passengers) were unknown. Some regulation is a blessing for all concerned."

During the late 1960s and up to 1977, Lorna flew Cessnas, Pipers, and various light twins including Aero Commander, Aerostar, and Beech-18.[7]

This was when the "fun flying" came. Lorna participated in a number of Powder Puff derbies, often winning "best non-U.S." prize. She flew in the Greater Burlington Centennial Seaplane Race and a few Angel Derbies, and did some "satisfying recreational gliding."

Then the battles began.

Desiring some stability in her career, in 1974 Lorna applied for a job with AirTransit, a crown corporation that flew Twin Otters between Ottawa and Montreal. In her application she emphasized her several thousand flying hours, including time on Twin Otters and other STOL (short take-off and landing) aircraft. The company thanked her for her application, but said that other applications had come in from pilots who had time on more sophisticated aircraft. Then, they hired Lorna's ex-students. Later, she heard some of the reasons cited for not hiring her—from the people who were hired: she had too much time as a copilot; not enough captain time; she was too short; and they didn't design uniforms for women.

"I was so angry! I raised a flap about it," Lorna says. "Especially in an editorial letter to *Canadian Flight* magazine in 1974, protesting evidence of discrimination against women pilots by AirTransit, which was a subsidiary of Air Canada. The article attracted national media attention."

Even though people began talking about the situation, nothing was done

Powder Puff Derby, 1971, from Calgary, Alberta, to Baton Rouge, Louisiana. (L-R): Lorna deBlicquy and Betty Jane Schumerhorn, who also flew together in 1972, sponsored by Bradley Air Services Ltd. *Lorna deBlicquy Collection*

to improve it. Whenever job openings came up with the DOT, Lorna doggedly continued to voice her concerns, and to keep applying, in the belief that the Flight Training Standards division of Transport Canada seemed the most likely area to hire civilians, especially female civilians. "DOT was manned—and I do mean manned—with mostly ex-military personnel," Lorna says.

Colleagues agreed, however, that there would be little change to hiring policies until the implementation of the findings from the report on the "Royal Commission on the Status of Women in Canada," (tabled in the House of Commons on 7 December 1970). The report contained 167 recommendations, based on fundamental principles that assumed equality of opportunity for Canadian men and women was possible, desirable, and ethically necessary.

Lorna managed to get an interview with the DOT, but found that the questions concentrated on personal matters: What would her husband think of her taking the job? What would she do about her daughter?

She kept applying and almost made it, but a man with more experience was hired as Number One. "I was Number Two on the list, perfectly legitimately."

But men weren't the only ones who seemed to expect women to follow, and be satisfied with, traditional roles. Never being the type of woman who wore "pink puffball dresses," Lorna was distressed by these societal expectations.

"Worse still, the climate of opinion in which I grew up, in many not-too-obvious ways, imprinted in women's minds that we were in a competition to attract the best mate," Lorna said in a recent talk to a women's aviation seminar in British Columbia. "The competition was other women. And it was women who criticized other women. The point is, we tend to blame the climate of opinion on that other half of the population—men. I don't want to do this. We *people* create the world around us."

After the Status of Women committee began to gain influence, she sent it a copy of one of her inquiry letters to DOT asking for hiring policy clarification. Until then, all Class I instructors had been notified of openings. Then she stopped receiving the notifications, but new people were being hired. Why?

Her correspondence with Mrs. Florence Bird, an Ottawa journalist and broadcaster who had chaired the Royal Commission on the Status of Women in Canada, marked a turning point, and 1977 brought about a major achievement in Lorna deBlicquy's career: she was the first woman to be hired as a DOT inspector for Air Regulations Division, Ontario Region, on Beech Baron 55s, DHC-6s (Twin Otters) and Cessna 182s.

"I became the first female inspector with the great and glorious 'Department of Trouble,'" Lorna says. "By the time I had the job, I didn't really want it, but I stayed for over two years and have subsequently had a few contracts with them." She also worked as an inspector for personnel licensing, and Flight Training Standards, until 1979.

Lorna believes there are now approximately 50 female DOT inspectors across the country. "Still, you run into the strangest interpretations of what your behaviour should be as a female in this industry," Lorna says. One time when she and another female inspector attended a CUPE (Canadian Union of Public Employees) meeting and happened to sit in different areas of the room, someone asked out loud, "What's the matter? Can't you get along?"

Lorna continued to work diligently to ensure a future for female pilots in the aviation industry. When Canada endorsed ICAO's (International Civil Aviation Organization's) policy to list pregnancy under the category of "a disease," Lorna served on the 99s (International Association of Women Pilots) committee to monitor how pregnancy might relate to a pilot's medical standards. As a result of the committee's work, some leniency was allowed on the usual loss of a Category I medical certificate during a pilot's pregnancy.

"As far as marriage and motherhood with this career goes, a person cannot do it all," Lorna says. "But, if one doesn't have too many children, it's certainly possible to take a little time off and do some of it in an effective way.

But the other challenge for women who want to become successful in the aviation field—job equality for men and women—goes back a long way, and will not be solved overnight.

"I invite you to think about this," Lorna says. "I was born in 1931. Had I started as a bank teller out of high school, I would have had no chance to become manager of the bank. So it wasn't just flying.

"Also, I had the advantage of having a husband behind me. I know it would not have been possible, or as easy in those days, had I not been somebody's wife. I was rather fortunate."

In 1986, Lorna journeyed overseas to fly a DHC-6 for Air-Serv International to assist in famine relief in Addis Ababa, Ethiopia. "As recently as 1986, believe it or not, the major airlines were recalling their crews laid off in the minor recession of the previous year. As a result, AIRSERVE, a sidekick of Missionary Air Freight, asked Dick and me to fill in flying famine relief in Ethiopia. Not fun. But interesting flying."

Their trips were usually made from the end of the road in to almost-inaccessible small plateaus in the high country where every inch of arable ground was intensively cultivated by the burgeoning population, Lorna says. Erosion was horrendous. "In 12-minute legs in a Twin Otter, the elevation of the land under us could be as low as 3,000 feet ASL (above sea level) to a height of 8,000-plus feet ASL. The aircraft was refuelled with engines running, and loaded through the open door with sacks and sacks of a wheat-like grain called 'teff.'"

Teff is very fine-grained, and until De Havilland advised against it, pilots flew with a rear door open to save loading and unloading time. Their approaches would be steep, to rough, hilly stone-covered strips. Often the population would be sitting, cross-legged, on the edge of the strips, busy splitting the large rocks into smaller stones to accommodate their landing. "As the flaps were extended, the tiny grains of teff would exit the loose woven sacks and whirl forward into the cockpit," Lorna says. "I'll bet there are not too many people who've landed a Twin Otter at 9,000 feet IFR in clouds of teff."

Lorna did not complete their two-month scheduled stay in Ethiopia. Problems included "life in a converted henhouse where no one had told the hens about the conversion." She also found difficult the trips down the Blue Nile to evacuate malaria cases, or watching the bugs swim in the water in their room at the Addis Ababa Hotel. "A week or two after I got out of the country, ill with dysentery, Dick came home with typhoid."

It was humbling to see the work done by so many dedicated people under such appalling conditions, Lorna says, "but I cannot convince myself that this is the way to better our world. Famine biscuits may keep some alive in some state for some time, but long-term solutions are another matter."

The deBlicquys also spent some time in Saudi Arabia. Lorna travelled as a passenger while Dick flew to various areas of the country. There, they saw sites ranging from Lawrence of Arabia's train, which had been derailed in 1917, to Arab and Bedouin camps.

This experience was followed, again, by working for Transport Canada, as a CAI-3 (Civil Air Inspector) in their Inspector/Engineer Training and Development sector.

The marriage of Lorna and Dick deBlicquy was, unfortunately, dissolved in 1992.

The last five years of Lorna's flying career have included working as a DFTE (Designated Flight Test Examiner) out of the Carp Airport west of Ottawa, and part-time instructing for the Ottawa Flying Club.

To date (1993) she has a total of 10,000 hours accident-free flying, which includes 5,500 hours instructing, 1,000 on multi-engine aircraft, 750 on floats, 400 on skis, approximately 150 hours testing instructor candidates, and 1,300 hours testing candidates for private, commercial, and multi-engine licence endorsements.

Although Lorna is modest about the awards she's accumulated throughout her flying career, the list itself is anything but modest. In 1970 she won the Amelia Earhart Scholarship sponsored by the 99s, followed in 1972 by the President's Trophy from the Ottawa Flying Club. As well, she's won several air-race and competition trophies, including Best Non-U.S. Racing Trophy, B.A. Scott spot landing, Powder Puff Derby, and local rally trophies. Then came the major awards: the National Transportation Week Award of Excellence in June 1992 for her more than 40 years of outstanding contribution to transportation in Canada, and the prestigious Transportation Canada McKee Trophy in 1993.

The McKee Trophy, first awarded in 1927, is named after a wealthy American sportsman pilot, J. Dalzell McKee. It annually honours a Canadian pilot who the committee feels has contributed the most during the preceding year to the advancement of Canadian aviation.

Lorna deBlicquy, at 61, was the first woman to receive the trophy in its 66-year history.

Lorna's work toward advancing the cause of women in commercial aviation, as well as her achievements in being Canada's first female high-latitude pilot, and the first female civil aviation flight-test inspector, were cited as exemplary. The Governor General's Award in Commemoration of the Persons Case, given annually in recognition of outstanding contributions to the quality of life of women in Canada, followed in December 1993. And, in 1994, Lorna deBlicquy received the Order of Ontario, the Ottawa YWCA Annual Women of Distinction Award, and was named top alumnae of the year, the David Duntan Award, from Carleton University.

Lorna has taken the time to repay the community that has provided her life with such variety and excitement through active membership in aviation organizations.[8]

In August 1993, Lorna attended a Women's Aviation Conference in Vancouver. "There, I saw competent, self-assured people, who happened to be women, doing all sorts of jobs in the aviation industry," she says. "It's an encouraging trend, despite the fact that most of the major airlines have had to lay off their female employees who are pilots because of the system 'last hired, soonest fired.' But I think a good many doors are opening. It's mainly economics, that's the problem now, not discrimination.

"I come from an earlier generation when aviation seemed romantic and interesting," Lorna says, in evaluating her long and varied career as a pilot. "I still believe it's very interesting, but perhaps there's not as much space for the romance as there once was. That's as it should be, I suppose.

"I've done flight tests on a couple of students who will be part of the next crop of Canada's astronauts. I think that's where the romance is coming next."

Although she says sometimes she wished she'd possessed "more of a business head," she is managing fine. "I really have had a very satisfying life, and I can't imagine doing anything much else. I live in a sort of house that I was planning to use as a summer cottage, though it's a perfectly decent house. I love doing things like chopping my own wood with a wedge and a good sledge hammer. I enjoy the outdoors, and I can't imagine being imprisoned in an apartment or on a boat or something like that. That's probably a legacy from the time spent in northern Manitoba, for which I thank my lucky stars.

"But," she adds, "sometimes I wish I hadn't been on the fringes of the average life.

"Looking back, though, I've seen a lot of the world. I've had the opportunity to meet all kinds of fascinating people—and I haven't quit yet. Life is still very interesting for me because of my flying. No regrets."

Notes

1. In a precautionary approach, a pilot throttles back, descends, and flies approximately 500 feet above the ground in slow flight to examine the area below (lake, river, field, etc.) to check if it's safe to land.
2. An examiner might place a card or sheet of paper over the instrument panel to force the pilot to fly the airplane entirely by attitude. The pilot should be able to sense how fast he/she is flying by how quickly the aircraft is moving over the landscape, assess the angle of bank or climb by evaluating the relationship between the nose and wing to horizon, sound of airplane in air, and know if he/she is slipping or skidding in a turn, etc. It has been explained as the difference between "flying with your head inside, or outside, the cockpit," with the latter being the sign of a competent pilot able to judge such factors by "feel" and logic rather than relying on instruments.
3. A constant speed propeller will change its pitch automatically according to whether the aircraft is cruising, ascending, or descending. A fine pitch is required when climbing (such as during take-off) when the aircraft needs as many rpm as possible. A coarse pitch is required when the aircraft has levelled out and the engine is running at lower rpm.
4. Shirley Render, *No Place for a Lady, The Story of Canadian Women Pilots 1928–1992* (Portage & Main Press, Winnipeg), 1992, 187.
5. Waco CF-BBQ was left to expire on the shore of a lake for a number of years, then purchased by a U.S. collector in the mid-1970s. It is now an immaculately restored vintage airplane.
6. Render, 189–90.

7. Lorna deBlicquy has flown many different aircraft, including DC-3, Beech-18, Bell 47, DHC-6 (Twin Otter) and DHC-2 Beaver with Tundra Tires, a DHC-1 (Chipmunk), Aerocommander, Aerostar, Waco ZKS-6, B-55 (Beechcraft Baron), Apache, Cessna 195 (crosswind gear), DH-82 (Tiger Moth), and various other singles and twins.

8. Lorna deBlicquy has been a member since 1949 of the 99s International Association of Women Pilots, serving in various chapters and section offices; belonged at one time to the Whirly Girls #131 (an organization for female helicopter pilots, similar to the 99s); is an honourary life member of the Ottawa Flying Club, and served on its board of directors in 1975-76. She is a member of COPA (Canadian Owners and Pilots Association), has served on the consultative committee of Ottawa's National Aviation Museum, on the advisory committee on Algonquin College's aviation faculty, is a member of ATAC's (Air Transport Association of Canada's) Flying Training Committee (1975), and was a representative on the 99s committee for Transport Canada's study of "how pregnancy related to pilots' medical standards."

Rebel with a Cause

*O*KAY, *SAME DRILL, TERRY,* take her up as far as you feel is a good target for yourself, and then let her roll."

"Roger."

The bird-dog's voice crackles on one of four radios he's monitoring from the Beech Baron, flying high over the fire that's raging through Saskatchewan's once-green forest.

"Not too much active along that line right now, just hanging in there, a lot of smoke."

"I got one off the far corner there, Don, in Big Spruce."

"Yeah, it looks like a good one. Nice open flame."

"Bird-Dog Three, Bird-Dog Two."

"Go ahead.

Static, background noises, jumbled jargon, fragmented messages. The tape is indecipherable—but not to bird-dog, Don Hadden, who later translates the back-and-forth conversation taped in the aircraft while fighting a forest fire at Meadow Lake in 1993.

A pilot's voice comes on: "Ah, it's just that close turnaround, I'll pick out

The bird-dog aircraft: Beech Baron B-55. *Don Hadden Collection*

a new lake there but I'll wait until you do your thing because there's going to be sharp end-turns close in."

"You've got to get an ear for the radio," Hadden laughs. "The guy said he was going to pick out a better spot because it was a kind of tight turnaround in there, with helicopters dropping and all that."

"Oh, there she goes. They let her get away again. Helicopter Three Five, Bird-Dog Two. We check that you are at 6,000 with 3002 on the altimeter . . ."

"She's looking pretty orange in there now, eh?"

"It is, yeah, damn orange."

Up to four radios were being monitored by the bird-dog. He admits that it can get a bit hairy while fighting a fire if all four radios come on at once—which can happen. He has to know instantly who is saying what, from where, to whom, and on which frequency. But to the uninitiated, the voices sound like a bunch of barking seals.

"You know what's going to happen, you sort of know the name of the game. I'm simplifying it, I suppose, but for myself it's like, 'the carpet's there, walk on it.'"

Fighting forest fires from the air has always been Don Hadden's occupation. And, even though he's supposed to be retired, taking it easy, he's still up there pitting man and machines against nature.

Donald MacKenzie Hadden was born in Nipawin, Saskatchewan, in 1936, and grew up on a farm nearby. At age 17, he joined the military and ended up in the airborne artillery, where he learned to parachute. This experience helped him land a job with the Saskatchewan Smoke Jumpers unit. Hadden worked from their base in La Ronge, Saskatchewan, for the next 10 years.

In the early 1940s, Saskatchewan's Department of Natural Resources (DNR) studied methods of forest-fire suppression being practised by the U.S. Department of Agriculture in the Nez Perce National Forest in Idaho and at Missoula, Montana. The Montana enterprise was dramatized in a 1952 movie titled *Red Skies of Montana*, starring Richard Widmark and Richard Crenna.

The Saskatchewan Smoke Jumpers program was further developed by the DNR with assistance from an Edmonton company, Hargreaves and Dick, who trained parachutists for search and rescue work. In June 1947, a mockup of an aircraft fuselage, set on a "tower" 20-feet in the air, was constructed in the corner of an old World War II hangar at Prince Albert airport for use in their first six-week training course.

At that time, qualifications for smoke jumpers included "passing a tough medical examination, being between 22 and 32 years of age, weighing from 170 to 180 pounds (although Hadden says that men were hired on either side of the guidelines), and being temperamentally stable."[1]

As soon as smoke was reported, the smoke jumpers' mandate was to attend the forest fire and to extinguish or contain it until regular firefighters could get there. They did this by being dropped from airplanes and parachuting in to a fire site. The crews who took over from the smoke jumpers set up a base at the nearest lake or water source, and packed in overland on foot.

The organization was later based in La Ronge, where the smoke jumpers' building, called "the barracks," housed the men, and had a room for parachute packing, and a tower for hanging parachutes to air and dry. The cry of "Jump Fire!" over the speakers became a familiar sound, and it brought the inhabitants to immediate action.

Don Hadden had heard of the famous group when he was still a kid. He found the idea of jumping out of airplanes into fires tremendously exciting.

It was not difficult to get hired. "The qualifications when I joined the smoke jumpers were that you just walked in off the street, and if you were physically fit they would train you. I had a bit of a head start because I already had my wings, as such, and experience at jumping."

He was hired in 1957, but in a position called "the fifth wheel," which meant that the onus was on him to prove that they should keep him over somebody else. "They had too many right then. One person had to go. But I'd always been in good physical shape, I had the training—and just enough arrogance—so I fit in."

The men trained in a self-contained classroom at the Prince Albert base. Instruction included basic firefighting techniques, with a focus on forest fires. They also did some jump training at Prince Albert, but in June moved to La Ronge to finish the program. There they used a 40-foot tower—a mockup of the airplane doorway that the men would be jumping out of—to perfect the technique of jumping from airplanes. Following their jump, they would slide 100 feet on a gradual slope down a cable until they hit the ground.

"It was a quick training course," Hadden says. "If you were in there a month before you went on your first fire, that was about it."

Many smoke jumpers ended up taking flying lessons. It was the thing to do, Hadden says. "You'd go out in the morning and take an hour here and a half-hour there. I started taking flying lessons in 1957, but I decided I didn't like it. It was just a glorified taxi-driver's job, I thought, so I never finished. I quit in 1958."

Hadden says that now flying courses are more stringent, "but back then they'd throw you into an airplane for 25 hours and give you a licence. Sometimes, if you were fairly good at it, they'd tell you to solo in two hours. Christ, you were hardly familiar with the thing!" So he chose to become a professional smoke jumper, rather than a pilot.

A typical day for the smoke jumpers would start with breakfast in their dining room, followed by calisthenics for an hour, and then a five-mile run. The training was relatively rugged. "If you weren't in top shape, you'd have to fake it awful good! But anybody who was in decent shape could do it. You just had to want to do this crazy thing."

Most of the candidates were in their early twenties, with the odd one in his teens. Some had been soldiers in the Korean War. A man would usually stay in the organization for three to five years, then he'd move on. By staying 10 years, Don Hadden became a veteran.

Full-time, year-round employment was never guaranteed. Hadden found off-season work with the forestry branch. "I always cruised timber in the winter, and then I'd smoke jump in the summer. And actually, cruising timber, because I was always out snowshoeing some place, kept me in good shape for the spring training.

"As a result, I ended up doing a lot of the physical training for the organization, because you could rise there relatively fast on your own initiative, if you had the go-ahead to do it."

The smoke jumpers were encouraged to do "free work for the town on government time." "Back in those days money wasn't rolling in to communities like it is nowadays, for programs and stuff, so we would work, gratis, on projects such as cutting firewood, scrubbing brush out of the cemetery, painting and putting up signs, cleaning campsites, cutting portages, and various other things when we weren't on fires."

But when the men heard the words "Jump Fire!" over the loudspeakers, a designated four-man group would race back to the base, get into their uniforms, grab their parachutes, climb into the airplane and be gone.

One of the airplanes used by the smoke jumpers was Norseman CF-SAM, which has been restored and is now on display in the Western Development Museum at Moose Jaw. In later years they had a Single Otter (CF-JFJ).

"JFJ was a lot nicer than SAM," Hadden recalls, "because we could throw our parachutes and gear inside, and dress on the way to the fire; we wouldn't have to pre-dress. We thought that was quite a step up. Plus, with JFJ we left the bomb tanks on the floats—and they could bomb the fire for us while we were working on it, help us out, whereas with the Norseman they didn't have such a thing.

"The Canso water bombers were coming into being then, and they were the greatest things ever."

Inside the aircraft were the jump master (or a designated foreman), four smoke jumpers, and the pilot. "The adrenalin was always flowing. Quite often, the guys would be joking around, giving each other a punch on the shoulder, talking a lot; then as we approached the fire, quiet. Everybody was inside his own head at that time. It was really strange."

They would jump with two men to a "stick," two guys going out, one right after the other. One guy would jump, then the next, through the door or through a hole in the belly of the plane. "When we were on wheels we'd go out the door, when we were on floats we'd go through the 'trap-door' down between the floats. They'd put in a sort of chute so we wouldn't hit any of the critical parts of the airplane.

"They would drop two guys, then two more after the first stick came around into view. When they'd dropped down to a low level, out would come the cargo, which was our firefighting equipment: sleeping bags, ration box, stuff to sustain

Smoke Jumpers, two men to a "stick," jumping from Norseman CF-SAM to a fire site. *Saskatchewan Archives Board*

ourselves while we were down there. And the radio, of course.

"As soon as we hit the ground, we'd take off our parachutes and our protective equipment, and head for the 'drop zone,' where the equipment was going to be dropped. Once the equipment was down, the foreman got the radio going and from the airplane they'd give us a compass shot as they flew toward the nearest lake. We would take our compasses out of our belts and take a shot on them, and that's where we'd walk to, after we'd put the fire out. Three guys would immediately hit the fire, fighting it whichever way we could. Then the foreman would join us."

It worked like this: the airplane would drop equipment such as two shovels and two "pulaskis" (an axe with a blade on one side and a pick hoe on the other, used to hook and hoe, or to chop). They also had two Waterman packs that held five gallons of water, and were operated by small hand-spray pumps, commonly known as "piss pumps." These would be filled with water from some place, and used for spraying the fire.

The fires ranged from small bush fires to raging infernos. "So, occasionally they'd drop us a regular motorized pump and hose."

"And that was it—that was the extent of our equipment."

To get the water, they would dig a hole in muskeg, or find a creek or a waterhole. They'd fill up the pumps, then walk back to the fire and spray away.

No special fire-retardant suits were worn by the smoke jumpers, Hadden says. "We had nothing whatsoever—just regular pants and jackets. If you were in the fire, you were in the fire." But the men did wear special outfits when jumping. They consisted of helmets and boots, pants with low reinforced webbing to cushion crotches caught on tree branches, and matching jackets. Hadden wore everything but the jacket, preferring instead his trademark black leather jacket. "I was Fonzie jumping out of that plane."

The firefighting method used was to stand pointing a hose at the forest fire. "But if it got to the point of saving your own ass, you'd hang in near the water in case you had to dive in," Hadden says. "I've been burnt out a couple of times. Once we literally had to run and jump into the waterhole while the fire burned over us and went about another 15 miles. This was in the Cumberland House area, south and east of La Ronge about 110 miles."

The situation got pretty scary, Hadden recalls. "We jumped into a slough and had to keep ducking ourselves under the water to keep from burning."

They watched as the forest around their slough burned black. "When the little willow leaves at the edge of the slough literally turn brown-black, and crisp, you know it's pretty hot," Hadden says. "We had to keep ducking under the water, keeping good and wet, with our faces close to the water because there wasn't much oxygen left, it was all smoke. We'd lift our heads a little bit, gulp some more air in and duck under."

The actual timespan was short: it took no more than five minutes for the fire to burn around and past them. "Once it starts rolling like that, it can really move." But being in the aftermath of a forest fire was the worst part, because they couldn't breathe. "It was mostly smoke, and any of the oxygen left was being sucked into the fire. We did a lot of gagging and dry heaving and throwing up, stuff like that. That was scary—we couldn't get air. We were no longer threatened by the fire, but we were threatened by something we couldn't do anything about."

Hadden cannot recall seeing animals try to escape from a forest fire. "No, that's something we never saw too much of. Maybe they have an awful good sixth sense. The odd time we'd see some rabbits running like hell. And the time we bailed into that water hole, there were quite a few garter snakes in there. They'd come into the water to get away from the fire, too—or maybe they lived in there, I'm not really sure."

Sharing a slough with the snakes was not a pleasant experience, but for one of the smoke jumpers it was a nightmare.

"We had one individual who was deathly afraid of snakes. He'd had a bad experience in Korea with poisonous snakes.

"The day he dove into the waterhole with us, he knew there would likely be snakes in there but it was the lesser of two evils. He sort of survived that in his mind, and just got out of there as soon as he could."

Another experience that sticks in Hadden's mind took place at Nistowiak Falls in 1962. It had started out as a typical day for the smoke jumpers.

"We'd been sent out to Nistowiak Falls to cut out a nice clean portage,"

Smoke jumpers (L-R): Barry Motyer, Don Hadden (in black leather jacket—"I was Fonzie jumping out of that plane"), Frank Tompkins, George Cox, George Horne, and Gordon Brown, getting ready to board aircraft CF-ECF. *Saskatchewan Government Dept. of Industry & Information*

Hadden recalls. "We'd been there about a week, and the airplane (Norseman CF-SAM) had come in daily. The wind would be howling down the gut, down the river, each time the airplane came in, so for take-off we'd have to turn the tail around and push it off from shore. We'd get him facing out into the lake, and he'd taxi out and take off.

"This particular day he came in to pick up the whole crew and take us back to La Ronge. For some strange reason, the wind was blowing from the opposite direction. The guys got into the aircraft, and another fellow and I pushed him off from shore. Then we jumped onto the float preparing to get into the airplane. But the wind caught the plane and started turning it toward the river. We knew a small set of falls, six or eight feet high, were just downstream. We heard the engine hesitate, it didn't want to start too good, then the pilot got it started again and he drove it up on shore, onto the rocks.

"Then it slid off the rocks, and over the falls—with everyone inside, or clinging onto the outside like we were."

Hadden, who was the crew foreman, was left hanging on to the outside of the strut with his feet on the float. For a split second, it appeared as if the airplane was going to fall on top of him. It crashed down the falls, and came to rest on the rocks, rupturing a float.

The other fellow had fallen off the float, and swam to shore, still hanging onto a one-quarter-inch tie rope. He tied his end of the rope to a tree, and threw the rope back to Hadden, who secured the airplane. The crew began to evacuate the aircraft, clinging to the fine rope as they cautiously made their way to shore through the swift water.

Before they jumped into the water, however, they removed their boots, and put their wallets, matches, and cigarettes inside, tied them up and threw them to shore. Without matches to light a fire—and to provide other creature comforts such as a smoke—they could become pretty cold and miserable before rescue.

"We were stranded," Hadden says, simply. "The aircraft radio wouldn't work on the ground level."

Hadden and the pilot, Herb Gratias, were to be the last off the plane. But just as the third-last man left to swim to shore, the rope loosened and away went the Norseman again. Both the pilot and Hadden fell into the river.

The water was swift and cold, but worse, they became caught in an eddy. Around and around they swirled—and the pilot couldn't swim. He grabbed Hadden around the neck—"scaring the hell out of me." Hadden gave him a push that sent him out of the eddy and into safer waters, and he somehow managed to scramble to shore.

Although Hadden was a good swimmer, the fact that he was wearing a buckskin jacket and his boots—"I'd put my cigarettes and stuff in somebody else's boot"—made it extremely difficult to stay afloat. He finally made it toward shore, but when he looked back he saw the airplane bobbing downstream toward a bend in the river. He dived back in.

"My plan was to get to the airplane, clamber inside, start it up and drive it on shore again. But by the time I got in there I was so puffed out from swimming in that swift water, that I couldn't think straight. I just kicked the water rudder over, so it helped me steer a bit, then I grabbed a paddle out of the back and I went out on the float, and just started giving 'er. Then I remembered a big set of falls downstream. The 50-footer.

"The guys ran down along the shore to watch the airplane go over the big falls, and there I am out on that float, just a diggin'.

"Then one float hooked on a submerged rock—lucky for me or I wouldn't be here today—and I got it stopped just a few feet ahead of the main falls."

Although Hadden had known the waterfall was there, his only thought was to save the airplane, which he admits was pretty stupid.

When Hadden secured the airplane, one of the guys started to swim out to help him set up the radio. "He was a strong swimmer, he swam daily, but he nearly missed the airplane and went over the falls.

"He lost most of his clothing because he'd taken some off halfway across the river. It was kind of amusing because when he got to the airplane, he still had on a t-shirt and his shorts, but by the time he got to the far shore, when he was taking the antenna back over—we had to string these long wire antennas up in a tree, and I kept the radio over on the rock where I was sitting—he'd even lost his shorts! He had a t-shirt on, is all, and there were a million mosquitos out, and they were doing a real number on him."

The fellow nevertheless managed to climb a tree and string up the antenna. Hadden called in to La Ronge, and received an immediate answer to his emergency rescue call. "I told them to send an airplane out with flotation gear because the Norseman was sinking."

The fellow who had strung up the antenna was now stranded on the far side of the river, with no matches to light a fire on this cold autumn day, and wearing only his t-shirt. The other guys were sitting on the opposite shore with a little fire going. And Don Hadden was sitting on a rock in the middle of the river, with his waterlogged leather jacket and boots.

Their rescue wasn't long coming; the station sent out a Beaver, along with a motorized canoe. They secured the airplane so it wouldn't sink overnight by tying a couple of empty 45-gallon drums to the floats. They flew back to La Ronge, and the next day a crew returned to repair and bring out the Norseman.

John Finch, then superintendent of maintenance for Saskatchewan Government Airways, describes the rescue: "We hauled it to shore, took off the wings, and then cut a portage about 25 feet wide and one-quarter mile long. We put the plane on beaching gear and winched it back to the upper side of the falls, reassembled it, and then flew home."[2]

Hadden may be credited with saving the airplane, but it's not a feat he brags about. "I guess I did, inadvertently. But it was stupidity, really. We got rescued, and got hurrahed for it all because we were so stupid. It wasn't really our doing—we were just being picked up."

In 1962 Don Hadden was honoured for being the first member of the Saskatchewan Smoke Jumpers to make 100 jumps—which translated into "falling about 100 miles." He was presented, on 16 October, with the first charter membership ever given in the Saskatchewan Smoke Jumpers' Century Club. His 100th jump, which took place at La Ronge, was documented in a film entitled *Diary of a Smoke Jumper*. Although the local newspaper reported that the most serious injury Hadden had yet sustained was a broken ankle during a ground-party timber-cruising operation, he also recalled a recent "close brush with misfortune" during a helicopter pickup in Pasqua Hills. When the winch used to reel him into the aircraft stuck, it left Hadden dangling 500 feet above the ground, hooked to a 90-foot cable.

Before helicopters became commonly used to deliver and pick up the ground firefighters, the smoke jumpers had to walk out to the lake from their drop-off, or from the fire site. The first helicopters used were small two-place machines. One time the smoke jumper team found itself trapped, with the fire burning all around them.

"We weren't really in dire danger, but we were stuck in the middle of the fire," Hadden says. "Jim Munro, an old-time helicopter pilot who works for us

Don Hadden receiving the first charter membership ever given in the Saskatchewan Smoke Jumpers' Century Club, presented by jump master Frank Tompkins, 16 October 1962. The 100 jumps translated into "falling about 100 miles." *Saskatchewan Government Dept. of Industry & Information*

in Prince Albert right now, decided to come in and save us. He found us, came down, and plucked us one at a time from this fiery place."

Not everyone associated with the smoke jumpers is remembered in positive terms. Hadden recalls a former director whom he describes as being "right out to lunch."

"We had a huge fire, it had a two-mile front on it and was just rolling. They dropped four smoke jumpers in front of it—and expected us to stop this fire. Forget it!

"But of course, we're mindless idiots, we don't think. We jumped—and suddenly realized we were in the middle of hell. They dropped us a pump and some hoses and stuff. There was a small lake, so we set up the pump and we saved it, ourselves, and our adjacent 100 feet or whatever it was, and that was it. The fire went on by us. I said to myself at that time, 'No way anybody's going to push me out of an airplane in front of something like that, ever again.'

"But we didn't do anything about it because, as I say, we were mindless idiots and we didn't stick up for ourselves. This was expected of us, and we honoured the old 'esprit de corps' and all that stuff."

The guys did stick together, but the individuality of some of the members made it difficult, at times, to practise the spirit of brotherhood. Hadden remembers one of their members as being "a little squirrely, never really suited to the organization."

"The first jump he ever made, we had to throw him out of the airplane because he just wouldn't go. He'd get white every time he had to jump; he was scared of it. He was always a pain in the ass.

"We used to pack all our stuff out of the fire sites, and all told it weighed about 70 pounds. One day this fellow is dropping back and can't carry his pack, so one guy says, 'I'll take your radio,' and another says, 'I'll take this,' and another, 'I'll take that,' until we're packing his stuff on our backs along with our own load.

"We get out to the lake and he's being awfully secretive, won't let anybody touch his pack. So when we finally get back here to La Ronge and are doing repack, he goes off into a corner. So somebody gets curious. They grab his pack and find he's hiding a bunch of old drill cores! He thought he'd found a fortune out in the hills—and carried all these rocks home. We were ready to kill him."

Smoke Jumper Stan Schneider, suited and poised on the wheel mode of the Norseman. *Courtesy Rosemary Nemeth*

Hadden explains that a jump master was supposed to organize the jumpers' evacuation from the airplane and then drop the cargo down to them. One time Hadden was left in charge. A number of men had days off, which they normally didn't get, as they were expected to work the entire summer without a break. As well, one guy had been injured—he had broken his foot in an unrelated accident.

"He was hanging around, along with two other guys, and myself, which didn't really constitute a crew but was better than nothing," Hadden says. "I was supposed to go out with the pilot, and drop these two guys in a fire when we got the call. I decided in my mind, 'I'm going to suit up and go with these guys. I'll get this other fellow with the broken foot to chuck the cargo out to us.'

"So I lined up everything, dropped the guys, and jumped out behind them. I did that a couple of times, when I was just supposed to manage the jumping operation, not be one of the jumpers. Caught supreme hell for it, but I did it anyway.

"I also carried that into the air attack end of it. G.T. Rowan, the chief pilot, gave me hell a couple of times because the Baron was down for repairs, we had a fire call, so I jumped in the lead tracker and I bird-dogged from there. We did the drop from it, and then used it as the bird-dog aircraft.

"Then about three years ago I jumped into one of the CL-215s and bird-dogged from it. He was angry because it involves insurance and all sorts of MOT [Ministry of Transport] stuff. You're just not supposed to do those things."

Although most risks were "calculated," there was one time during Hadden's days as a smoke jumper when he was sure he was a dead man.

Fighting fires in Saskatchewan, 1978. Three Grumman Trackers on a Ferry Flight from Prince Albert to La Ronge. *Don Hadden Collection*

"They misjudged, and they dropped me into a lake," he says. "I had on my main parachute, my reserve parachute, protective equipment, helmet, harness, the whole bit, about 70 pounds total. And it weighed even more when that stuff got wet. I was sure I was going to drown.

"I was quite a way from shore, but luckily it was a shallow lake. I ended up chest high in water. If the lake had been deep, I could never have gotten out."

The Saskatchewan Smoke Jumpers has an amazing record. "We never lost anybody, ever," Hadden says. "I think the worst injury was when George Horne broke a leg and an arm. He landed on a tree and the top broke off; when he went down he broke his leg, and then the top hit him and broke his arm. But that happened before my time."

During Hadden's time a few guys got sprained ankles, broken toes, or other minor injuries, but that was it.

For Don Hadden, being part of the Saskatchewan Smoke Jumpers was a dream come true. It was exciting work, he was well-paid, and the boys were kings of the country.

"I started off in 1957 making $288 a month, which was a phenomenal fee after coming away from the military making $76 a month," Hadden says. "I didn't really know what to do with my money, at the start, but I soon found a few ways to spend it.

"One of the things about smoke jumpers, when we moved into town here, we owned it," Hadden continues. "We were the 'head honchos,' more or less. We did what we wanted to do. Back in those days, it was funny but we used to carry pistols and stuff. Didn't have permits. We each had great big Bowie knives or something on our hips—we carried them for our parachuting in case we got into trouble and had to cut the lines. That was the last resort, of course, but we did have to carry these big hunting knives, and a lot of us carried pistols, but kind of halfway hidden."

He admits the police must not have known, "or else they'd have had us hauled in." To this day, he doesn't know why they carried this artillery, except, "It was the thing. Everybody did it." In general, Hadden feels that the smoke jumpers conducted themselves well. "We were never malicious. We didn't wreck things. We didn't unnecessarily harass people. We sort of had a code. We policed each other. If someone got out of line, we'd take him aside and give him a talking to. Sometimes it came to blows, but . . . "

So, then, what happens after it all ends? Does the camaraderie continue for a lifetime?

"It would be there, I suppose, if we could all meet again. I very seldom ever see someone I worked with then. But when I do, everybody else is excluded."

There are still some men living in La Ronge who were smoke jumpers, but Hadden sees them only occasionally. And the rest?

"A lot of them are dead from aviation crashes and stuff."

They were once going to have a reunion, and Hadden has compiled a list of names, which he has passed on to Rosemary Nemeth of the La Ronge Fire Centre. She is collecting photographs and memorabilia of the smoke jumpers' heyday, for a display at the Natural Resources Museum at Spruce Home, north of Prince Albert.

"The Saskatchewan Smoke Jumpers was a good organization; it served its purpose, but then, like anything, it had to go its way. Helicopters took over and things of that nature."

In 1966, during Hadden's 10th year with the smoke jumpers, the "mock tower" almost did him in.

"All the equipment broke on me, and I went straight through and right into the ground. It knocked me out for three days and left me paralysed for a while, and quite a few other things."

Hadden, as training instructor, had been doing a "demo-drop" for the students when the cable broke. He fell 40 feet, face-first on a gravel road.

He was transported on an emergency flight to Prince Albert, and wasn't expected to live. "They called the family in and said I wasn't going to make it,"

Hadden says. "They called my sisters in from BC and relatives from all over the country. I sort of floated around for three days, I went to heaven, I went to hell, and neither one of them wanted me, so I came back."

He had contusions, and a concussion from the whiplash-effect when his face had hit the ground and caused his head to snap back. "I hit the road face-first. I had a mask on, otherwise I'd be flat-faced. But all I got was a big cut on my forehead. The rest was paralysis from the whiplash."

Strangely enough he didn't break a single bone. Twenty-seven years later, some of the injuries are surfacing, including nerve damage and a hernial disc in his back.

He was walking eight days after the accident, but the physical problems were less serious for the moment than the psychological effects. The accident changed his personality and attitude. "I'd come from a real athletic background, and all of a sudden I was told I'd be a vegetable. I went into a deep depression over the whole thing. I just couldn't handle it.

"The doctors told me, 'You're never going to do this again, you're never going to do that again,' and they had me brainwashed. Finally, one doctor came in, 'subbing' for another, and he checked me over and said, 'Sure you've got bad injuries, but why don't you join society and quit feeling sorry for yourself?'

"I was a little bit ticked at him. I went home, and then I decided to go to work on it. I started by picking up my hand—one arm was paralysed—and I'd say, 'Today I'm going to move a finger.' I tried that for several days, and one day I got twitching one finger, and I never looked back."

The accident, needless to say, brought about his immediate retirement from the Saskatchewan Smoke Jumpers.

The smoke jumper program ended in 1966, after being in operation for 19 years, but Hadden never did receive the golden handshake. He was in the hospital, and it was 13 months before he worked again.

"I didn't really 'work' at my new job," Hadden says. "DNR just put me back to work as therapy, figuring it was better for me to be among people I knew and doing something. So I built all these communication towers and forestry lookout towers in the province. There's hardly one that I haven't been on, or that I haven't built."

The steel towers were ordered from Dominion Bridge in Winnipeg, and would arrive in a "package" like an giant Erector Set. It fell to the smoke jumpers to set them up out in the bush.

Don Hadden married his wife, Maryann, in 1962 when he was 27 years old. At the time, he was employed building towers with the smoke jumpers. "I was married but I was always on the road, always some place else. When my son was born, I didn't even know about it for four days. I was building a tower.

"My wife lived in La Ronge for one year. Then she lived at her parents' place on the farm—we had a house there for a couple or three years—and then we moved to Prince Albert. We've lived there ever since." The Haddens now have three children and three grandchildren.

Following his "therapy" work building towers, Hadden went to work in the La Ronge Fire Control shop for six years, followed by 19 years in the Air Attack division.

"I became a resource officer, and that's what I am today, although retired. But still working. Reinstated."

As air attack officer, Hadden directs the manoeuvres of helicopters, Twin Otters, CL-215 skimmers, Cansos, and

Don Hadden, La Ronge, 1993. *Collection of the author*

Grumman Trackers at forest fires. He does this from the bird-dog airplane, a Beech Baron. He works out of the Forest Fire Management Centres (formerly called the "Fire Cache") at Prince Albert and La Ronge, which serves six districts and the sub-districts of Sandy Bay, Uranium City, and Wollaston.

Hadden is proud of the improvements he's seen in forest fire-fighting techniques.

"We've got new technology, and new and better equipment. You don't have to be Superman to carry a pump now. It sometimes took two guys to carry a pump, but now you can pick the new ones up in one hand and they do the same job—better. There are new ideas. Retardants, foam. We drop foam out of these CL-215s and Cansos." Hadden says that the CL-215 was a great improvement in firefighting aircraft, and its capabilities are continually being upgraded, but at a cost. "One turbine-equipped airplane costs $13 million. The ones they now have are worth $7 million each."

Hadden estimates that a Grumman Tracker, once converted—which means taking a straight tracker from the military and putting in the tankage and computers to make it a forest fire-fighting unit—would probably run close to $1 million. The Trackers are basically an initial attack machine, which means they go out when the fire is first spotted, and lay a line of retardant around it.

"You'd probably be able to buy a decent Canso—but I'm just guessing—for $100,000 or $150,000, but then you've got your conversions to put in. We couldn't do without the Cansos. They are a little slower than the Skimmers and carry a smaller load, but they're extremely accurate in hitting targets.

"The CL-215 Skimmers are the king machines because there are so many lakes; with them, you can pick up water almost any place, and we've also got foam capabilities in all the machines now. When it comes to sustained action, which means the fire is getting away, the Skimmers are the machines for the situation."

Hadden emphasises, however, that even with all the multi-million-dollar machinery, it is the firefighter on the ground who controls or extinguishes the fires.

"We in the air don't put 'out' fires, we put them 'down,' and keep them down, allowing the guy on the ground a given time to put out the fire. He's the one who does the job. Joe Firefighter from off the street."

At one time, the system in place to recruit firefighters consisted of cleaning out the bars by saying, "There's a fire—get out there."

"That's what we used to do but now we have fire crews, people who are trained during the year," Hadden says. "There's a basic firefighters' course going on right now over at the Fire Centre. We train them, give them a card that says they're a trained firefighter, and they're the ones we'll hire first."

The main difference between the old system of firefighting and the present system is that the smoke jumpers actually jumped. Now helicopters can carry them to a chosen site and pick them up—but the fire is still fought by an individual standing on the ground. And the firefighters still wear blue jeans—although some might wear orange coveralls so they can be seen by the fire-bombers. Their equipment is basically the same, too—the old shovels and axes, except for the newer pumps.

"We've become real professional as opposed to haphazard," Hadden says. "Now we have bird-dogs to command the thing, and we're accountable for everything we do and say. We have debriefings when we come back from a fire, to see what we might have done differently, things of that nature. We have duty days, we can't fly beyond a certain number of days, we've got to have time off. Whereas before you could work for 24 hours and nobody said anything."

But regulations also mean restrictions, and that doesn't always sit well with the former smoke jumper.

"In some cases they're for the better because they make you keep an eye on people who are getting burnt out, so to speak, but in other ways they really foul the system in that we can't work as long as we'd like to finish the job.

"MOT regulates it, but we police ourselves because MOT will jump on us and close us down if we don't."

He says he works as well with the Ministry of Transport as anybody can. "MOT is sort of a stigma to a lot of people because they're always in there trying to put the pinch on you for some reason. Regulations, regulations, regulations. But, I guess they're for the best or else we wouldn't have them."

Hadden's family has remained in Prince Albert during his lifelong career with the Saskatchewan Government. He retired in the fall of 1992 after 35 years. "But I sat around all winter and looked at the wall and decided that retirement was not for me," Hadden says, "so I came back to work." He prides himself on continuous learning, and returned to school at age 37 to finish his grade 12.

Hadden still spends a good part of each year, the summers anyway, out on the territory, but usually only as far as La Ronge or Buffalo Narrows "I'm just an air attack officer—I go to the base I'm assigned to."

Hadden loves his work as a bird-dog, and real retirement seems far away.

"You get in the Baron when you get a fire call, and you're in command of the group. You tell them how you want the fire fought. The pilot is busy looking after himself, plus knowing where the other aircraft are. And the bird-dog takes care of the firefighting aspect of it: where he want the drops, what type of drops, things of that nature."

A Canadair CL-215 making a practice drop near La Ronge, 1990. As air attack officer, Hadden directs the manoeuvres of helicopters, Twin Otters, CL-215 skimmers, Cansos, and Grumman Trackers at forest fires. He does this from the bird-dog Beech Baron, working out of the Forest Fire Management Centres (formerly called the "Fire Cache") at Prince Albert and La Ronge, which serves six districts and the sub-districts of Sandy Bay, Uranium City, and Wollaston. *Don Hadden Collection*

Don Hadden has learned many things about fires in his long career, but he still acknowledges he doesn't have all the answers to what a fire will do, and how it will do it.

"I learned—or I think I've learned, because this may be disputed by other people—that when you go to a fire, you go with a blank mind. Each fire has its own individuality, is different from another in some way due to weather conditions or fuel conditions—like the trees and stuff, what's burning. There are so many variables. How many lakes, which way the wind's blowing and what it's blowing into, and what kind of fuel it's going into, how it's burning—sometimes it will burn intensely, other times it won't—things of that nature.

"I would say—and I'm not trying to blow my own horn—that there is nobody in Saskatchewan right now working for the government who knows more about fire control than I do. There are probably some Native fellows up north who do know as much, but there's nobody who's spent 35 continuous years in forest-fire control.

"They usually come in for a short stint and go out, or up to higher things. I've stayed with it continuously. I've worked them on the ground, I've worked them from the air. And I guess I've probably seen them all."

By 1993, Hadden had personally worked on nearly 1,000 individual forest fires. "I have 799 as an air attack officer and I've got about 100 as a smoke jumper, so I'm approaching 1,000 fires some way or another.

"It's sort of like a chess game to me. I beat this one. I beat that one. And then I weigh that against how many I lost. If I've lost one or two a year, I'm really mad at myself. I should have done something different!

"I'm still a bit of an egotist when it comes to that—I've got to beat the fire or else I'm mad at myself. I'm not mad at the people who work with me."

But when he reflects on his firefighting career, he can't help but feel some regrets about his own performance. "When I look back I think, if I hadn't been such a renegade—that's really what I was—I probably would have risen to the top and been director of Fire Control long ago. But I wouldn't play the game.

"Right to this day, there isn't a person around that I've worked with that I haven't told to go to hell one way or another, regardless of what his rank is. That's the way I grew up, and that's the way I went through life. And it set me back a few times."

It also gave him the guts to do what he's done—that "little bit of arrogance" that has seen him through many hot spots. From smoke jumper to air attack bird-dog, Don Hadden has been a rebel—*with* a cause.

Notes

1. *Wings Beyond Road's End*, Saskatchewan Education, Northern Division, La Ronge, Sask, 1992; 77–79.
2. *Ibid.*, 95.

Flights and Fights
of a Pioneer Pilot

*T*HERE HAS BEEN A FIGHTER in Joe Irwin's aviation career. But it was not an airplane; it was Irwin himself. Although he turned 86 in 1993, the years haven't quelled the spirit of this lifelong warrior. Like Popeye the Sailor, with one eye shut he laughs and scowls in the same look, shifting his cigarette from lips to fingers to make a point. On his bookcase is an inscribed wooden plaque that captures his lifelong battle cry: *Illegitimati Non Carborundum*, which Joe translates as "Don't let the bastards grind you down."

Irwin's stories, backed by 28,600 hours of flying everything from an open-cockpit Waco to a super-smooth De Havilland Dove, through wartime and peacetime, lay bare Canadian aviation history. His expressions, both facial and verbal, reflect a range of emotions as he thinks back over the last 50 years, and his stories, substantiated by a fine collection of aviation photographs and memorabilia, bring to life wondrous recollections of flights and fights not found in conventional annals of history.

Irwin points to a picture on the wall: Bellanca Air Bus, Fort Smith, 1942.

Joe Irwin with Canadian Pacific Airline's Bellanca Air Bus, Fort Smith, 1942, at start of Canol Project. *Joe Irwin Collection*

"I took the first load of Canol pipeline personnel in with the Bellanca, from Edmonton to Norman Wells," he says proudly, "and I was one of the first into Yellowknife on wheels, flying a 'Bark 'n Growl' (Barkley-Grow)."

Bruce Gowans, editor/author of aviation books such as *Wings Over Calgary* and *Wings Over Lethbridge*, states: "I doubt if I have known of another pilot in Canada with the variety of flying experience in civil aviation that Irwin has." In his assessment of Joe Irwin's career, begun as a prologue to a longer work, Gowans lists Irwin's achievements as a barnstormer, flying instructor, bush pilot, test pilot, spray pilot, airline captain, and corporate pilot. "During his 37 years and 28,000 hours of flying, Irwin never had an accident, yet few Canadians or even Albertans have ever heard of him."

Born at Eburne, BC, Joe Irwin grew up on a half-section of land at Brant, on the Little Bow River, near Vulcan, Alberta. Joe met his lifelong friend, Phil Lucas, in the one-room school they attended, and the two began dreaming about becoming pilots. When Great Western Airways of Calgary started a satellite school in Vulcan in the summer of 1929, Joe and Phil were among their first students.

Later that year, Irwin moved to Calgary and took on two jobs in order to pay for his pilots' licences, one working in a banana-ripening room, and the other as a parkade attendant. He even opted to walk to the Calgary airport to save a nickel each way on the streetcar fare. His rewards came in 1930 and 1931, respectively, when he earned his private and commercial licences, and in 1936 he qualified as an aircraft maintenance engineer.

Joe Irwin's first solo, April 1930 in 60X Moth, Great West Airways, Calgary. *Joe Irwin Collection*

He later took his instrument work at the RAF instructors' training school at Bowden, Alberta (allowing him to fly IFR—Instrument Flight Rules), and earned a Public Transport Licence, which qualified him to carry passengers on scheduled airlines.

Irwin began his flying adventures by barnstorming, and it was here that he met the risk-takers of the air. With Lloyd Comba's "All Canadian Air Tours," Irwin flew from town to town throughout Alberta, Saskatchewan, and Manitoba with such people as W.A. "Red" Sherman in a De Havilland Gipsy Moth (CF-AGJ); their feature attraction was a Montana parachute jumper named "Wild Irish" Haddock.

A group of aviators at Rutledge Hangar, Calgary, Alberta, prior to leaving on barnstorming tour of Alberta, British Columbia, Saskatchewan, and Manitoba. (Back row, L-R): Gil McLaren, Charlie Tweed, Ken Kendall, Albert Smith, Lionel Vine, "Sandy" Sandgate, Joe Patton, Cecil McNeil, Kirk Kirkham, Homer Carr, Herbie Hobson, Bruce Waddell. (Front Row, L-R): Chet Culberg, Lloyd Comba, Fred McCall, Howard Ingram, Frank Haddock, Ernie Boffa, Red Sherman, Joe Irwin, ? McFadgen, and Eugene Hogan. *Courtesy Glenbow-Alberta Institute/NA-415-1.*

Over the next few years, Irwin helped with the fall harvest on his family's farm, but barnstormed during the summers, flying rented aircraft: Scotty Love's old OX-5 Waco (CF-AOI) and Phil Lucas's American Eagle (CF-AHZ) and others. But barnstorming was not much of a living; it was done more to build up hours and experience, so Joe went looking for work.

In 1933, Irwin moved to Edmonton where he met Jim McIntosh. McIntosh ran a trading post and a commercial fishing operation in Calling Lake, 35 miles north of Athabasca, and needed a pilot to fly his fresh fish to market. So Irwin took on the job with a ski-equipped De Havilland Puss Moth (CF-APE).

"We were flying in from Athabasca 10 to 12 trips a day in the summertime.

Joe Irwin in his fur-lined flying suit with American Eagle, Calling Lake, Alberta, 1934. *Joe Irwin Collection*

There were only winter roads. There was a muskeg area about halfway out, and in that muskeg were three moose. The first dozen times I flew in, the moose would run. From then on, they paid no attention at all."

In the old days in the North, it wasn't a question of the weather being "iffy." No matter what the weather, you flew.

"Remember the famous flight that Wop May made in to Fort Vermilion, in an open cockpit airplane at 30 below?" Irwin asks. "Well, I never knew airplanes had lids on them until 1936! I never flew a cabin airplane except the Puss Moth for one month of the winter of '33, and then a Curtiss Robin at Calling Lake for four years after 1936."

The next year, Joe Irwin made his first of many leaps into business by teaming up with Eber H. Van Valkenberg, an Edmonton designer and builder of airplanes who had started a business called Van Valkenberg Aircraft Limited. The company's latest design, the BM-3 Byamo (CF-AON), constructed with steel tubing, had a light aluminum fuselage skin with wood and fabric wings, and was powered by a Kinner 125-horsepower engine.

"I did the test work on Van Valkenberg's little four-place cabin monoplane. We planned to take it to Ottawa to do further tests and to certify it." The venture left Irwin broke—and far from home—when "Van" ran out of money in Sault Ste. Marie.

The airplane was mortgaged to the Soo Garage Limited while Irwin and Van Valkenberg headed to the United States to seek financiers for the project. Finding none, they returned to Ontario and went into partnership on a little plant that manufactured acetylene generators for welding equipment.

"And then old Van ducked out on me," Irwin says. "The garage man seized the airplane, and I was stuck in Sault Ste. Marie with no money and no aircraft. The acetylene generator business went the way of all flesh, too, of course."

Irwin stayed to pay off the bills, which took a couple of years. The bright side was that Joe was able to build up his experience on various aircraft, and explore the lakes and bush country of Ontario.

He eventually made his way home again, and got into another partnership, this time with Jim McIntosh in a charter operation, Calling Lake Air Service. They used a Curtiss Robin (CF-AMA) that "Mac" had bought from Consolidated Mining. "Mac bought the plane, and I ran it." Their operation called on the remote northern Alberta areas of Wabasca, Grouard, Fort Vermilion, Birch Hills, and Chipewyan Lake.

By this time, Irwin had his A & C engineer's licence. "When I was up there, I had no engineer—I was my own engineer. We got up at five in the morning, poured the oil back into the airplane, put the batteries back, and set blowpots under the engine."

Since they were on floats in the summer and skis in the winter, spring break-up and fall freeze-up were the only times they were unable to fly. During those periods they lived very isolated lives. "During one break-up, when I needed to take a propeller to Edmonton for servicing, I packed it out by packhorse. We slogged knee-deep through water and muskeg."

Joe married McIntosh's daughter, Jeannette, in 1937; their son was born a year later (and their daughter in 1947).

The next few years were demanding but rewarding. Then the war intervened and Calling Lake Air Service operations came to a halt when fuel became unobtainable. (Irwin did not serve in the armed forces because "we were all frozen in our jobs, the airlines needed us. And I was over-age for the air force anyway.") Irwin moved his family to Edmonton, and, in 1940, found himself in the employ of Canadian Airways, based in Edmonton and Yellow-knife.

At times, when he had to stay overnight on one of his remote charter flights, Irwin camped with the Indian residents.

"Many of them had damned good cabins. I learned some very interesting things from these people, like the way they used to prepare duck. About 45 miles west of Fort Simpson, on the duck and goose migration flight line, the Indians used to gather to get their winter kill. They'd shoot ducks and geese, and have a fire pit lined with local clay. They'd cut the coarse feathers from the wings, tails, and legs, and roll the ducks in balls of mud—guts, feathers, and all—and bake them in the fire. They were just like rocks when they came out. Then they'd throw them up on the roof of the cabin. When they wanted duck, they'd crack one open. The guts would have dried up completely, and the feathers and stuff would be stuck in the clay. Nothing but duck. Beautiful!"

Later, in the winter of 1940-41, Jim McIntosh received an allotment of 20 to 30 barrels of gas because he was moving a food product. This enabled "Mac" to hire one of Irwin's former barnstorming partners, Reinhold "Walter" Kiehlbauch, to fly for him.

On 6 February 1941, Kiehlbauch went missing with the Curtiss-Robin while on a flight north of Calling Lake. Irwin asked for, and got, a leave of absence from his job with Canadian Airways to join in the search.

Walter Kiehlbauch's personal aircraft was a Fairchild 24 (CF-BQL). Irwin contacted the Kiehlbauch brothers about using this airplane in the search. But it was in a hangar at the Kiehlbauch farm at Chipman, on wheels, and there was two feet of snow on the ground. They got a team of horses, put the main gear up on a couple of stoneboats, and brought the airplane into town. Irwin took off from the main street on wheels, flew the Fairchild in to Edmonton, put it on skis, and went on the search.

The 11 February 1941 Edmonton *Bulletin* read:

> [A search is underway for] Walter Kiehlbauch of Chipman, whose plane was located from the air Tuesday. The craft, missing since last Thursday, is down in the bush 15 miles north of Calling Lake, and ground parties were proceeding toward the plane through heavy bush country.

"This was the first sighting, then they lost track of it," Irwin says. "The Observer's School went out on the search. Two Aussie chaps thought they had seen it. They had—it was hanging in a tree at the time. But a heavy snowstorm came, the airplane fell down and was covered with snow, so they couldn't find it again.

"I was in about a week the first time, and we didn't find anything at all. Some trappers found the airplane that spring, in the Pelican Mountain area.

"Canadian Airways then sent me in with the Department of Transport people because I knew the area, I knew the situation, and was interested in the thing, naturally. We flew into Rock Island Lake, and went from there with a team of horses to the crash site. The Kiehlbauch brothers were with us—they figured they had a lawsuit they could pursue. The bears, meantime, had been into the load of fish that was on the airplane, you know, and the fish and Walter were pretty well gone. When they tried to gather up Walter's remains, all the police were interested in was the skull for identification, as proof of death. So the police brought the head out and that was it."

They also brought the remains of the Robin out of the bush, but it was good only for scrap. That was the end of the Curtiss-Robin, and Calling Lake Air Services.

Thus ended Irwin and McIntosh's business venture, but Irwin's flying career was taking off. He spent the summer in Yellowknife flying a Norseman for Canadian Airways.

When the U.S. and Canada signed an agreement to build a 577-mile Canadian Oil (Canol) pipeline in 1942 to carry oil products from Norman Wells, NWT, to Whitehorse, YT, Irwin took the first load of personnel in to Norman Wells with a Bellanca (CF-BKV) on floats. His route followed the Mackenzie River, mainly to and from Norman Wells.

"We flew a variety of stuff: we had the big Bellanca, three Beechcraft, Beech 18s, and the 'Bark 'n Growls'—we had all the Barkley-Grows at one time. [The Canadian registry lists that only eight were ever made.] Then, when the Observers School shut down, we got their Boeing 247Ds for the airline. When they built the airport in Fort McMurray they started running a Boeing 247D from Edmonton to McMurray, so I added that to my territory. By this time the airport at Fort Smith was done, and I started shuttling from Yellowknife and Fort Smith down to Fort McMurray with the big Bellanca on floats."

Canadian Pacific Airlines, who had bought Canadian Airways and many other flying companies across Canada, was now Irwin's employer; in 1943 Joe became one of the first pilots to land in Yellowknife on wheels.

"A fellow named George Gilmore, who retired from CPA flying 748s, was the first Barkley-Grow in, and I was 10 minutes behind in mine. Charlie Robinson was the first one in with a Boeing on wheels.

"They had just started moving up to the new town from the rock down below. There was no airport there at all, just a cleared strip," Irwin recalls.

"It was rough as hell but we could land on it on wheels with the airplanes we were using at the time, the Barkley-Grows, the Twin Beech, that stuff. Then later we got the stripped-out C-60 Lodestars."

Irwin had long been considering operating his own flying service, and in 1946 he applied to the DOT (Department of Transport) for a licence to operate a charter service and flying school out of Grande Prairie, Alberta. His main school would be based in Grande Prairie, with satellite schools intended for Peace River, Alberta, and Dawson Creek, BC. "Then it was wait, wait, wait—you know, the stuff that broke the scales—" for his licence to be approved. He had left Canadian Pacific Airlines and was forced to take on temporary flying jobs to tide him over.

While waiting for the licence, he bought—and sold—several aircraft, finally retaining one "Tiger-Schmidt" (Tiger Moth) CF-DFG. Still no licence. Then he bought a Mark V Anson (CF-DOT), thinking it would be useful for both charter work and fish hauls. The Anson was one of the few World War II training aircraft to be adapted for commercial operations. Irwin's was one of the first sold out of the RAF station at Penhold after the war.

When Grande Prairie Flying Service finally got underway, Irwin's 24-hour work days began. He ran the flying schools, as well as flying the Anson himself on commercial fish hauls and carrying freight to and from Norman Wells.

"I eventually hired a guy to run the flying school in Grande Prairie, but I still had to fly back a couple of times a week to look after stuff. Mike Zubko, a pilot-engineer who was waiting to get his charter for Aklavik, came to work temporarily for me as an engineer, which relieved some strain."

That summer he also hired pilot Doug Ireland to haul fish with the Tiger (DFG) from Calling Lake to Athabasca, on wheels. But alas, Ireland flipped the aircraft onto its back in a field of long meadow grass. Although DFG was eventually rebuilt, Irwin bought another Tiger (CF-BMP) to finish the job. Then he left BMP parked east of the lake when the fishing season closed.

"When we went to bring BMP back to Grande Prairie, we found that cattle had damaged it," Irwin says morosely. "They'd licked it, and had bust some trimming edge off the lower wing.

"I then hired a pilot from Calgary who'd been an instructor in the air force.

Tiger Moth CF-BMP at Calling Lake, July 1947, before the fire. *Joe Irwin Collection*

He turned out to be a hopeless case as far as the Anson was concerned, but I thought surely he could fly a Tiger Moth.

"I got all the stuff ready to put on BMP—a brand new pair of skis and a new prop—and at the end of the season, Mike Zubko flew the pilot to Calling Lake." Irwin's last words of instruction were for them to buy a bolt of canvas from Jim McIntosh's store, and have someone make up a tarp to keep the wind off them while they were working on the airplane. Two mornings later he received a telegram: BMP DESTROYED BY FIRE.

Irwin went up the wall.

Instead of buying the canvas and having a tarp made, Zubko had borrowed DC-3 silk wing-covers from CPA at Grande Prairie to use for a tarp. The firepots had ignited the silk wing covers, and the whole airplane had gone up in flames.

Irwin tells the story in highly indignant tones, leaning forward in his chair and pinning his audience with a nicotine-yellow forefinger and a squinty one-eyed glare. "Not only that," he adds, "but I'd given them my *Five Star eiderdown sleeping bag*, and my *fur-lined flying suit*. I'd paid a lot of money for those things in the '30s when I was flying the open-lid aircraft! They were in the front seat of the airplane—with the *fire extinguishers*, by the way."

Yes, Irwin admits there's something funny about the fire extinguishers burning with everything else. "You can say that again!" But he's not finished yet. "They were all on the front seat of the airplane—*on top of which*, they'd put on the new propeller and a pair of skis before they burned it up." He sits back, the irony and the ignorance of the situation overwhelming him.

"McIntosh never got through kidding me about it. He said he could have burnt it for me, to get insurance or something, if that's what I'd intended. I wouldn't have had to hire all that high-priced help!"

Joe Irwin snorts as he finishes this story—which is all he can do about it now.

"I've never seen that pilot since. Mike said he got on the bus and left the country."

So that ended Irwin's Tiger Moth, BMP. Insurance gave him back "about what I had into it." Irwin recently heard that the restored aircraft is now at the Canadian Museum of Flight and Transportation, in Surrey, BC.

His Anson got it next. In the early winter of 1947, Irwin broke through the ice of Sandy Lake, north of Calling Lake, damaging a wing-tip. He salvaged the aircraft and brought it in for repair, but by then there was no work for it.

About that time, his entire business bit the dust.

Irwin explains that flying schools were commonly run by flying clubs, and the clubs weren't required to be licensed as schools. Soon after Irwin got his licence, however, the ruling was enforced so that every flying school, whether or not it was a club, had to have a licence.

"I believe I was the first operator in Canada to receive a flying school licence," Irwin said, "but the Air Transport Board sold me to the wolves.

"With the charter, your territory was well-protected because they were so hard to get," Irwin explains. "At the school in Grande Prairie we didn't have all that many students, but our satellite school in Peace River had lots of business. We spent two days a week at the satellite school in Peace River, then three days in Grande Prairie."

Irwin lights his hundredth cigarette of the day, and leans forward to tell what happened next, in his usual manner: colourful, indignant, and graphic.

"A guy named Ronnie Page bought a 'Super Snoozer' (Cub Cruiser), and managed to wrangle a licence to operate out of Peace River."

With a competitor now authorized to bring his airplanes in for use by the Peace River students, Irwin lost his one profit-making location. It knocked the base from under Grande Prairie Flying Service, and everything seemed to fall apart at once.

"I'd had about 12 students soloing in Peace River at the time. Ronnie Page rented his aircraft to my former students to allow them to build up their hours, then he buggered off to Hay River to work on the fish haul and do general charter work. Peace River came to me crying that they now had no airplanes. 'Go get one from Ronnie Page. You broke me!' I said. Meanwhile, the civil aviation authorities granted a charter licence to a guy in Dawson Creek, and our hope for another satellite disappeared. I thought, to hell with this."

Irwin produces a newspaper article (*Insider*, 12 November 1990) that recalls how people felt about the flying school fiasco:

The committee [Air Transport board] granted a second licence [for a flying school] in Peace River, and there just wasn't the room for two. Like most pilots who survived the period before the government saw fit to regulate it [the operating territories], Irwin developed a deep mistrust toward the new governing body. Older and wiser than some of their regulators, it was difficult for some pilots to adapt to the hard line taken by the government, said Irwin.

But Irwin still possessed his fighting spirit, and luckily another opportunity presented itself.

Ted Holmes, pilot and owner-operator of Westland Spraying Service Limited in Airdrie, Alberta, contacted Irwin about crop spraying with a Lysander. So in the spring of 1948, Irwin moved south to Airdrie to join Westland.

Four ex-air force pilots formed the company in 1947. They purchased four surplus Lysanders (CF-DGI, CF-DRL, CF-FOA, and CF-GFJ), two-place high-wing monoplanes powered by 900-horsepower radial engines that could carry payloads of up to 1,400 pounds. Westland was the only company in the world to operate Lysanders commercially.

Westland Spraying Service's Lysanders. *Joe Irwin Collection*

"Ted and I, in 1948, did the first liquid aerial crop-spraying in Canada," Irwin explains. "Prior to that, in '47, they had dusted, but we were rigged for liquid spray. We used 2,4-D mainly, which is now restricted, on weed control, and did some brush work with 2,4-5-T. It had just come out in 1948, and is now banned except for some specific uses. We used it to get rid of willow brush and stuff in pasture land up in the ranch country. We did that, and roadside weed control and work of this nature."

Between 1948 and 1949, Irwin designed and built all the spray equipment for his two Tiger Moths (DFG and a more recent acquisition, CVJ). They were the first ever so equipped.

He was proud of designing the spray equipment and its installation in the airplanes. Frank Barchard, an aeronautical engineer, had done the stress analyses and drawings, and the equipment subsequently received DOT approval. In 1949, Irwin incorporated his new business, Irwin Spraying Service.

He was in it 10 years too soon. "It was hard to sell," he says, philosophically. Moreover, he discusses today's chemical restrictions, and how everyone is suing about "drift" coming over onto their property. "It makes it pretty rough on the spraying business.

"The environmentalists are crazy. Just 'who' is it who finds the chemicals dangerous?" Indeed, Irwin has established a strong point of view on the subject, and he's sticking to it.

"Damned right. There's a lot to be said, both ways. We didn't spray indiscriminately—we sprayed where it was necessary. You did have occasional drift from the chemical onto other properties, but it didn't do that much damage. They have used 2,4-D for years in Prince Edward Island and New Brunswick, in potato country, to defoliate the potatoes to enhance their growth."

He cites an incident that occurred when he was with Westland Spraying Service, working near Drumheller. A farmer had a patch of potatoes planted in the middle of his wheat field. Irwin had asked him if there was anything out there, and he'd said no. "As I went by—with the Lysander we sprayed at 150 miles per hour and you didn't have all day to look around for stuff—I saw, Christ! there was a potato patch. So I asked him about it when I came back. He said, 'Oh yeah, I forgot about them. But it won't hurt them.'

"I purposely went back that fall and checked, and you never saw potatoes like those in your life! They had been sprayed right after they'd bloomed, which took the foliage down, which takes away energy for growth of the tubers, and he had the damnedest crop of potatoes you ever saw in your life."

However, Irwin does recall another incident connected with the spray service that contradicts its positive side.

"Talking of 2,4-D and various chemicals, they (Westland Spraying Service Limited) had one duster in their outfit, and three sprayers. The dust they were using then was Aldrin, for pest control. The trees south of Midnapore (near Calgary) along the highway were badly infested with aphids so they hired Westland Spraying. That was the first year I had my own outfit, so a fellow by the name of Frank Hawthorne went flying for them to do this dusting job later after the spraying season was over.

"Frank was a very conscientious guy and a damned good pilot—very cautious with chemicals—moreso than any of the rest of the guys in the outfit. He went in there and dusted those trees.

"It killed him, just the way it kills the bugs. It destroys the central nervous system. The dust used to come back into the cockpit, but that had nothing to do with his demise, apparently. They figured he got it into his system when he relieved himself afterward; the dust had got on his hands, and it had gone in through the penis into his bladder. We set up various collections and sent him down to the Mayo Clinic, but there was nothing they could do. Two or three years later, he died."

By early spring of 1949, Irwin had completed the repairs on his Anson. He'd fixed the broken wing-tip, installed a brand new set of Hamilton props at a cost of $600 each, and test-flown the airplane. It was now parked at the side of the hangar with just 55 minutes on the spanking new props.

In May, he got a call from Ernie Boffa, a widely known and well-respected pilot (who, in 1993, was inducted into Canada's Aviation Hall of Fame).

"A lot of things stick in your mind that you'd sooner forget," Irwin says, reflectively.

"Ernie Boffa asked if he could rent my Anson."

At the time, Boffa was flying for CPA, and an Arctic explorer named Washburn had asked CPA if they could take him and his wife in to Reid and Holman islands to do surveys of flora and fauna. But CPA had already shut down its flying operations for the season—mild weather meant the ice was breaking up earlier than usual.

"When he was told that CPA couldn't take him in, Washburn was upset—if he didn't get in now, he'd have to wait another year. Ernie Boffa, knowing I had the Anson, came to see me about leasing it so that he could fly Washburn in independently.

"If it had been anybody else but Boffa, I would have said no. But I thought, 'What the hell? Safe, like in church!'

"The sticker was," Irwin recalls, "he was supposed to be going in on wheels. But he borrowed a set of skis from T.P. Fox and Vern Simmons, who ran Associated Airways in Yellowknife, and he goes in on skis. This greatly reduced his range—you don't travel so fast and you don't go so far on a tankful of gas. But anyway, gas had nothing to do with it. Read the book about Ernie Boffa, and his version of what happened the only time he didn't finish a trip, when he'd leased an airplane off a guy. Well, this is the guy."[1]

Meanwhile, Irwin was at Drumheller, spraying, when he got a call telling him that his airplane was missing, and Search and Rescue wanted him up there. "But by the time I got into Calgary they had found the Anson, so there was no point in me going any further. I left word for Ernie to get in touch with me right away because I was concerned about the salvage, then I went back to Drumheller. Ten days later he still hadn't phoned me.

"I later caught up to him in the King Edward Hotel in Edmonton. I said, 'Why the hell didn't you get in touch with me?' He said he was embarrassed, and felt bad about the whole thing. I said, 'You don't feel half as bad as I do! How about getting it out of there before break-up?' He said, 'Oh, there's no chance. It's out on a little lake about 10 miles back from the shore. Once the ice went out, it was gone.'

"But it was found right on the shore at Cape Krusenstern! He would have flown by it every day that he made a trip that way to service this camp.

"I later heard the story from Pete [Paul] Gibb. Pete was an ex-air force pilot who had intended to instruct for me at Grande Prairie, but then the air force had called him back. In fact, he was the oldest jet pilot in the RCAF, and flew F-86 Sabres over to Germany on that leapfrog operation. When my Anson went down, Pete was on an RCAF search and rescue mission out of Fort Nelson."

About a month after the accident, Joe was talking to Pete and told him about losing the salvage on the aircraft. Pete said 'What the hell are you talking about?' He then told Joe that the air force had brought in a DC-3 equipped with Jato (jet rockets to assist take-off) from Rivers, Manitoba, and with it had taken out the downed crew—Boffa and his engineer, Fred Riley. The Washburns had stayed at Holman Island. At that time, they also took out the loose stuff such as sleeping bags, snowshoes, and other portable goods. The RCAF took a picture of the Anson down on the ice.

But sometime after that, somebody had taken out the salvage: instruments, batteries, wing covers, engine cover, radio, all the tools, emergency rations, bush seats, firepots, all this stuff, and had brought them to Yellowknife.

"I found out that Mobile Oil had later bought one of the engines from Morrie Keith, who ran an aircraft supply business in Edmonton, for a spare for their Beaver. I know this for a fact because I had recorded the serial numbers—when you buy surplus stuff it's recorded in the temporary log book. But I couldn't claim it as stolen goods, because once you abandon an aircraft or a vessel it's public domain.

"And I got nothing! Not a damned thing!

"Yeah, a lot of things stick in your mind that you'd rather forget," Irwin says, again.

When the spraying season of 1949 came to an end, Irwin returned to the farm. Then Franz McTavish, who operated Chinook Flying Service out of Calgary, called and asked if he could help him fulfil his contract of supplying and flying a Mark V Anson for the Sun Oil Company. Irwin agreed to take the flying job on a temporary basis, fully intending to return to crop spraying the following spring.

McTavish explained that Chinook Flying Service had been doing the flying work for Sun Oil. A series of pilots had been hired to fly for the company, but the system had not proved satisfactory.

"The final straw," Irwin recalls, "was that Sun Oil had some brass come up from their head office in Philadelphia. They were headed for Steen River, north of Peace River. There was heavy smoke in the country at the time. This kid took off, got himself lost, and finally wound up in Fort Nelson with about half a gallon of gas left. Well, that tore it. They told Franz McTavish, 'Fly it for us yourself, or get someone on the airplane who knows how to fly it!'"

Irwin flew their Anson for two months, at which time the company decided to buy their own airplane, and asked Irwin if he would come on staff as their pilot. He agreed, but on the condition that come May he could quit to operate his own business, Irwin Spraying Services, using his outfitted Tiger Moths.

The company officials strongly encouraged him to consider their offer of full-time employment, and offered him an airline ticket to Toronto to meet Mr. Raymond Higgins, manager of Sun Oil's aviation department. So Irwin went to Toronto, and was interviewed for the position of assistant chief pilot of Canadian Operations.

Mr. Higgins, ever the executive, looked Joe over. "We don't normally hire a guy over 35 years of age."

"Good," Irwin said "I don't want to get hired! I told you I'd only fly for you during the wintertime. Come May, I'm gone."

"Well now, just a minute."

Mr. Higgins went on to explain that because Irwin was over age, there might be problems with the pension plan. Joe just sat there.

Finally Mr. Higgins leaned back. "You know, the more I look at the other applications we've got here, the younger you look! Yes, you'd better come and fly for me."

But Joe was adamant. "No—only until May and that's it."

He took the job, reluctantly, and started flying on a full-time (although still temporary) basis for Sun Oil in 1950.

"My wife was kind of putting the pressure on, too, about the good paycheque coming in once a month, so I thought, well, I'll try it for a year."

He still had the Irwin Spraying Service business, and the Tiger Moths. Because Sun Oil was reluctant to let him go, and because he did have a pretty good job with them, when Chinook Flying Service asked to lease Irwin's spray-equipped airplanes in 1950, he agreed to do so.

The contract was a share agreement between Franz McTavish's Chinook Flying Service and Irwin Spraying Service. Irwin stipulated that the contract include the agreement that Franz McTavish himself, or Mary Wilcox, who was flying for them, or Gerry Stauffer, flew the airplane—nobody else.

Unbeknownst to Irwin, Chinook had a number of students working for it, who were building up their time by ferrying the Tigers from one job to another. A student was ferrying one of Irwin's Tigers (CVJ) one day when he decided to do a little "playing with spraying." He got into the crop and flipped the airplane.

Wrote it off. End of CVJ.

Shaking his head at the memory, Irwin recalls his experiences being his own business manager:

"That first year, 1950, I operated on my own and Chinook supplied all the operating expenses," Irwin says. "We had a 50/50 split. We did $87,000 worth of business.

"When Chinook came into the operation, in 1951, our gross income was $113,000. But somehow, when it came time for year-end pay-out, I'd lost an airplane and I wound up $300 in the hole, for my share!"

Irwin stomped downtown to see an accountant. What he was told made him even more furious. "You should hire this bookkeeper for yourself," the accountant told him. "It's all there, I can show you real easy where the money went, but you can't do a damned thing about it. Tell this guy to drop around, we'll give him a job. Everybody should have a bookkeeper like that."

So Irwin was down to one airplane (DFG), but its demise was already in the cards.

"The next spring, Bobbie Smeed was on the loose, nothing to do, and had 5,000 or 6,000 flying hours with TransCanada Airlines. I knew Bob really well, a good pilot, ex-TCA, so I thought I'd try 'er one time more. I took a couple of days off my job at Sun Oil to get Bobbie started. I had the airplane (DFG) out at Airdrie, actually an airplane and a half, if you want to count the one that kid had tore up on me (CVJ), so I took Bobbie out."

By then, Westland Spraying Service was out of business, and Irwin Spraying Service was lining up jobs through a booking agency. Their first job that season was in an area that was among the first in Alberta to put in rural electrification, and the single-wire power lines became the nemesis of spray pilots. Spaced a pole-and-a-half apart, there was considerable sag in between, making them nearly impossible for a pilot to see.

Irwin carefully explained to Bob how to watch out for these power lines. "Don't look for the line, because you won't see it," Irwin warned. He pointed to the rows of poles on both sides of the road, electric power poles opposite from telephone lines. "Fly by the pole lines—don't try looking for wires."

Irwin waited at the airport. Twenty minutes later Bob hadn't returned. Half an hour later he hadn't returned. Irwin began to worry. Surely he was through by now. He got into the truck to go look for him. Before he reached the airport gate he saw a vehicle coming. Bob got out, turned around and said, "Kick me right there!"

"He'd hit the power line," Irwin exclaims, "not from here to the bloody wall from where I'd been showing it to him! He'd tried to fly under the wire, hooked the rudder counterweight on it, and yanked the fin and rudder off the airplane. He landed in the pasture, hit a badger hole with one wheel, ducked a wing in, and tore a lower wing off as well.

"By the time I'd got Field Aviation to fix the airplane, the spraying season was over. That was my last Tiger."

The following year, a man from Acadia Valley came in and wanted to rent the newly repaired airplane. "The only way you can have it is to buy it," Irwin told him. "Then you can do what you like with it."

So he sold it, and Joe Irwin was out of Tiger Moths, and the spraying business.

Sun Oil was very pleased to acquire a pilot of Irwin's qualifications—a seasoned pilot/engineer with vast experience on numerous types of aircraft in varied climates. The company's offer, to come on staff as assistant chief pilot and set up their Canadian Aviation Division based out of Calgary, was too good to turn down.

The first aircraft acquired by Sun Oil was a new De Havilland Beaver (CF-GQV). By 1952 it was obvious that they needed a larger aircraft, so they purchased a De Havilland Dove (CF-GBE). It became one of Irwin's favourites; he logged more hours (over 11,600) on that Dove than any other single pilot had put on Doves throughout the North American continent, "and I believe in the

Joe Irwin flying De Havilland Dove (CF-GBE) from Calgary to Banff, 1954. *Joe Irwin Collection*

Western Hemisphere," he says. For the next 11 years, Irwin flew the Dove on trips to and from the company's headquarters in Philadelphia, and to other centres throughout the United States and Canada.

Irwin won unprecedented awards while in the employ of Sun Oil, among them a certificate for One Million Miles of Safe Flying. The citation is effusive with the company's praise for his service.

A *Calgary Herald* newspaper article, headlined, "Top Pilot," itemized Irwin's career:

> A Calgary pilot who started his career barnstorming at fairs and sports days was honoured Monday night (11 September 1961) by Sun Oil for whom he has flown more than One Million Miles without an accident. Joseph W. Irwin was presented with a special award at a dinner at the Palliser Hotel celebrating Sun Oil's 75th Anniversary. He has logged more than 20,000 hours flying since he became a pilot in 1930.

But nine days after his Million Mile achievement, tragedy struck. Irwin's son, John (Jack), was a pilot with Canadian Pacific Airlines. When he and a fellow pilot were temporarily laid off, they decided to take seasonal jobs crop spraying—called "top dressing" in New Zealand—for James Aviation, based in Hamilton, New Zealand.

Irwin explains that the soil in New Zealand requires phosphate to promote growth. Aerial applications of phosphate, which is now banned, produced amazing results.

At that time, the government's Department of Reclamation was reclaiming land, debrushing it—getting rid of the gorse brush—applying fertilizer and seed from the air, and fencing the property. Then it was auctioned off as a going concern either as a cattle or sheep station.

Jack wrote home, describing the airplanes they were flying, Fletcher F-24s, as "abortions." But, he added, they flew, and they were enjoying their jobs.

"He had been there six or seven weeks and was flying near Rotorua, New Zealand, when he had a structure failure on the airplane," Irwin says. "He lost about 12 feet off the end of the wing, and he was killed."

The Irwin family was devastated.

When he received a copy of the accident report it didn't make sense to Joe, whose knowledge of aviation made him suspect a cover-up. He set out to discover what he could about this airplane that had taken the life of his son.

He learned that Fletcher had built the airplanes for European armed-service competitions. They were actually a reconnaissance airplane, built for observation and flight supply, and could be constructed from a kit. The New Zealand government had bought, and now owned, every Fletcher F-24 ever made, and Joe Irwin discovered that they had lost a lot of them.

"Apparently when Fletcher was pushing this thing as a sprayer he'd turned two airplanes over to the Applicators' Association in California to do an evaluation on them.

"The people in California told me that the airplane had been categorized generally as 'a mess,' and the Applicators' Association had turned thumbs down on it. The control system was a real Rube Goldberg. Not only had they recommended that it not be licensed, but that there be a restriction on its use. Phosphate is highly corrosive—all materials used in spraying are very corrosive—and this was one of the reasons that the Applicators' Association had turned the thing down. It was an airplane that would do the job—which it did until it got eaten up with corrosion. That's what happened in Jack's case."

Irwin decided to go to New Zealand, and, although it took him two weeks, he finally got an appointment to see the head of the Civil Aeronautics Authority. Joe told him the accident report had holes in it as big as those in the airplane, and he needed some straight answers.

"I know you had 110 of these airplanes in the first place, and you've got about 27 of them left. About two-thirds of those accidents have caused fatalities. My son was one of them, and I want to know why."

Irwin was told that although the CAA had grounded the airplanes on a regular basis, the restrictions were usually lifted within 24 hours. Apparently, the Department of Reclamation contended that because the airplanes did not carry freight or passengers for hire, if the pilots didn't want to fly them, they didn't have to.

Irwin admits that, although the pilots were not told this directly, it was common knowledge. "Everyone in the country knew about the fatalities and accidents with top-dressing flights.

"Jack would have had this knowledge, but when you're 21, 22 years old and something makes a lot of noise, that's a good airplane.

"Meanwhile, the New Zealand CAA was doing development work on the airplane. They eventually made a hell of a fine airplane out of it, and it became the prime aircraft in the top-dressing business there."

The Irwins feel that their personal investigations in New Zealand did help bring about some changes, in attitude as well as in structural improvements. "They didn't dump the Fletchers, but continually improved the structure as they repaired them."

While the Agricultural Aviation Accident Summary acknowledged, with regret, the high accident rate, the report Joe received related that "it was up to the pilots individually to make a firm resolution to avoid all occasions which could result in an accident."

"Of course," Irwin states, "you have no control over the wings falling off."

Joe tries to explain what actually happened in Jack's case, and produces photographs of the crash site to augment the story. "Jack was doing a turn after his first run, and the wing-tip split from the airplane in mid-air because of the serious corrosion problem. The wing was hanging by the control cables, which was what brought the airplane in as flat as it did. He was thrown clear, out through the canopy, but was killed on impact. Following the crash, the aircraft partially burned."

The photos are graphic and terribly disturbing. The aircraft is a mess of burned peeling paint and broken wings. The engine is lying out on the ground. But the crash site looks so small, a black burn scar on a pastoral hillside in a faraway country.

"The people who owned the place let us erect a plaque where the plane went down. And I planted that Manitoba maple tree," Joe says softly, pointing to the photograph.

Joe Irwin continued to fly with Sun Oil, and was within 200,000 miles of attaining his Two Million Miles of Safe Flying record when he left the company in April 1966. His resignation reflects many things about Joe's personality. The rumour still circulates that Irwin "decked a Sun Oil v.p. [Higgins] when he made a comment about know-nothing Canadian pilots."

"Negative!" Irwin replies when asked about the story's authenticity. "The manager of the aviation department for Sun Oil Company did make a remark about dumb Canadian pilots. I sort of—corrected—him on it, but I didn't deck him. I just corrected him verbally, shall we say?"

Irwin does not admit that this argument hastened his retirement, but "it didn't decelerate it, either. There was a little smoke.

"In the morning, there was a change of management, and I was not it. That was in April, and I was due to retire in October."

He did get his pension, but the golden handshake was a long time coming. Sixteen years, to be exact.

Sun Oil's Beech Baron; (L-R): Red Rogers, Ray Higgins, and Joe Irwin, 1962. *Joe Irwin Collection*

Joe Irwin stands up to display a belt buckle portraying the image of a De Havilland Dove.

"See my gold belt buckle for 15 years safe flying service? The Safety Dinner, where this was to be presented to me, was the evening of the altercation. I told him, 'Just keep the sonofabitch, and tell me in the morning.' So in the morning they told me they wanted me to go to the Wetaskiwin office and fly an Aztec out of there—a demotion. I said, 'Oh no, it don't work that way at all.'

"So, he didn't give me the buckle, but he left it so I should have to come and ask for it. I told him he could stuff it where the sun don't shine.

"About six months after my dismissal, they fired the guy who managed the aviation department in Philadelphia. And the chap who took over finally found the buckle and sent it to me—16 years later.

"I wouldn't have asked for it," Irwin says, "but I wear it, and I'm proud of it. That's a $150 buckle!"

After Irwin retired from Sun Oil, he never flew again. He left Calgary after the breakup of his marriage, and bought a quarter-section of land in an area he'd always liked, northern Alberta, 30 miles south of Athabasca, near the hamlet of Rochester. There he teamed up with other creatures that defy all odds to pursue flying—bees. He operated an apiary for six years, until he sold his land and the operation, and bought an old Lutheran church that he fixed up and called home. Then he married again, and moved into town.

When asked what his biggest thrill was in flying, or if there is one accomplishment he remembers with great satisfaction, he has to take time to think about it. "I've got quite a few of those things."

He cites the development of his sprayers as a noted achievement. The flying thrill goes to the Lysanders. "I liked flying those almost as much as the Dove, they were beautiful little things. The Lysanders were observation airplanes during the war and you could do some pretty miraculous things with them."

When he's with other pilots and engineers, the stories tumble over each other, and laughter accentuates almost every tale: "Christ, we were pigging it, steamboating down the Athabasca River at 50 feet, and it was 40 below outside . . ." and one story melds into the next: discovering, enroute from Fort Nelson to Fort Simpson, remnants of a Japanese paper balloon that had carried incendiary and antipersonnel bombs onto Canadian territory. "It was hanging just over the ranger station at Simpson. The Signal Corps and U.S. Army guys had perforated it with rifle power, just enough to get it onto the ground and defuse it. When I came in it was deflated like a long string bag, with a gadget on the bottom like a manhole cover."

Irwin's career included working out of Winnipeg as relief pilot with Canadian Airways, flying into northern Manitoba, to the Arctic as far as the Boothia Peninsula, and to Cambridge Bay and Coppermine. Down the Mackenzie River, to Aklavik and Tuktoyaktuk, "and all that country." Throughout northern BC from Fort Ware to Whitehorse, Yukon.

Joe Irwin, engineer Howard Yancey, and pilot Bill Watts the day of Phil Lucas's funeral, 22 April 1993. *Collection of the author*

He was in northern Quebec when they built the dam at the iron mine north of Baie-Comeau. With Sun Oil he flew personnel to the Mines Ministers' conferences in St. John, New Brunswick; to the head office in Philadelphia; and to Houston, Beaumont, Dallas, and Jacksonville, Mississippi.

When Irwin is asked if he's ever won awards for his flying, in addition to the One Million Mile award, his response is immediate: "Hell, no! What do you win awards for?"

How about 28,600 flying hours, without putting "any scratches on an airplane, or dents in people, either, while flying all over the country"?

Except for fighters—and except to war—Joe Irwin has flown nearly everything, to nearly everywhere. That, perhaps, is reward enough.

Notes

1. Florence Whyard, *Canadian Bush Pilot Ernie Boffa* (Alaska North West Publishing Co., Anchorage, Alaska, 1984), 78-81.

The Has-been

Olden Bawld (a.k.a. Charles R. Robinson)

I marvel at the changes I have seen down through the years—
from open-cockpit crates to jumbo jets;
and though I'm now a "has-been," and the game has passed me by,
when all is said and done, I've no regrets.
I've known a lot of pilots, some were old and some were bold,
but through the years I found this to be true:
The old ones were not bold ones—and the bold ones were by far
much younger than the old ones that I knew!

I've never flown around the world, I never won a race;
I've never tried to reach the speed of sound;
No epic flights—no daring deeds—nor have I thrilled the crowd
with trick and fancy flying near the ground.
My name is not emblazoned in the books of flying lore,
nor in the Aviation Hall of Fame;
But when my log is tallied up, the pages will reveal
I've done a lot of flying, just the same!

No one can slow the march of time, nor stay the hand of fate,
and certain things we have to understand:
No flight can cruise forever, soon we all must throttle back
and drop the wheels and bring her in to land.
And me? I'm turning final and the cockpit check is done—
and while the runway lights slide swiftly by
I'll dream beside my cabin by the lake amid the pines,
and watch the jets lay contrails in the sky.

(Composed at Bending Lake, Ontario; September 1976)

The Red-headed Stranger

I'VE *ALWAYS FELT* that women should get ahead on their own merits, without any special consideration," states Catherine Fletcher. "I have never been involved in women's groups. The only way you're going to be accepted is if you're qualified and you do the job. You can legislate quotas, but you can't legislate acceptance."

Catherine Fletcher's personality exudes confidence. She leans forward as she makes these statements, and others, then sits back to discuss ways in which a northern pilot must prepare her/himself for the challenges of flying the frontiers. Although she is smiling, she speaks with knowledge and authority, and a listener can tell she's been there, personally, and has met those challenges head-on.

Born on 27 March 1954, in Burnley, Lancashire, England, Catherine Margaret Fletcher (nee Simpson) immigrated to Canada as a child when her family settled in Oshawa, Ontario. By the time she was 24 years old, she had a reliable career in laboratory sciences. But to Catherine, this vocation simply provided the financial base for her true avocation: flying.

Aviation has always fascinated Catherine. Although girls could not join the Air Cadets when she was a high school student, she eventually became one of their instructors through the Civilian Cadet Instructor's List of the military reserves. "Weather was a pet subject of mine, and I had taken various courses on it, so I was teaching meteorology and aerodynamics to Air Cadets as part of their flying scholarship training. By the time I started ground school at Mount Hope, in Hamilton, I had a reasonable knowledge of aircraft subjects through this involvement."

While in the reserves, Catherine also participated in winter and summer survival camps. "I took a winter survival camp at Jarvis Lake, Alberta (near Hinton), and a summer one at CFB Borden where I learned to snare rabbits and squirrels, build a lean-to, a signal fire, perform emergency first-aid, and shoot rifles."

In 1973 she married Tom Fletcher, a Chemical Engineering student at McMaster University. Then, in 1978, as Catherine was completing her ground school training, Tom was offered a job in Edmonton. They began to prepare for the move west.

Catherine had no trouble finding a job in Edmonton, but as it turned out, the opening date was six to eight weeks away. Meanwhile, she decided to finish her pilot's training with the Edmonton Flying Club.

At the end of "a fast eight weeks," she had a private pilots' licence. Then she began working for the University of Alberta, as a chemistry lab supervisor.

"But I wasn't comfortable with just a private licence–I wanted more," Catherine recalls. "So, to boost my own confidence I would say, I took my night rating and then, over the winter months, went on to take my commercial."

By mid-1979 Catherine realized she was spending all her time and money flying–home or leisure activities were almost nonexistent. Catherine and Tom concluded that she should simply concentrate on flying. She quit her job and took an instructor rating through the Edmonton Flying Club.

"Six weeks later I had my instructor's rating, and the following day I was offered a job at the Edmonton Flying Club–well, that afternoon, actually. I did my ride in the morning and I had a job that afternoon."

Catherine then began her full-time aviation career with *ab initio* (beginning, first level) instruction for pilot training. She continued to upgrade her qualifications, eventually reaching Class 1, the highest level in an instructor rating. "I also had upgraded to multi-engine, taken my instrument rating, did all my senior commercial examinations and ATR examinations, and got an Airline Transport rating.

"I was still instructing at the time, and was flying 'on the side' for a private oil company taking parts here and there across the country. I did a Forestry contract, flying infra-red photos up into the fields using their airplanes. Also when I was at the flying club I did traffic patrols–you know, like The Flying Tiger, in a fixed-wing aircraft–all sorts of odd jobs."

Based on her excellent record as an instructor, in 1982 Transport Canada offered her a position as a Designated Flight Test Examiner, to test pilots for their private licences.

Catherine and Tom had now been married for nine years and decided the time was right to begin having children. But when Catherine became pregnant, she was afraid to tell her employer.

"At that time, if you became pregnant the Aviation Medical Officer at Transport Canada automatically cancelled your medical," Catherine says. "You were grounded for the full term of your pregnancy, and until a reasonable time after your pregnancy. Those were the standards. So, I was very reluctant to tell anyone."

When she did inform her medical examiner, his response was surprisingly positive. "I don't see any reason you shouldn't fly. You're young and healthy. I'll write a letter to Transport Canada stating that I feel you can still fly."

The letter allowed Catherine to fly until the "brass" of Transport Canada had debated the issue. Then Fletcher waited for news of the waiver that would allow her to retain her Category 1 medical status.

"I just dreaded that call!" Catherine says. "I fully expected to be grounded.

Six to eight weeks later, the call came. They had decided to give me a temporary medical on a monthly basis. Providing I remained in good health, I could continue to fly with my commercial medical. I was thrilled! But some of the other pilots didn't take it too kindly."

Catherine cautiously explains that "there are a lot of attitudes out there."

For one thing, women in aviation weren't that common—and now a pregnant one? "At that time, a country-wide test program was being undertaken by Transport Canada, Aviation Medicine, that allowed certain women to fly while they were pregnant," Catherine explains. "They kept a record of my progress to be used for documentation as a test case. I talked to the aviation medical doctors every four weeks and received a new medical licence every month."

Shrugging off the criticism of some fellow aviators, she continued to do flight tests until she was seven months along, then quit flying and limited herself to teaching ground school. Six weeks after the birth of her son in 1983, she requalified for her instrument rating.

The situation now, Catherine says, is that as long as a pregnant pilot is in good health, she can fly without a special dispensation. "I was one of the first in Canada to be allowed to do that. Now it's more commonplace."

The only two female inspectors Catherine knew of at the time had been hired under a special employment program. "There was a huge void in the information available about other female pilots," Catherine says. "I knew only my immediate female colleagues. Things are different today. You hear about other female pilots and their accomplishments."

In December 1984, Catherine began working as an examiner for Transport Canada Air Regulations. "I was looking for a calmer lifestyle, because I had been flying weekends and late at night, and now I had a young child. I wanted something more predictable."

"Predictable" is a word that often comes up when pilots discuss improvements they'd like to see in their jobs. Unfortunately, it is very elusive. Catherine found this niche with Transport Canada.

"I'd always had a good relationship with Transport Canada. As a pilot I worked with them all the time, and they'd renewed my qualifications regularly. For this job I had to apply in an open competition, and it was difficult to get hired. It took me two tries."

Catherine's qualifications and endorsements, her more than 3,000 flying hours, and her confident manner, brought her success. Her new job with Air Regulations involved examining pilots' instrument ratings, doing air carrier checks on both pilots and companies involved in commercial flying, pilot proficiency checks to ensure maintenance of flight training standards, and issuing licences.

Because she would be flying in sparsely settled areas of Canada's Far North, she continued to take survival training courses with Transport Canada.

This composite photo (it is actually two photos) of a Twin Otter—Catherine's "most favourite airplane ever"— was taken at an abandoned airstrip at Fort Selkirk, NWT. The only people to land here any more are the RCMP who tend the graves of deceased officers. Here Catherine and her coworker are assessing whether the runway could be reopened as a means of accessing the old fort. *Catherine Fletcher Collection*

Emergency equipment and rations were kept on board as a matter of course. With her training and familiarity with emergency equipment, she believes she could survive on her own, if she had to—an important skill for anyone who ventures over the trackless northern landscape.

The North country in winter is dark and silent, and holds a few surprises for a southerner. "In most northern communities, caribou is the main source of food, and their deepfreeze in the wintertime is simply 'outside their door,'" Catherine says. "So when you walk around in the community, you see all sorts of dead caribou stacked up; they look like they're standing and really alive. Some still have their eyes open, but they're frozen solid.

"One guy had a bunch of them all stacked up, and he'd put a sled behind them and attached Christmas lights. There they were, all propped up, standing on their four legs, decorated for Christmas."

Catherine found the lifestyle in the North to be welcoming and hospitable. Not even the food is out of the ordinary. "There's a lot of air service, and the hotels are very pleasant. You don't have to eat weird things. I've had musk ox, caribou, and Arctic char, and they're some of my favourite foods. I had the offer of muktuk one day, which is blubber. They assured me it tasted like candy, but I still haven't been brave enough to check that out yet. But I really enjoy the Arctic islands."

Dealing with the social aspect of her work was another challenge for Catherine. Her first test came when she met the Natives of the North—and they met her.

"I got stared at!" she laughs. "They weren't used to seeing red hair. And a woman jumping out of the left seat of an aircraft was somewhat uncommon up North. But the people have such delightful senses of humour."

One day she and a male copilot landed at Sachs Harbour. The copilot began to refuel the airplane while Catherine went in to talk to the airport radio operator.

An Inuit man, who had watched with amusement as this woman with the wild red hair emerged from the cockpit, decided to satisfy his curiosity. He approached the copilot.

"You fly this airplane all by yourself?"

"No. The pilot is the woman who just walked past."

The Inuit man began to laugh.

"She's the pilot. I'm the copilot."

The man laughed until he nearly fell in the snow. Women with red hair–flying airplanes! What next?

Northern hotel accommodation also presented a bit of a conundrum.

"In Coppermine, the hotel is just delightful; it's one of my favourite places," Catherine says. "But I learned very quickly that I should ask the booking agent to identify me as a woman, instead of just listing my initials. You see, when you reserve accommodations in the North, you don't necessarily get a room–you get a bed. There aren't that many women who travel up North and they assume that you're a man and so allot you one of maybe three single beds in a room.

"When I showed up they said, 'Oh my goodness, you're a woman!' I didn't understand what the problem was–but I soon found out."

Catherine had arrived at the same time as a group of Americans who were hunting musk-ox. The accommodation problem was resolved by finding her a room in an annex, a building detached from the main hotel, which itself was a collection of Atco trailers or small buildings put together. A frozen caribou was propped up against the back door to the annex. "It certainly added flavour, and unforgettable memories," Catherine laughs.

As Catherine prepared for bed, she began to plan the logistics of the morning parade to the lone bathroom at the end of the hall. The hosts had informed her that breakfast would be served at 8 o'clock in the dining room. "I'll set my alarm for 5:30 A.M.," she thought, "quietly have my shower so I won't disturb anyone, and get out before the guys wake up."

The plan went ahead, but just as she was tiptoeing back down the hall an American hunter emerged from his room and began to make his bleary way toward the bathroom. With his "soap on a rope" swinging from one hand, and his towel and toothbrush clenched in the other, he was oblivious to anyone else's presence. Obviously, for he was stark naked. He didn't notice Catherine until they met face to face.

The American looked up. "Oh! Sorry, little lady! I forgot you were here," he said with a big smile and a southern drawl–and just kept going toward the bathroom, while she continued on to her room.

Catherine laughs at the aplomb with which he handled the situation. "Oh, he had a lot of class, that individual!"

In 1986 she decided she wanted a job change, and applied to Air Navigation Services. She was successful in the competition, and has been there ever since. "I went to Aerodrome Standards, which ensures that the airport environment is safe for pilots to operate in. I worked there until 1992 as an inspector, and then I became the supervisor."

She is presently in charge of Aerodrome Standards, inspecting all the airports, heliports, and ice strips that have commercial air carrier operations, or those located in the built-up areas of cities or towns.

Catherine flies in this helicopter to complete heliport inspections. *Catherine Fletcher Collection*

Her job covers the Western Region, west from the Saskatchewan border to the BC coast, south from the U.S. border to the western half of the Northwest Territories and all the Yukon. It includes northeastern BC and all of Alberta. In the Arctic, she travels east to Cambridge Bay, and west to the Alaska border. "I'm usually away one week a month."

She now has almost 6,000 flying hours to her credit—"But I don't keep up my log book, I'm terrible."

Catherine and Tom have two children, James born in 1983 and Graham born in 1988. Catherine continued to fly during her second pregnancy as well, while carrying on her regular work for the Department of Transport in Aerodrome Standards.

Over the years, numerous organizations have asked Catherine to join them but she was always reluctant to do so, until she came in contact with the Alberta Stepping Stones program, sponsored by the provincial government under the Minister for Women's Issues. This educational program sends successful candidates to talk to young boys and girls in junior and senior high schools about various nontraditional job opportunities.

"It is important for young people to know what's available in a career such as the one I've followed. That girls realize aviation is a career possibility for them, and that boys also come to recognize that aviation is an acceptable profession for a girl. The only way you're going to overcome prejudice, bias, and stereotyping is through education, so I felt this was a good program."

Catherine Fletcher is a good choice for such presentations. "I was the first female inspector with Transport Canada's Western Region to come in under an open competition; that is, I wasn't accepted under a special employment program. I competed against my peers to get the position."

Catherine has some well-founded theories on why few women have taken up careers in flying, especially as bush pilots. "There are definitely some physical requirements for working in that environment that make it tough, just like there are for female firefighters and such. For one thing, the work is physically demanding, often involving loading and off-loading heavy cargo.

"That requirement still occurs, even today. I'm not a bush pilot, nor was I. I fly in to northern airstrips to ensure that they're safe for those pilots who work in the North.

"It was a pretty horrendous job opening up the North. It really was. Some of the stories are amazing," Catherine says. "Still, women have always been pilots, even during the Second World War. Women aviators played an incredible part in history. But bush flying seemed the hardest, so women more often became instructors or worked for airlines. Some were interested in becoming bush pilots, all right, but it wasn't a profession that was highly

The nose of this Transport Canada DC-3 has the name "Mel Bryan" painted on it. Mel was an aviator and training pilot. Although Transport Canada retired the aircraft from service four years ago, and Mel no longer flies (he is now blind), Catherine has a soft spot in her heart for both the aircraft and the man she fondly refers to as her "mentor." *Catherine Fletcher Collection*

Inspector Catherine "Kate" Fletcher. Supervisor Aerodrome Standards and Certification. *Catherine Fletcher Collection*

acceptable for a woman, and not too many years ago. Luckily, things have changed a bit, and women are moving into these rugged jobs."

Catherine is optimistic about the advancements aviation has brought about in the North. "Airports are being developed; there's more access, bigger aircraft going in; communities are getting larger with modern buildings, modern technology, nursing stations, and so on. There are some major schools such as in Yellowknife, where students come in from various communities. In the 10 years I've been flying up there, a lot of development has occurred.

"There's a lot of bush flying, to the fly-in fishing and hunting camps that are active, also to survey and mining sites. Now we're seeing the advent of more modern, quicker aircraft going in to the sites. Medevac facilities are much farther ahead. You can get on a Lear jet now out of Cambridge Bay."

Flying has given Catherine Fletcher a career she could once only dream about, when girls were not encouraged to enter the profession. But when the opportunities came she took them, and created new ones, and that determination has made the difference.

"I love it! I think for anyone who flies, it's a passion. You live it and breathe it. It's not a job. It's an avocation as well as a vocation, and you do it regardless of any problems, you just enjoy it so much."

The red-headed pilot is no longer a stranger to the North. She takes the "perks" of her job in stride, whether they involve being served muktuk, meeting a frozen caribou with Christmas lights blinking from its frosted horns, or running into a happy-go-lucky buck of another sort in the narrow hallways of an Atco trailer hotel. She shifts easily from North to South, from work to play. One day she had flown for 12 hours, stopping only to refuel coming back from Tuktoyaktuk, eager to arrive in Edmonton on time to attend her husband's company party. As soon as she landed the Twin Otter in Edmonton, she rushed into the airport washroom, shucked off her heavy parka, boots, and jeans, then pulled from her suitcase a party dress and high-heeled shoes. She quickly brushed and styled her hair, added some jewellery, and examined her manicured nails. Then she threw her work-clothes into the suitcase and emerged from the washroom, ready to join her husband at his formal party, ready to meet the southern folks.

The Queen's Engineer

B ILL LAW HAS BEEN ASSOCIATED with some of the best-known names in Canada's aviation history, and acknowledges that he has received as much joy from participating in their careers as he has in achieving his own goals. He has few photographs, or other personal memorabilia, to mark his own career path. "I realize now that I'm the one who was always taking the pictures, and over the years I've never asked anyone to take my picture. So, that explains the sparsity," he says, apologetically.

When asked to tell his story, it was difficult to get Law to talk about his achievements, shrouded as they were in his pride at the successes of his old friends, Weldy Phipps and Lorna deBlicquy. But, finally convinced that engineers were indeed an integral part of Canada's aviation history, he relented, and out poured the tales.

Bill Law has always been interested in airplanes. He built models from the age of 12, and read everything about aviation he could get his hands on, from fiction stories about aviation hero Howie Wing, to nonfiction articles that described wonderful aircraft such as a Payne Knight Twister with a 12-foot wingspan, which he decided he'd build one day. Thus the plans to become an aeronautical engineer, as well as a pilot, took form. But Law had a struggle ahead of him to achieve these goals.

Bill was born on 18 April 1927 and grew up in Cobalt, Westboro, and Ottawa, Ontario. During the summer of 1941, while still in highschool, Law worked at Uplands (now Ottawa International) Airport for Laurentian Air Services, overhauling Jacobs L6MB aircraft engines. Though Bill quit school for a while after the death of his father, he later returned, and managed to win a scholarship, which factored heavily in his being accepted at Queen's University. "About 20 students out of 300 were not veterans at that time. Only the top students from high schools were considered, usually based on those students winning scholarships."

Weldy Phipps, meanwhile, had served in the RCAF as a flight engineer, was shot down, taken prisoner of war, escaped, and returned home to Ottawa. In the summer of 1945 he decided to go back to high school and was enroled in grade 13 when he was 23 years old. Weldy and Bill were in the same class.

"The school had the fuselage of some aircraft in the basement," Law recalls.

"Some of the students told me that they had seen Weldy sitting in the cockpit talking to himself and pretending to fly. They thought he was nuts!"

Bill Law, however, formed a friendship with Weldy Phipps, one that would last a lifetime and would significantly influence Law's career.

"Weldy had little interest in school and was always in trouble for smoking, which was not allowed. A student who openly smoked was considered to be a bad influence on other students. I found out that Weldy was spending most of his time learning to fly, since this was covered by the veteran's program. In the spring of 1946 he had his licence and arrived with it at school. He was quite proud, and invited me for a flight. I had never flown before, and within five minutes, Weldy was doing a spin! I decided then and there that I would have to learn to fly, also, so I could scare someone else the same way."

Law had a summer job at the NRC (National Research Council) in 1946, but would go out to the airport every weekend to help Weldy. Law's work at the airport was reimbursed in flying time, rather than wages, and his instructor was none other than Weldy Phipps. "Weldy only had a few hours and no instructor rating at the time. Completely illegal, but in those days, who cared?" Law went solo on 11 August 1946, just before he was to begin his university studies.

Bill Law first recalls meeting Lorna Bray (Nichols deBlicquy) in the summer of 1946 at the McGuire Flying School, which had an office in Laurentian's building at Uplands. "I will never forget a little freckle-faced 14-year-old girl with auburn hair, standing behind the gates leading to the airfield. The gate was closed to keep the crowds off the apron, away from the propeller blades of an aircraft used to give rides to people who wanted to fly over Ottawa and view the parliament buildings."

Law remembers the young girl trying to stop some people from getting through the gate by yelling, "You can't come in here without a ticket!" One man claimed he wanted to go to his aircraft parked on the apron, but the young girl obliged him to get someone from McGuire's to vouch for him. Bill Law laughs when he thinks of how, 46 years later, he was instrumental in getting "that little girl" nominated for the prestigious McKee Trophy and hopefully to Canada's Aviation Hall of Fame.

In 1946, Law applied, and was accepted, to study engineering at Queen's University in Kingston, Ontario.

"I remember flying down with Weldy Phipps to register and buy my books and find a place to stay. My mother had packed me a lunch. On the trip back with Weldy, we had to weigh my textbooks before boarding the Piper Cub (J-3) to make sure we were not overweight. The ride was so rough coming back that I spilled prune juice all over my new Chemistry text."

Law got his private pilots' licence in June of 1947 and spent weekends during the summer holidays barnstorming with Weldy, flying the J-3 within a 70-mile radius of Ottawa to Shawville, Maniwaki, Pendleton, and Smiths Falls. They charged $2 for a long circuit, which lasted five to seven minutes.

Bill Law with Piper Cub, 1947. *Bill Law Collection*

Law had to carry their fuel supply, which consisted of up to five five-gallon cans of gas, balanced partly on his lap. One particular takeoff from Uplands required about 1,000 feet of runway to get airborne. After that, they decided to cut their fuel supply from five to four cans to reduce their weight.

"Weldy was an artist at getting into short fields," Law says, "which no doubt prepared him for his Arctic work later in his career. His method was to approach low and slow, just on the point of stalling; then, in a violent side-slip, he would keep the wing down until it was just about to touch the ground, then level off and apply full brakes with the stick right back. I learned to fly this way, too, and so scared everyone who flew with me."

The stories of Bill Law's and Weldy Phipps's flying adventures would fill a book.

"I remember one take-off from a ploughed field when I had to get out to push the plane to get it moving, then scramble aboard. The aircraft was still not airborne when we approached a fence, so Weldy pulled back on the stick. The aircraft just cleared the fence and settled on the other side, and continued rolling on the ground in the next field until we finally got airborne.

"Many times after landing, we had to clear the field of debris in order to operate. On one occasion we hit a piece of cable with the propeller. Weldy looked it over and flew for the rest of the day. Then we headed back to Uplands where the propeller was scrapped because of the extensive damage.

"Once we landed in a grain field and had to have the farmer cut a path for takeoff at a cost of $20, which was a lot of money in 1947. We left the cans of gas, which may still be there."

Some of their adventures in those days resembled the antics of the Keystone Kops.

During the barnstorming days, Weldy, Lorna, and Bill often took people up so they could view their farms from the air. One day, two men came over and paid for tickets, but Weldy could see they were drunk. He tried to dissuade them, but they insisted, so he let them into the airplane. Once they were airborne, the unruly passengers began to grab at the controls. Weldy picked out a cluster of buildings below. "Oh, there's your farm!" Weldy cried, pointing. The men looked down, figured it must be right, and so Weldy was able to return after a very quick circuit.

A while later, the men realized they couldn't possibly have reached their home place in such a short time because it was a fair distance away. Angered at being deceived, they jumped into their car and came roaring toward the field intending to crash into the airplane. They drove off the road, ploughed through the ditch, but were momentarily stopped by the wire fence. Weldy and Bill made the most of the opportunity by jumping into their airplane and taking off, with the car pursuing them down the field.

They left Lorna and the others to make their way back to Ottawa as best they could, by car. As Law says, at moments like that, "the aircraft came before chivalry!"

One day Weldy and Bill were out flying near La Malbaie (Murray Bay), Quebec, looking for a camp that might need some supplies brought in by air. They landed in a little lake surrounded by hills on all sides. When it came time to take off, the Seabee aircraft didn't lift off in one direction, so Weldy simply tried again in the opposite direction.

"Well, we just cleared the shore," Law says. "Unfortunately, the hills rose at the same rate as our climb. The top of one spruce tree passed between the float and the fuselage. On the later modifications, there was an added strut which would surely have been hit by the tree. Anyway, there we were with no indication of airspeed on the 'clock' and my hands on the switches ready to cut them as soon as we started hitting the trees, and Weldy shouting, 'Come on, baby!'"

Law recalled that before leaving La Malbaie he had urged Weldy to carry a bit more gas on board; Weldy had replied they'd be okay, and anyway, they didn't have time to refuel. "The added weight of an extra 20 gallons of fuel on board might have been the difference between life and death," Law concludes.

The trees "mercifully" levelled off, and they made it. "We shook hands. Weldy said in later years that was the closest he ever came to being killed."

The adventurous young pilots faced several other life-and-death situations. One time they were barnstorming at Shawville, Quebec. Law was designated to "swing the prop." It was customary to give the prop a couple of swings prior to turning on the switches to let gas into the cylinders. Weldy got into the aircraft. Law casually swung the prop twice, then yelled, "Switches on!" Weldy yelled back, "The switches are already on!" With the next swing of the prop, the engine started. Again, Law says, he escaped death through pure luck.

In the summer of 1947, both Lorna Bray and Bill Law were taught the art of packing a parachute and parachute jumping. Their teacher was Bill Bennett, "a man who has made thousands of jumps." Law made several jumps in 1947 and Bray made a jump in the spring of 1948. "As such, Bray was the first woman to make a parachute jump in Canada, at age 16."

That summer, Atlas Aviation, which was located "across the field" from Laurentian, began operating a flying training school. Law would see Bray bicycling out from downtown Ottawa to save the bus fare, so every penny could go towards her training. She expressed her anger to Bill that boys could learn to fly for nothing through the Air Cadets, while she had to pay for every minute in the air.

Bill Law completing a parachute jump at Carp Airport (near Ottawa). *Bill Law Collection*

In 1947, when Law had less than 15 hours total flying time, Lorna asked him to take her for a flight, which he did ("again, completely illegal") with his log book hours padded a bit. Thus, Lorna became Bill Law's first passenger.

When Weldy and Law were barnstorming in 1947, Lorna sometimes showed up with a car and gas so they could continue flying.

"Lorna once arrived at Gracefield, Quebec, to watch us fly," Law says. "When we were finished for the day, she wanted to fly back but I said I was and she could drive back. She hit me so hard on my right ear that I still get an earache in the winter each year! Quite a way to keep her on my mind over the years. Since I started talking to her again—after about 45 years—I came to realize how important flying was to her. That flight from Gracefield to Ottawa could have amounted to weeks of her working after school to pay for air time, and I was going to rob her of it."

Bill Law continued his engineering studies, and Lorna went on to begin her career in aviation. In 1953 she married geologist Tony Nichols and moved to northern Manitoba, and the two old friends lost contact. Over the years, however, Law would clip newspaper and magazine articles chronicling Lorna's achievements. In 1992 he presented her with the filled scrapbook, to help her research when she writes her memoirs.

Upon his graduation from Queen's in 1950, with a BSc (Honours) in

Mechanical Engineering, Law was hired by Spartan Air Services. His friend, Weldy Phipps, was already working there.

Not only did the team of Phipps and Law begin to design and develop innovations for pilots and airplanes, but they had a lot of fun doing it.

"Some time in 1952 or 1953, Weldy decided he needed a pressure suit in order to fly at 35,000 feet," Law says. So Law and Maurice Giroux, who was a radio man at Spartan, undertook the task of covering Weldy's naked body with plaster of Paris in order to get a mould for a perfectly fitting suit. After an hour the plaster hadn't set and Weldy complained that he was freezing to death. "We had to cut him out and thereby destroy the cast," Law laments, "so that idea never came to fruition."

As the only engineer then employed by Spartan, Law "did everything around the place," from "bucking" rivets to building offices. Sometimes he even did what he was trained for: stress analyses and engineering drawings. "For seven years I never had a holiday. I worked until midnight every day except Sunday, because my mother said she would like to see me for one meal a week."

Having a pilot's licence, says Law, allowed him to speak with greater knowledge to people in the aviation field. "I'm sure that being a pilot, in addition to an engineer, opened a lot of doors that otherwise would have remained closed."

Bill Law with P-38 "Lightning," 1950. *Bill Law Collection*

Spartan had Ansons, P-38s, Mosquitos, Yorks, Lancasters, Venturas, PBY 5A Cansos, a DC-3, a Dragon Rapide, a Sea Hornet, and a Super Cub. "In fact, they had any war surplus or other aircraft that they could buy for next to nothing."

During his seven years with Spartan, from 1950 to 1957, the company modified these aircraft for aerial survey, high altitude photography, magnetometer, and scintillometer surveys. The modifications ranged from rather simple jobs such as radio installations with trailing antennae, to major structural changes such as enlarging the nose of the P-38, which permitted a person to sit upright and both navigate and operate the camera.

"Nearly every Spartan aircraft had a hole cut in the belly for a large vertical camera," Law explains. "Some, such as the Anson and Canso, had winches so you could reel a cable in or out. The end of the cable attached to a trailing 'bird' for magnetometer or scintillometer surveys." This was needed to keep the sensitive magnetic pickups in the bird away from the magnetic influences of the aircraft.

The aerial survey work resulted in the mapping of large areas of Canada and the discovery of major mineral deposits. The scintillometer was used for locating uranium deposits.

"I did stress analyses on all of Spartan's aircraft and I doubled as a mechanic. So not only did I design the modifications, and make the drawings, but I would help build them and stress them, then go to Toronto to get DOT approvals.

In a speech Law delivered at Spartan's reunion in 1988 in Ottawa, he tells of some "amusing methods" used at the time.

"So here I'd be, ready to carry out modifications on military aircraft that were even then rather sophisticated," Law says. "There was only one problem—no drawings or any structural engineering data were available. The modifications we carried out should have necessitated a large engineering and shop staff, and have taken several months to complete. Well, I was the lone engineer, and the shop staff consisted of four metal-bashers, two of whom had recently been in the Luftwaffe. And we had days, not months, to complete the jobs. I would be told that an air crew would be arriving in a few days, and the aircraft was to have a camera installed and be ready to go. Since the company was run by ex-air

The shop at Spartan's hangar at Uplands Airport, 1950. "It's hard to believe, but sophisticated modifications were done to P-38s and Mosquitos in this mess!" says Bill Law. As the only engineer then employed by Spartan, Law did everything around the place, from "bucking" rivets to building offices. Sometimes he even did what he was trained for: stress analyses and engineering drawings. *Bill Law Collection*

force personnel, we were not allowed to say there was no way the aircraft could not be ready on such short notice. This was still World War II mentality, with an operations room and with the ops board already showing the aircraft and its departure date.

"The first thing we'd do was to go down to the aircraft with a saw and cut a hole. Any formers or stringers in the way were also removed. 'Engineering analysis' consisted of hopefully replacing the strength lost by making a reinforcement around the hole. Usually, my engineering experience was considered secondary, so I often spent the days bucking rivets; the engineering and drawings had to be done in the evenings or on weekends. During the first couple of years, the only space available for me to set up a drafting board was in the no-longer-functioning World War II women's toilet.

"I got married in 1957 to Audrey (Muffet) Horn, and just took a long weekend for a honeymoon."

Law will never forget the stress analysis he and Weldy carried out on the major nose modifications to the P-38: "Weldy climbed to 20,000 feet, and, with the dive brakes extended, we dove at terminal velocity. The stress analysis consisted of me holding one finger against the inside of the plexiglas nose with instructions to let Weldy know if the plexiglas was showing signs of failure. These test flights were usually conducted the day before the aircraft was to leave.

"All that remained after the tests was to get DOT approval. I would catch the overnight train to Toronto and arrive at their offices with a roll of drawings in my hand. Meanwhile, back in Ottawa, the Spartan crew would be arriving at the hangar, waiting for my telephone call to say the drawings had been approved."

The meeting with DOT would go something like this:

"Have you flown the aircraft?" Law would be asked.

He knew if he said yes, it would be admitting an illegal action, but to say no would mean "NO APPROVAL."

He took a deep breath, said, "Yes," and the drawings were stamped APPROVED.

Next, DOT officials said they had to inspect the aircraft to see that the work had been completed in a satisfactory manner for the Certificate of Airworthiness. Law would plead that the aircraft was urgently needed for a job, and ask if they could inspect it sometime later. Like, how about when the aircraft returned in the fall?

In almost every case, Law says, the answer was "Okay." He would then rush to the telephone and make that all-important call to the hangar. Only once, when a major modification had been done, did DOT insist that they must inspect it prior to granting approval. "I remember this particular instance," Law says, "because I had to tell DOT that the aircraft had already left the day before for Dawson City, Yukon. So again, with reluctance, we got approval."

Law believes the reason they got away with it was "DOT felt most of the people who flew Spartan aircraft were rather crazy bastards. And, since only the crew was allowed to fly in the aircraft, and since these aircraft always flew over uninhabited terrain, it didn't matter much if anything did happen!"

By 1957, Law was manager of the research and engineering division, responsible for the design and fabrication of extensive modifications to aircraft to adapt them to aerial survey, and in charge of all machine and metals shops as well as the engineering personnel.

At that point, his service with Spartan Air Services was put on hold and a new phase began when he was seconded to De Havilland Aircraft of Canada for two years—which turned out to be fifteen—as special projects and senior research engineer. But the professional and personal relationship between Law and Phipps continued.

"Back in the early 1950s, Spartan had obtained a J-3 with Whittiker tandem gear, and I'd designed a track made out of conveyor belting that went around the two tandem wheels," Law says. "Lorna deBlicquy later told me she had flown the tandem gear—but not with the belts—since even though it worked well—you could climb up on a snowbank or land in deep hay—there was always the danger that one of the belts would slip off.

"In 1952 in the hangar at Spartan, Dave Bell of Transport Canada had suggested the subject to Weldy and me—of using large diameter tires 'like were used in the 1930s.'" Then, when Weldy came into contact with geologists E.T. Tozer and R. Thorsteinsson of the Geological Survey of Canada, the men discussed systems that would effectively bring Arctic geology and flying together to the benefit of both.

In 1958, Weldy asked Law to do a stress analysis on a J-3 with 35-inch diameter tires. The design came about, says Law, "through a slow evolution. Much later, in 1963 at De Havilland, I came across a 1930s tire catalogue that showed these very tires. And in 1963-64 I corresponded with a Count Bonmartini in Italy who had, around 1951, designed a somewhat similar device except he had used an inflatable track. So several people were responsible for the idea of big tires."

Weldy successfully flew the Whittiker configuration up to the Arctic, Law says. "I still have the map Weldy marked with his trip in a J-3 to Cape Columbia (where Peary set off for the Pole). We flew down to see Piper Aircraft to show them the versatility of their aircraft."

In 1959, Law did stress analyses and drawings for 45-inch diameter tires for the Beaver, and also for 60- and 71-inch diameter tire configurations for the Otter.

"In 1964, Weldy asked me to investigate the possibility of oversized tires for the Twin Otter. De Havilland wasn't interested, so I had to do it on my own, utilizing De Havilland's stress analysis of their Twin Otter without their knowledge! Anyway, I designed a 45-inch diameter main wheel and an oversized 35-inch diameter nose wheel with a special fork to clear the oversized tire on the nose. Weldy had this configuration on the Twin Otter when he bought it."

While at De Havilland, Law went on to design 45-inch mains for the Caribou aircraft, which were being bought by the U.S. Army. The Caribou were large two-engine freighters with a rear-loading door big enough to drive a car into. The large tires were shipped to Vietnam to be installed on the Caribou, "but were conveniently lost by the United States Air Force until the war was over. There was so much rivalry between the U.S. Air Force and U.S. Army. The air force didn't want the army in the flying business," Law says. "The oversized tires would have allowed the army to operate in unprepared terrain and the USAF would not have been needed as much. What a way to run a war."

De Havilland Caribou with 45-inch diameter tires designed by Bill Law, 1964 *De Havilland Photo*

Throughout the years 1963 to 1970, Law supervised many tests on unprepared terrain, model and full-scale, and participated, with Weldy Phipps, in some Arctic tests by McGill University. A number of the tests were done on a "soil track" at McGill while others were done in the Arctic, to determine the reduction in takeoff roll on soft terrain provided by the oversized tires.

"So, I'm the one who did all the engineering for Weldy and De Havilland on the oversized tires," Law says. "I have boxes of data on the tires." This material, of great significance to Canada's aviation heritage, will be deposited with the archives of Canada's National Aviation Museum in Ottawa.

Innovations were Law's specialty. At De Havilland, he worked on other special projects such as wind-tunnel model designs, and conducted noise measurements and tests for soundproofing of aircraft. He received a patent for his design of an all-weather STOL (short take-off and landing) port.

"Unfortunately, the environmentalists, who were more concerned about possible noise and air pollution, thought the idea of aircraft operating from the tops of buildings—my idea—would be too noisy, so the idea was never adopted."

Law's education was augmented through the years by courses on Value

Engineering, Instrument Flying, Management Skills, and Micro-Computer literacy. He was always interested in new ideas, and the people who were pioneering them.

His work from 1972 to 1976 for Transport Canada, on the Toronto Area Airports project (Pickering Airport) included forecasting passenger and aircraft movements, airport layout, and everything from general aviation planning to noise studies.

Law concluded his career as principal aviation engineer with DOT, Province of Ontario, providing expertise for the minister. Another significant achievement was promoting area navigation systems (in particular, Loran-C) for both enroute and nonprecision approaches, and developing the Ontario Airport System Plan.

Throughout his career, Law has published dozens of articles, on subjects as diverse as downtown air services, ditching tests for the U.S. Army AC-1A Caribou, investigations of slipstream flaps at low forward speeds, and propeller noise.

Bill Law, 1985. *Bill Law Collection*

For Transport Canada, his published papers covered surveys of Toronto's regional aviation airports, "Probability of an Aircraft Hitting the Pickering Nuclear Power Plant" (1972), to analyses of winds and runway capacities, and studies of U.S. and U.K. air carrier aircraft, airport zoning requirements, and ceiling and visibility conditions.

Law is a member of the Association of Professional Engineers of Ontario and the Canadian Owners and Pilots Association (COPA).

And then Law found a new challenge. In February 1991, he was leafing through ATAC's (Air Transport Association of Canada) monthly newsletter when he read that "Women in Transportation" was to be that year's theme for NTW (National Transportation Week). He immediately thought of Lorna deBlicquy, although he had no idea what she'd been doing for the past 45 years, beyond what he'd read in newspapers and magazines. When Law contacted NTW he was told that the nomination date had closed but they would make an exception if the form was received within two days. He quickly got updates on Lorna's achievements, "put together a one-page terrible letter and sent it to Bill Peppler, manager of COPA, who had agreed to second my nomination. Well, the result was, no cigar."

But Law persevered, and in the fall of 1991, Peppler's wife, Isabel, wrote "a better one-page letter." Lorna deBlicquy won the NTW Award of Excellence, which came as a complete surprise to her. Law accompanied Isabel and Lorna to Montreal in June of 1992 to see Lorna receive her award.

Through Isabel's letter, Law learned of the work Lorna had been doing to champion women's rights in aviation, and also that she had spent over half of her 10,000 hours of flying time teaching others to fly. Bolstered by this information, in the spring of 1992 Law decided to go a step further and nominate Lorna for the Trans-Canada (McKee) Trophy.

"I was to retire in April 1992 and I thought this was a good project." Again, he decided to keep the nomination secret from Lorna while he solicited the support of "fourteen of the top people in aviation." But, he needed more detailed information, which only Lorna could provide. When he told her of his plan, her response was, "Don't be foolish!" She did agree, however, to send him a CV that ran for seven pages, covering aspects of her career that Law hadn't known about.

But, how was he to convince the jurors for the Trans-Canada Trophy to award it to a woman? It would set a precedent—one that may not be welcomed by some of the old stalwarts of aviation, an industry that had been a male bastion for years. Law resorted to "reverse psychology." In his nomination of Lorna, he stated, "I am not a supporter of women's liberation, but Lorna's accomplishments certainly qualify her for entrance into an up-to-now all-male club." In spite of mutterings in the ranks, the idea took hold: why not a woman? And Lorna certainly was a bona-fide candidate.

As a result, Lorna deBlicquy, in 1993, was the first woman to win the prestigious McKee Trophy. Law has now set his sights on Lorna being nominated to The Order of Canada and to Canada's Aviation Hall of Fame. His energy, plus his conviction that she richly deserves this recognition, will hopefully result in success. "I am confident that soon Lorna will have received many more awards," Law says. "She has just received the 99's Award of Merit, the Governor General's Award in Commemoration of the Person's Case, and the Tissandier Award presented by the Federation Aeronautique Internationale of Paris. All these are prestigious awards, and all richly deserved."

When contacted to reveal his role in helping to bring about the recognition of his friends, Weldy and Lorna, Law was modest. "I appreciate the opportunity to tell my side of the story as far as the big tires are concerned," Law said, "and for helping Lorna get the recognition she deserves."

Then he added, with his usual sanguine energy, "Hey! Maybe I will get my name in your book and that will be as good as getting a medal.

"Well, almost as good!"

Tales from the Log Book

*P*ILOT RALPH LANGEMANN has no love for airplanes.
"I was a typical small-town kid—I'd have done anything to get out of our small jerk-water town," Langemann says.

The air force presented a way out. "Unlike many people, I never had this great burning desire to be a pilot from when I was in three-corner pants. It was a cold-blooded, logical decision."

Because the air force was in the business of flying, he figured that if he was accepted he might as well be a pilot.

"My attitude drives other pilots crazy. They think that because you're a pilot you should love airplanes. To me, they've always been just a piece of equipment, and most of them are poorly designed and poorly built equipment; they're garbage. We would not accept cars that are built the way aircraft are built. We stopped riveting cars together in 1928! We're still riveting aircraft."

Ralph Langemann was born 7 March 1936, in Coaldale, Alberta. He joined the air force in 1955. "'Join the air force and see the world!' That's where things went wrong," he laughs. He did his basic flying training in Claresholm, Alberta, and jet training in Portage la Prairie, Manitoba. Then he returned to Claresholm as a flying instructor. When that base closed in 1958, he was transferred to Penhold, Alberta, where he stayed until being transferred to Calgary in 1961. "I started counting up how many airports were left in this province, and realized I could do a whole air force career in Alberta. I got out at that stage."

Ralph Langemann's log book reveals that he has flown 40 different types of aircraft and has over 5,000 hours of accident-free flying to his credit. These statistics are augmented by photographs and quotes that bring to life the bare facts of aircraft flown, places visited, and times clocked.

"This log book is like a diary. I flip through, read about the airplanes I've flown, people I've flown with, and I wonder where some of them went, what they did."

"January 1956. First instructor, first trip, showed me how to leave wheel tracks on the tops of snow-covered haystacks."

Langemann recalls the story.

"We were in a little Chipmunk trainer built by De Havilland Canada.

Really, it was a streamlined Tiger Moth with only one wing—a monoplane; the Tiger Moth was a biplane. They were nice little airplanes.

"I was sitting there all bright-eyed in the front of the airplane. My instructor went roaring over this snow-covered haystack near Claresholm, then pulled up and around and, sure enough, there were two wheel tracks across the top of the stack. If he'd hit too hard, it would have torn the wheels off. The haystack would be pretty solid in the wintertime, and we were doing over 100 miles an hour.

"It was one of those make-or-break deals. If you were going to get scared by that I guess they wanted to know right away."

Langemann admits that he learned that trick well. "Oh, yeah. I got court-martialled for something like that a few years later."

The pilots then graduated from Chipmunks to Harvard trainers. "I did a lot of time on Harvards. We had fun on those big suckers. At the time we all felt we were the last of the red-hot fighter pilots; we were going on to bigger and more wonderful things.

"Then two of us got caught low-flying in Harvard trainer aircraft. They measured us at 27 feet off the ground, two airplanes in close formation. I think what really bugged them was that we were upside-down."

He was based in Claresholm and had been to Penhold for lunch. On the way back he and another pilot were jacking around, flying in formation over a field, and one thing led to another. What they didn't know was that a couple of senior officers from Penhold were scouting for a possible satellite field, and were on the ground doing survey work. When the two airplanes went by between the trees—upside-down—they immediately measured the height of the trees.

The lead pilot was demoted one rank, and Langemann received a $125 fine, which at the time was a sizeable sum from their paltry air force pay.

"But you know, the air force at that time still had very much of a World War II mentality, where human beings were expendable," Langemann explains. "They'd deny it, but it was really true. We were told what *not* to do, but the way in which we were told, we knew that if we had any guts at all we'd go out and do that. And so they had all kinds of people trying all kinds of rather foolish things."

He tells of his first day of instruction on jets, at the Portage la Prairie, Manitoba, base, "back in the days when jets were still kind of dangerous, I guess. There was a pretty high death rate at the time.

"We were all standing out at the flight line when four jets took off in formation. Just as they got by the end of the runway, Number Four rolled over and crashed. Big explosion right in front of us. Ball of flame! And that was it. The pilot was dead. That was our introduction.

"The chap who was giving us the briefing looked at the flaming plane, said, 'Humph!,' turned around and kept right on briefing us. The attitude was very different."

But, Langemann says, they were young, and wanted to be part of the game.

"We all thought we were fantastic, we were going to be better than everybody else. It was the poor pilots who got killed—good guys like us never got killed! That guy had made a mistake, and if you were good, you wouldn't make those mistakes. A psychologist once said that the difference between pilots and, as he put it, 'normal people,' was that when a normal person does something that scares the hell out of him, he says, 'I'm not going to do that again!' When a pilot, especially the military type, does something that scares the hell out of him he says, 'That was fun. I'm going to do that again.' And, you do. The bottom line was to never lose one's courage."

When Langemann looks back on his jet training in 1957, he's amazed that so many of the students survived. "We did our basic training at night. Theoretically it was daytime, but when you take off at seven on a January morning in Portage la Prairie, it's night—I don't care what they call it—and frequently the last flight didn't land until six-thirty at night. That was all considered day flying, because we hadn't had a night checkout yet.

"They gave us the feeling there were whole hangars full of airplanes that hadn't been used, and there were great line-ups of people behind us. If we couldn't handle it, get out of the way, somebody else would take our place."

Langemann turned 20 while he was in Manitoba, in the spring of 1957. His instructor was a year younger than him—a 20-year-old student paired with a 19-year-old instructor.

At that time, the airmens' hopes were to fly single-seat F-86 Sabre fighter planes in Europe. "Every pilot worth his salt was going to be an F-86 pilot with NATO (North Atlantic Treaty Organization). The RCAF had four bases over in Europe; others such as the American air force had many more.

"Then, horror of horrors, instead of sending me to fly jets, they decided I should become a flying instructor. I bitched, moaned, screamed, complained, threatened. It didn't make any difference at all.

"A flying instructor's course was 16 weeks. I finished it in 10. I think they hurried me through just to get me off the station because I was being such a miserable swine."

The 21-year-old airman's next job was to instruct NATO students at the base in Claresholm. Canada had taken on the role of training pilots from various NATO countries, and the base received students from Norway, Denmark, Germany, Holland, Belgium, France, Greece, Turkey, and the U.K. "They were all just mixed together. We had entire courses that had no Canadians in them at all. They had all gone through an English language school but some learned English a little better than others—it was really an interesting situation."

The NATO training course was the first place Langemann started to notice cultural differences.

"The Italians were lovely guys—terrible pilots—but the nicest people in the world. As soon as something went wrong, they lost all their English, went back to Italian, let go of the controls and waved their arms in the air when they were supposed to be flying the airplane.

"The Norwegians and the Danes were just the opposite; they never seemed to get rattled. I had a Danish student once who screwed up most awfully. He was in the back seat doing basic instrument flying. We came out of this wicked contortion at 300 feet above the ground—we'd started about 4,000 feet— and the only thing he said was, 'Vell, I guess I do that again, ya?'

Ralph Langemann (in middle) between two German students, Lt. Kronester and Lt. Hoermann, with Harvard trainer aircraft. *Ralph Langemann Collection*

"The Turks, I learned very quickly, had a different attitude toward life than did Christians. The Christians knew they were going to go to heaven, but just in case, they were going to hang around as long as they could. The Turks, as Muslims, firmly believed that if they died while in uniform they automatically went straight to heaven, and it really showed up in their flying. The motivating force in teaching someone to fly is, 'Don't do that or you'll kill yourself!' We were now dealing with students who . . . didn't care. Heaven was better.

"Lovely people, delightful, great guys on the ground, no mechanical experience at all. While driving a car many of them couldn't figure out why you couldn't take a right-angle corner on a gravel road at 60 miles an hour. After all, you turn the wheel, why didn't the car go where it was pointed? And we were teaching these guys to fly airplanes! That got quite exciting at times. It was always a fine-line problem for an instructor to judge just how long to give the student to pull out of a scrape."

From the job of training NATO students on Harvards, Langemann went to the maintenance hangar as a test pilot, "and that's not as fancy as it sounds." It involved test flying aircraft to define exact repairs needed, or testing them out after routine maintenance before they were sent down the flight line. It was not a dangerous occupation if you were careful.

Ralph Langemann was in the regular service for six years, and in the reserve squadron for just under four years, flying aircraft almost every day. Although he was never officially sent on any missions, some of the airmen "sent themselves" on a few long-range training trips to Montreal, after getting checked out on the twin engine Beech 18. "I had 36 hours total multi-engine time, and away I went from Claresholm to Montreal! Talk about being early in the learning curve. They encouraged us to do this, actually, because it was a morale-booster."

Langemann left the regular air force in 1961, as a flying officer. His first commercial pilots' licence was issued in Edmonton in June 1961. "I never flew a plane or anything. I showed the DOT (Department of Transport) my log book, that I was an air force pilot, wing standard, and they said that was fine. So I flew for years without ever taking a test."

Although Langemann's 5,000-plus flying hours are few when compared with some others, "airline pilots particularly," after leaving the regular air force he flew only part-time. This allowed him to choose the kind of flying he wanted to do. "I didn't have to do what the air force told me, or anyone else."

Langemann has flown on wheels and skis, but not floats. "I'm a prairie pilot. Water is for showering in, and putting in Scotch. No landing on rivers or lakes for me—I'm not interested in that type of stuff at all."

In September of 1957—the same year he was court-martialled—Langemann married a school teacher who later developed a second career as a visual landscape artist. His wife and their two daughters soon got used to Ralph flying off to remote camps during the summer, and living at home in Calgary during the fall, winter, and early spring. "Daddy disappeared for the summer, and showed up in the fall," was their attitude, Langemann says.

While attending the University of Calgary—Langemann holds an undergraduate degree in English and a graduate degree in Cultural Geography—he was a flight lieutenant in the RCAF's local reserve squadron until it closed in 1964, as well as doing some flying for various commercial companies in the summer.

During his tenure in No. 403 Air Reserve Squadron, Langemann made his one and only trip to the Arctic. Hay River in the Northwest Territories was flooding and the townspeople had to be evacuated immediately. Langemann's squadron rushed to the rescue in a Single Otter on wheels, transporting people to safety in Yellowknife.

The air force also worried that the ice on one of the tributaries to the Mackenzie River might go out before the Mackenzie did, flooding Fort Simpson. And so, in Single Otters, they flew up and down the river on ice patrols, watching for and reporting changes in ice conditions. This was the last week in April, first week in May, and Langemann describes it as cold, wet, miserable, and uncomfortable.

"They had some poor army supply officer in charge of the base at Fort Simpson, and he'd been told that he should 'bustle,' whatever that meant," Langemann says. "This was his first command, and I think his last. He wanted us to stand by for inspection in the mornings, stuff like that, and we just said, 'Go play your games with someone else.' Two young army pilots with helicopters were there, and they had to sort of follow his instructions, but the rest of us, the air force types, could say, 'Go to hell, fella! We're here to fly airplanes.'

"He was supposed to go on these ice patrols and assess the ice, so we took him along. He got a little nervous about flying eight or ten feet over the ice—you had to go that close to see it well. We'd been there a few days when an army helicopter showed up. The helicopter pilot was in his mid-40s, and he found out that we young guys had been giving the army officer a hard time. He asked the man if he'd like to do his patrol in an army helicopter the next day, and he said he would. The army helicopter pilot assured him, 'I'll fly careful, not like these young fellas.'

"They parked him in the doorway of the helicopter, and put this big harness on him that was hooked onto the sides of the doors. Then they went up, very slowly, and flew along the river. He thought this was wonderful. But as they came back to the airport they got up a little higher. He was still sitting in the doorway, looking out.

"The crew on the helicopter, meantime, had very quietly extended his harness. The chopper pilot suddenly pulled the helicopter up over the base and laid it on its side—and the sucker fell out! He was still held in with the harness, but he was hanging about eight feet outside the helicopter. It scared the hell out of him. He thought he was a goner. When they got down, he wobbled into his office, pushed the desk and the filing cabinets up against the door, and we didn't see him for two days."

All told, they were in the far North for five weeks, enduring the simplest form of accommodation. Following that mission, the squadron went further north as far as Inuvik, landing on bush strips throughout the area. "We had to break the ice in a barrel of water to wash in the morning, and at the same time the damn mosquitos were so big that we needed a shotgun to protect ourselves from them. That convinced me that I didn't want to be a bush pilot in the Arctic. I like my creature comforts too much."

When the squadron closed down in 1964, Langemann took on civilian flying jobs during the summer after university classes had finished for the year. One of these was crop spraying, flying Piper Super Cubs and a Piper Pawnee for Frank Young of Airdrie, Alberta. "Frank was a bit of a character in his own right. He ran a spray outfit, partly from the Airdrie airport but partly from his back yard, which was close to the railway track. We used to land airplanes in his hay field, taxi them down the road to his porch, and work on them in his back yard."

Environmental awareness has caused the spraying industry to be more closely regulated now than it was in the past. "There was a time in the 1950s and 1960s where there were almost no regulations," Langemann recalls. "You just went out there and sprayed, and if two ounces to the acre was good, then four ounces was twice as good, so you just laid it on. And I know from crop spraying around Alberta we weren't all that careful with the stuff. We didn't know any better.

"We would keep all the bits and pieces of herbicides that were left over from doing farmers' fields and pour them into big tanks, then use that for brush clearing back in the foothills for the ranchers. We hadn't a clue what was in there by the end of the summer. They sure killed brush—and who knew what else they were killing? We had some pretty toxic mixes going in there.

"We were using an awful lot of what the military called Agent Orange. The farmers still do—it's just a mixture of two very common chemicals, 2,4-D and 2,4-5-T herbicides. Many farmers have their own airplanes. There are very different regulations if a professional company does spraying or if a farmer does his own spraying, so as a result, the farmers can use chemicals that the professionals can't. Any farmer is allowed to spray his own farm, and he can spray commercially without any licence at all within 25 miles of his own farm. And there are some of the *longest* 25-mile stretches!"

Langemann also worked a couple of seasons for a Calgary company called Rainier Development, cloud-seeding hailstorms. He enjoyed the job, which he describes as dodging around thunderstorms all summer long. For hail suppression work they used a Harvard military fore-and-aft trainer with canopy windows on top. Under the wings were flares mounted in rocket pods that the pilot could ignite from the cockpit. Silver iodide was inserted into the flares; as they burned, the iodide was released into the air.

A photo in Langemann's log book shows an open cockpit Stearman biplane, the first airplane he flew on fire-bombing jobs for Air Spray, a company based in Edson, west of Edmonton. "My goggles would get all steamed up on both the inside and the outside."

Langemann's flying has included air force manoeuvres, flight instruction, test-flying,

Ralph Langemann, 1965 with open cockpit Stearman biplane used for fire-bombing by Air Spray, a company based in Edson, west of Edmonton. *Ralph Langemann Collection*

aerial spraying, fire suppression, and flying for pleasure, but the strangest group he has ever been associated with are skydivers.

"I flew skydivers for a while, for one of the local parachute clubs," he says. "They had very different attitudes toward the value of human life, and almost no knowledge about how mechanical things worked."

The attitudes of the skydivers differed from pilots in that "no pilot will ever leave an airplane unless he absolutely has to. But skydivers think of the airplane as an elevator, something to get them up. They're paying for the airplane until it's back down on the ground, so they think you should climb at full power and fry the engine, and after they jump, take a screaming dive down.

"So, I didn't do that for very long."

Langemann was amazed at the trust the skydivers put in their parachutes to open properly. "One guy had just finished jumping when he realized that the next flight was going to be the last one of the day. He didn't have time to repack his chute so he just stuffed it into a shopping bag. He leapt out of the airplane with his parachute in the bag, pulling it out as he went down."

As the pilot, Langemann had nothing to say about it. "If he's dumb enough to want to do that . . . " He shakes his head. "Those guys were funny."

Langemann's log book also contains a photo of a Lancaster. It was taken 4 July 1964 at the Calgary International Airport, during the last flight of a Lancaster in military colours in the world.

"A number of us who were university students at the time became involved with two air museums: The Air Museum of Canada and the Alberta Aviation Museum, and the CIA–Calgary International Airshows–set up and organized by Lynn Garrison, who had been in the No. 403 Air Reserve Squadron at the same time I was.[1] We bought the Lancaster (KB-976).

"The Ministry of Transport had given permission for the Lancaster to be flown at the Calgary International Airshow under one of three conditions: the air force could fly it for us, we could get a certificate of airworthiness, or they would give us permission to fly it one trip only with a minimum qualified crew. So we went for the third one, because to get a certificate of airworthiness was impossible—and we didn't want the military to fly it. Damn it, we owned it!

"We went looking for somebody to fly the airplane, but we couldn't find anybody suitable. So we looked at each other and said, 'What the hell! It's got to be like any other airplane.'"

None of the men had ever before flown a Lancaster—"We didn't even have a book on it!" Garrison had flown P-51s, which had the same engines, but other than that, "we hadn't a clue." Garrison and Langemann got in, started it up, and then others jumped on board: an engineer, Jimmy Sutherland, who had worked on it; Joe McGoldrick jumped in the back; and Brian McKay, who was to be their radio operator (though none of the radios worked). "We had a little portable radio and the only way we could pick up the tower was to hold this thing out the window. So Brian did that."

With Garrison as pilot, and Langemann as copilot, they took off. Bruce Lebons, the announcer, came on the PA system: "Ladies and Gentlemen," he said, to the crowd of 40,000 people, "the amazing thing here is neither of these pilots has ever been in a Lancaster before!"

The announcement caught the fine-tuned ears of two Ministry of Transport inspectors, who "came and had words with us afterwards," followed by laying a charge for flying the airplane without proper authorization.

"We showed them the telegram we'd received from the Ministry of

The last flight of a Lancaster in military colours in the world. 4 July 1964. Lancaster KB-976 soars over a "grounded" Lancaster bomber resting on a pedestal at the Calgary International Airport. Photo signed by all crew-members: Lynn Garrison, Ralph Langemann, Joe McGoldrick, J. Sutherland, Brian McKay. *Ralph Langemann Collection*

Transport, giving us permission to fly it with a minimum qualified crew," Langemann says with a smile. "The telegram didn't have any punctuation in it, so there was no comma between the words 'minimum' and 'qualified.' When it came to the Hearing for Discovery, we argued that our qualifications were as minimum as they could be—we were totally unqualified—therefore according to their telegram, we conformed to their requirements. The judge must have had a sense of humour. It didn't get to a court case; it got chucked out at the Hearing for Discovery level."[2]

In the summer of 1966, Langemann started working in New Brunswick on the spruce budworm spraying project, and continued to be associated with this work for the next 17 years. "I became a New Brunswicker on the instalment plan," he laughs.

He initially flew for Skyway Air Services, which later became Conair Aviation Limited of Abbotsford, BC. The company's dual program involved spruce budworm spraying in New Brunswick during the early summer months, and then flying the airplanes back to British Columbia for forestry fire-bombing.

Skyway Air Services began in 1945 with pilot Art Seller's purchase of a Tiger Moth. Seller was soon joined by pilot-engineer Ed Batchelor. In addition to a flying school, they built up a crop-dusting business and then acquired a Stearman for spray work. The spraying business got its start in British Columbia in 1948 when major floods in the Fraser Valley brought out millions of mosquitos. The spruce budworm infestation in New Brunswick prompted further expansion of the company. From 1952–55, Batchelor shepherded Skyway's fleet of Stearmans eastward across the country each spring, then back in the fall. Eventually, larger aircraft were needed and Skyway purchased some surplus Grumman Avengers (TBMs) from the Royal Canadian Navy, to be used specifically on "Project Budworm," and as fire bombers.

By the mid-1960s, the company had grown from a small flying school into the country's largest crop spraying and water bombing company, with operations from coast to coast. Seller sold off the spraying and fire-bombing side of the business to Les Kerr, who set up Conair Aviation Limited in 1969. He was joined by fellow Skyway pilots Barry Marsden and Slim Knights. They started with 14 aircraft consisting of Stearmans, Grumman Avengers, and Douglas A-26 Invaders. In 1970 they disposed of the spray machines and concentrated on firefighters, and now operate the largest private fleet of firefighting aircraft in the world.

When Ralph Langemann began working for Skyway in May of 1966, the pilots would pick up the airplanes in Abbotsford, and fly through Cranbrook, Regina, Winnipeg, Duluth, Sault Ste. Marie, Ottawa, and into New Brunswick. Part of May and all of June would be spent spraying in New Brunswick. At the end of June they would fly back through Duluth, Winnipeg, Brandon, Regina, Calgary, Kamloops, and up to Smithers, BC, and fire-bomb throughout BC until the end of August.

By 1969, Langemann had completed his university degrees and had started teaching in the geography department of Calgary's Mount Royal College, but during the summers he continued spraying and water-bombing. "I enjoyed flying. It allowed me, while going to university, to make more money in three months than a full professor made in a year. So I didn't have to do the poverty-stricken student bit."

The seasons for spruce budworm spraying and fire-bombing dovetailed nicely, and Langemann found the work challenging. "The airplane I was flying, the Grumman Avenger, was a seriously big airplane, with a 1,950-horsepower engine, and weighing 19,400 pounds. We were running these things out of really soft unprepared strips, just barely long enough, bulldozed into the bush in New Brunswick, so it was interesting."

Following his years of flying from well-prepared air force strips, this job marked the beginning of Langemann's bush flying, and the adventures came nonstop.

He describes a typical day at the spruce budworm spraying camp: "We had tents, or bunkhouses of one sort or another. They'd shake us out of bed at four in the morning to go flying, and before they even turned the lights on in the trailer you'd hear the popping of beer cans. Some guys would have to have two or three beers to wake up.

"We'd be airborne about 4:45 and fly until the sun was up, about nine o'clock, then shut down for the day and not fly again until after supper when the air was smooth and stable, and then fly until dark.

"We had the craziest collection of spray pilots in New Brunswick at the time that the world has ever seen in one area. They were mostly leftover types from World War II, and they were largely—how do you put this nicely?—they were kind of the dregs of the flying world."

They didn't spray near the towns, but rather stayed in the wilderness areas. It was a good thing. Some of the airplanes that came up from the States were in such poor mechanical shape that the men feared to even walk under a wing in case some part would fall on them. At that time, one large contractor was responsible for bringing in all the subcontractors, resulting in the variations in calibre of machines and men. The pilots came from all over the continent. Some would pick up their airplanes in California, New Mexico, or Nevada, and converge in New Brunswick. One year there were 75 airplanes, with Conair Aviation Limited (formerly Skyway Air Services) supplying 14. Langemann states that Skyway/Conair had excellent machines. "They were world leaders in this, and they still are, even now."

Langemann gives examples of the antics that went on in this hybrid community when he began: "Three pilots were heading up to the spray project one year, flying above cloud. Although they didn't have any radios that were worth a darn or any instruments, they figured once they got past the cloud they should be able to see land. One guy was leading two wing men. The leader, or navigator, waved for them to come closer; they came in closer. He kept waving them in until they were right beside him. When they got tucked in, in close formation, he slid his canopy back and bailed out! So the two wing pilots were left flying along in formation with an airplane that didn't have a pilot in it. The wing men didn't have a clue where they were. The navigator had the only map, and he had parachuted out.

"It turned out he'd been losing oil pressure on his engine and knew it was just about to fail, so he thought he might as well have a little fun with these fellows. So there they were, flying along beside this empty airplane."

The unmanned plane flew until it ran out of oil. When the engine seized up it dove into the ground, out there in the boondocks. The wing men managed to get down.

"But there was always stuff like that going on."

The stories continue: "'Digger' Graves was a pilot from the States. One morning he had some ice on the wings of his Grumman Avenger. Most of us wouldn't go flying until the sun thawed the ice off, but the sun had just cracked the horizon, and Digger was impatient to get going. He got the nose up fine. The left wing flew but the right one didn't. He came down, and bounced so high that the first time around he landed on the left wing, then took a cartwheel off into the trees."

Because one wing had been in the sun, the ice on it had turned soft and had blown off. The other was in the shade of the fuselage and the ice on it was still hard. One wing had flown, but the iced one had pointed straight down.

"A little while later we saw him come walking out of the bush carrying his parachute, kicking his crash helmet, totally annoyed because he wasn't going to make any money that season. We got paid strictly on the amount of work we did, by the gallons that we sprayed—no guarantee, no minimum, nothing. And the airplane he'd been hired to fly was absolutely totalled. The Grummans were built like tanks, and that's the reason he wasn't hurt."

It is likely that at times Langemann got caught up in the devil-may-care mood of the people he was suddenly brought into contact with, but he stresses that his air force training had made him a pretty serious pilot. "A few of us there with Conair were ex-air force types, and we had a more professional attitude toward this because of our background. But the old hands at the time weren't very serious at all—it was a big lark as far as they were concerned."

Aerostar. Langemann's favourite aircraft, "designed by a pilot, for a pilot." He flew Aerostars while working in management for Conair in Quebec in the early 1970s. *Ralph Langemann Collection*

Langemann did, however, have some close calls. "I blew an engine and force-landed at Chatham, New Brunswick, but I was close enough that I could dead-stick in to the airport."

One time he was flying down the St. Lawrence River, trying to get in to Quebec City. It had fogged in behind them at Baie Comeau, and ahead of them at Quebec City. They tried to get south to Rivière-du-Loup, but it was fogged in there. "We were in this hole in the fog that was getting smaller. We didn't have any instruments on these airplanes for instrument flying, that was not an option. Then somebody remembered he had seen a small gravel bush strip at this place called Grand Bergeron—it wasn't even on any maps—so we went back in there. We were the first to ever land there; five airplanes sitting on their little strip.

"The whole town came out to greet us. We discovered that the town had built the airport, reasoning that if they were going to join the 20th century they had to have an airport—and here it was working. Here were five airplanes at their airport! None of the residents spoke English, and we didn't speak any French, but we were made so welcome. We were there for two days."

By the time Langemann had worked as Conair's summer pilot for a few seasons, he was in his mid- to late 30s—a seasoned "grey hair" among the assembly. At that point, he took over managing field operations as chief pilot for Forest Production Limited, the major contractor for the operation in New Brunswick, with the mandate to smarten it up. Now the pilots working for Conair, who was a subcontractor, reported to him.

Langemann's log book records the chaos that he inherited.

On 22 May 1974, a kid flying a Grumman Avenger experienced an oil leak after take-off. He came roaring back to the airstrip and "really blew it in," went off the end of the runway and ended up on his back. Langemann will always remember the kid standing at the side of the strip after they had dragged him from the wreckage, soaked in oil and gasoline and insecticide, and saying, over and over, "What happened? What happened?"

On 3 June, another pilot went off the end of the runway, "nosed up, no problem." Then, on 4 June, another pilot experienced massive engine problems and was forced to land at an old strip at Dunfey that nobody used. Langemann landed at that strip to make sure he was okay. He walked back to his airplane, a Cessna 182, and picked up the radio to report his findings on the incident to one of the guys in the air. When Langemann said "How are things going?" the reply was "The helicopters are at the crash now." Langemann looked up. No helicopters in sight. "What crash?" he asked cautiously. Another one of the pilots had ploughed into a swamp—two of his crew had gone down, virtually at the same time.

On 6 June, another airplane was written off at a strip called Boston Brook. "It got off the runway on him and he trashed it. Totalled it." On 7 June, yet another crash occurred at Sovegal in northern New Brunswick. "He was flying for a guy who didn't believe in putting on new tires, so his tires were showing about three layers of canvas. On take-off one blew. He'd just about got it airborne, it was that close, it was just staggering, and then a wing hooked on one of these huge fire extinguishers that airports used to have, two big cylinders on iron wheels—and it pulled him back down and he crashed and the airplane burned. Luckily, he wasn't hurt.

The pilot of this Grumman headed for a river after he noticed smoke coming from the aircraft. Later it was discovered that the airplane had not been on fire. The smoke was a result of a small oil leak into the exhaust pipe. *Ralph Langemann Collection*

"We forgot to tell the Forestry about the fire on that one, because we'd asked to clear some brush at the end of the runway, and they said we needed a logging permit. That's where he crashed and the forest caught fire."

On 13 and 14 June, one guy blew an engine and went into the trees. Another blew an engine and went down on the road.

"It was a real zoo there," he says, in an understatement. "Every night at suppertime you'd hear stories of who went down that day. It was just crazy."

He continues reading from the log book, which has come to resemble a proverbial "Diary of Fate."

"Another crash—the second one for this guy, but this one wasn't his fault. The propeller broke off and the engine literally fell out of the airplane. It had a three-bladed propeller; one blade broke off about 12 inches from the hub, and it was then so out of balance that the torque from the other two blades ripped the engine right out. Three of them did that within a few days. It took us a while to find out why this was happening, but we finally tracked it down to wrong parts being put into the propellers by the overhaul shops.

"This guy ditched an airplane doing a low turn right over the lake. Lakes in the morning, when there's no wind, are absolutely glassy. He was watching the wing man up above him and he stuck his other wing tip right into the lake.

"And that was all for that season. I stopped being chief pilot and I went down there just to train the fellows. I did that for years, training others on the Grumman Avenger, getting them checked out."

In a given six-week season, out of the 20 to 24 aircraft that usually made up

Grumman Avenger in a perfect three-point landing—two wheels and the prop. *Ralph Langemann Collection*

the summer's contingent, the average loss was three. Fortunately, there were very few deaths because the Grumman—the most commonly used aircraft for spraying because of its large holding capacity—was such a rugged machine. "As long as they went in right side up, even in the big timber, they would just knock down trees. The wings were strong enough on these military airplanes that they could cut through a 24-inch tree."

But gradually efficiency began to improve. "Our mandate, then, was to have it run much more professionally, which we did. Within a couple of years we had the crash rate down to zero, pretty much."

Environmental concerns about the spray program were also becoming an issue as people became conscious "of the gasses or the poisons we were using, and that this stuff was spilling all over the place," says Langemann.

They had used DDT for the spruce budworm program, then switched to "a family of chemicals called organo-phosphates, which are basically nerve gases. These pesticides were effective in the sense that, once mixed with water, they had a very short half-life [the time period required for a chemical to lose half its strength], about six hours for some of them. Within a short period of time they had no strength left at all, as opposed to DDT, which I think had a half-life of 6,000 years or something!"

The organo-phosphates didn't seem to affect small mammals, birds, or rodents "if we put them on at the right strength." Tests were taken continually, Langemann says, by provincial and federal government agencies, and by forestry companies. "There were so many monitoring agents working up there, that I swear at times in the bush camps we had more monitoring agents than we had people working."

By the 1970s, Langemann says, government agencies were "really testing the effect of chemical sprays, especially in waterways. These organo-phosphates broke down even more quickly in running water. The best place to get rid of them was to dump them in a stream, as the chemicals broke down and became harmless within a few hundred yards in running water. The public didn't accept that, although categorically it is true, but you have to work very carefully with public perception.

"I was always considered to be pretty careful. With my academic background as well as the flying, I really wanted to know what was happening, so our organization cooperated very closely with the government and research agencies."

Langemann considers those 17 years a very successful part of his career. "The mix of people in the camps was great. Anybody who does that kind of work is an interesting character. The Maritimers are excellent. The Newfoundlanders have the art of storytelling, it's beautiful. There would often be somebody in camp with a fiddle, somebody with an accordion, and some old gaffer who could play the spoons and step-dance. There weren't any women in the camps for most of those years. The men would get together and sing, and people would tell stories."

When he got into management, however, he found he was flying a lot less. "It's called minding the store—a glorified babysitter."

The latter portions of Langemann's summers were spent flying the Grummans on water-bombing missions for forest-fire suppression in British Columbia.

Grumman Avenger with wings folded. Parking fees were based the length of the aircraft multiplied by its width. With wings folded, the Grumman saved on space and fees. The fuselage was stubby, saving space when on navy aircraft carriers. *Ralph Langemann Collection*

The early years of fire suppression by aircraft were experimental, and the situations pilots found themselves in were often highly dangerous. Advice for pilots fighting fires included: never fly into the smoke because you can't see the trees (they were flying at only 20 feet or so above the treetops). Also, never fly uphill because you'd need enough power to climb the hill, or somehow get around it. They were also warned to watch for "widow-makers," grey old growth, very difficult to spot, that juts above the rest of the forest. "Hitting something like that can spoil your whole day," Langemann says, grinning.

One of Langemann's adventures in water-bombing attracted newspaper reporters.

PILOT SAVES AIRCRAFT

A 32-year-old water bomber pilot successfully landed a disabled Avenger aircraft at Smithers Airport Monday. Ralph Langemann of Skyway Air Services, on charter to the BC Forest Service, manoeuvred the single-engine converted Second World War bomber to a safe landing after an oil line or piston blew while he was starting a practice tour. Langemann was about five minutes away from the base when smoke billowed from the plane and crankcase oil splattered the windshield.

He radioed his plight, then flew back over the airport, cut his engine, and coasted to a safe landing. He rolled the 500-gallon capacity water bomber off the runway and into the grass to put the craft clear of any other traffic and jumped clear. Flying with a full load, the pilot had dumped the water and mud solution when trouble struck. Forest Service spokesman Fred Roe called Langemann's effort in saving the plane a terrific job.[3]

Langemann's log book notes for 30 June 1967 indicate that he blew number eight cylinder.

Langemann laughs at the serious tone of the article. "Now, this is interesting, because everyone said, 'Oh, saving the airplane. Great hero.' What they forget is, my ass was in that bucket! I cared *less* about the airplane. I didn't think about the sacrifice of the airplane, it was *me* that was important. I wanted to get *me* back down on the ground."

In 1970, Ralph Langemann set up a two-year aviation program for Mount Royal College in Calgary. In 1993 he assumed the chair of the Aviation Department. "The previous chair had been here for 10 years and he decided, 'I don't want to be sitting in this office—I want to be flying!' so he resigned and he's out there flying for us, instructing students. I've never wanted to be an instructor, so I don't mind flying a desk for a while."

For many years, however, he was associated to a larger degree with the Geography Department of Mount Royal College, and taught only a meteorology course for the aviation program. "I don't get involved with the flying training at all, even though the students comment that they like having an instructor who has actually been out there and done certain things," Langemann says. "After being an air force instructor, I was convinced that the prime ambition of every student was to kill the instructor, and failing that, at the very least to drive him or her crazy. I swore I would never become a flying instructor. Anywhere, at all."

The Aviation Department is busy turning out people with commercial pilots' licences, with the basic qualifications and a number of hours. It is, however, quite costly to take the two-year aviation course.

"It probably costs close to $30,000 for tuition, books, and flying," Langemann says. "That's where we start running into problems. We get students who've always wanted to be pilots, but it's hard for them because aviation is not subsidized by the government. And jobs are cyclical. Right now it's hard to find a job, but soon there will be a shortage of airline pilots.

"Only in aviation do students have to pay the full costs of the program. Why? We've been trying since 1970 to get an answer. In other programs the tuition fees are so low, the student pays only about 12 to 15 percent of the actual cost; the rest comes from the government."

The way Langemann and many other pilots got their training—through the air force—is also difficult now.

"The air force this year [1993], we understand, is going to take six trainee pilots, total, across Canada. The qualifications they look for are competitiveness, a good academic background—grade 12 with good math and physics—and an understanding of what aviation is all about."

At present, there are 30 students enroled in Mount Royal's junior aviation course, and 32 in the senior course; of this number, there are four female students in the junior year, and two in the senior year.

"It's not because females are not good at math and physics," Langemann states. "It's because someone has *told* them they aren't good at these subjects.

When I was hiring pilots in eastern Canada, I hired women over men. They're much better employees. If we had four or five days of rain, when we couldn't spray, the men in these bush camps would start raising hell, punching out the walls, getting drunk. They couldn't handle it. The women could always find something to do to occupy their time."

But Langemann acknowledges that it's hard for any aviation graduates to get on with corporate airlines, "mainly because you're talking about passenger-carriers that are worth at least $7.5 million and you want someone who is capable of handling them. So they want people with a lot of experience."

Following his many years of working for Conair during the summers, Ralph Langemann's next flying adventures came about in September of 1990 when he decided to do something completely different.

"Being an academic, I went to the university library and pulled out an international aviation directory that lists companies by the types of aircraft they own and where they fly. I picked one that flew airplanes that sounded interesting, in a location that sounded attractive, and I wrote to them.

"It was actually done in the most unromantic approach possible," he laughs.

Langemann was looking to fly plain old bush planes, "nothing particularly sophisticated, just something that would do for daytime flying, no fancy equipment on them at all."

The company to whom he made inquiries was called Aer Kavango, in the African country of Botswana. The aviation company immediately answered his query with a job offer.

He took an unpaid leave of absence from the college and flew via Air Canada to London, and British Airways to Gaborone, the capital of Botswana. Company representatives took him to write his pilots' licence exams, and then the company itself administered flying tests, which he passed easily. "I ended up as chief pilot there," he says. "Actually, the day I arrived I was made chief pilot, and a week later I was operations manager. They had some young pilots in their early 20s and they thought they needed a few grey hairs to keep these cowboys in line. They were good pilots, really great fellows."

He arrived in Botswana in September and stayed until December that first season. They were flying in the northern part of the country, near the Kalahari Desert.

"It's a delightful area. A couple of rivers flow out of the Angola highlands where there is a lot of rain, into the northern part of the Kalahari Desert, and then they just disappear into the sand. So you've got this combination of a desert and lots of water. It's just teeming with game. There's never been a poaching problem there, so the animals aren't particularly worried about people. You can get close to elephants and lions. Lovely, absolutely lovely."

Langemann did, indeed, discover paradise, but one poised on the fine edge of development. A *Calgary Herald* article dated 10 July 1993, titled "Botswana on Tightrope" describes the situation:

> Landlocked, beautiful Botswana wants to attract more visitors from overseas while protecting its fragile ecology from over-exploitation. "We need the foreign exchange, we need the jobs, but not at any price," says a Gaborone-based conservationist. Tourism makes up less than three percent of Botswana's gross domestic product, but it is one of the major employers in the largely desert country, home to 1.3 million people. In the remote northern area, which takes in Chobe Park and the unspoilt Okavango Delta, more than 40 percent of the jobs are linked to tourism.

Already, people from other, more developed, countries were moving in. Langemann discovered a multicultural mix from all over the world, congregated in one of the most beautiful climates possible.

"I was flying in Botswana, the Kalahari Desert, where it's hot and dry. I must admit I'm a bit of a desert rat, I don't like being cold and wet. The town of Maun in the northern part of Botswana is kind of a wild-west town; a lot of interesting characters there. It's like the Arctic in that sense, that you don't ask people too many questions about where they come from or why they're there. They're nice guys, and you treat them that way. Englishmen, New Zealanders, Australians, Canadians, South Africans, some Portuguese fellows from Mozambique—I think there was only one American—were flying when I was there. Totally relaxed—I don't know if anybody in the town owns a tie or a suit. It's a town of about 15,000 people, with maybe 300 whites."

Langemann's job involved "good old-fashioned bush flying." The main airport had no radio navigation facilities, and pilots were expected to take off and land from little strips out in the bush that served the safari camps. It was straight charter work, hauling people, food, supplies, beer, clothing, refrigerators, bottles of propane, sides of beef, anything and everything that could be stuffed into, or under, an airplane. "We flew two really good bush airplanes: Britten Norman Islanders, and Cessna 206s with belly pods, like cargo carriers attached to the belly of the airplane, which allowed us to load it with 300 pounds of cargo and still seat six people in the aircraft. The Islanders were nice planes—twin engine, 10-seats, can get off a short strip on a hot day, flies slow, about 150 mph. The Cessna 206s were single engine, six seat. It's a good working airplane."

Flying conditions differed from what he was familiar with in Canada. "It's very hot and so airplanes don't perform worth a damn. An airplane that could get off a 2,000-foot strip here will take 4,000 feet there, and you have to get used to that. Because the air is much thinner, it doesn't get as good a bite on the aircraft.

"The maps are inaccurate. You get to where, according to your map, this place is supposed to be and you start doing increasing circles until you find it. Then you update your map, get your pencil out and mark it.

"And it's absolutely flat, so in terms of navigating it's very different. You can't go by hills and valleys because there aren't any, no contours at all. The Kalahari Desert is covered with brush about 20 feet high, and so it all looks the same, mile after mile after mile, and the features that you can pick out are very subtle, very small. A river valley shown on a map may be 20 feet deep and 20 miles wide, and have no water in it. It may not have had water in it for the last thousand years, it's just a fossil river valley."

Each flyer, says Langemann, had his own way of navigating. With his background in geography, he evaluated the local geological patterns. A New Zealander he flew with navigated by recognizing varieties of trees.

His log book records that the day he arrived "I put up my four gold bars, signifying captain, on my white shirt and took a load of passengers from the main town to another one. It was easy enough to find because I had lots of fuel and I could follow a road."

He gradually worked into the more difficult places, catching rides with the other pilots when they had an empty seat, to check out the various areas.

If it became necessary to make a forced landing, he knew he would have to pick the place carefully because he would need a much longer strip to get off again, as the terrain was mostly sand. Also, in the northern part of the country there were no roads. "They won't let them build roads into this area, it's part of their environmental plan. Twenty-three percent of Botswana is national parks."

Botswana is home to a wonderful variety of fauna as well as flora, and this presented unique challenges to the Canadian pilot. "You start looking for different things," Langemann says. "You make sure there aren't any ostriches, elephants, or baboons on the runway when you land. The control tower in one airport in the north regularly reports, 'Baboons on the runway,' when you call up for landing, because there are all kinds of melons growing around the runway and the baboons run back and forth eating these things. You get used to that. Like moose or deer up here, I guess.

"You also have to watch that you don't run into piles of elephant droppings. They pile up three feet high, and the individual 'units' are as big as footballs. If you ever stick a prop into that you can do serious damage! Most of these new airplanes are designed for paved runways, so on a 206, for example, the prop is quite low.

"In some areas if you leave your airplane on a bush strip overnight, you have to cut thorn bushes to put around the wheels because the lions will come out at night and munch on the tires. Not that they want to eat them, but they're chewy, like a teething ring."

Elephants will also come out and play with the airplane. They apparently don't damage them, but simply "check them out."

"I've had elephants come right up to the airplane when I've been sleeping inside. I've flown into a strip where the clients are going to be away for four or five hours, so I'll just 'kip' out in the back. I'll wake up and there's an elephant looking at me. Elephants are really curious. They're really intelligent."

At one bush camp, when they awoke they discovered elephant tracks just outside the tent, where they'd gone through on the sand paths at night. Although the herd had walked within three feet of the tents, no one had heard a thing. "If you're awake, you can hear a swish, swish, swish, that's it. They can walk on a path about two feet wide without stepping off the edge."

Langemann found poaching almost nonexistent in Botswana. "Although it is a problem in other countries such as Kenya, they've actually got that under control. They tend not to admit how they're doing it, but basically they just shoot poachers. If you're caught out there with a rifle, they shoot you, and they don't make note of where they shot or who they shot. Bang. The hyenas will clean up the body by morning, and that's that. No repeat offenders. Poaching is way down."

The area where Langemann worked is very close to the setting for the film *The Gods Must Be Crazy*, the sandy terrain in northern Botswana where the bushmen live. Langemann was impressed by the bushmen he came to know, describing them as "delightful people. Bright and sharp."

He enjoyed being with the bushmen, and observing their zest for life. "I had one little bushman in the front seat of the Islander one day, on about an hour-and-a-half trip. He had some mechanical knowledge from working the water pump in his own village. We were about 40 minutes into the trip when he poked me and said, 'I know what everything is. Yep. I know what everything is.' I started asking him, and he knew what every one of the gauges on the airplane was all about, what it did!

"He'd watched me for 45 minutes, and picked it up, just like that. He even had the radios figured out, that I had talked to certain people when I'd taken off from an airport and then, by changing the numbers I'd been able to talk to people at another airport. He'd figured out how the radio compass worked. We had a beacon, and he observed that when we took off it was pointing straight down; then I had changed the numbers and it was pointing to the top."

Unlike some of the Indians Langemann had met in northern Canada, the bushmen knew from the air exactly where they were. "On searches in the North with Indians, we'd found that as long as they were on the ground they knew exactly where they were. If we were on a search and we weren't sure where we were, we'd land on a lake and then my guide would say, 'Oh, we're on such and such a lake.' Then we'd find it on a map and away we'd go. But once we were 500 feet up, they were lost. But these bushmen knew."

His log books record trips hauling everything from tourists to crates of crocodile eggs. "They'd gathered the eggs from their natural site to be taken to crocodile farms. In the wilds, only about 1 percent live to maturity because of natural predators and over-hunting, so the government was allowing these people to collect eggs to be hatched at the farms."

The eggs were packed in picnic coolers and warm sand to be flown to the crocodile hatchery. The pilots had to ensure they didn't travel too high because the pressure decrease from sudden changes in altitude could destroy the eggs. They stayed at about 500 feet—pretty low flying, but in the flat country there was nothing to run into.

In 1992, Langemann started flying for another company, Okavango Air Charter of Africa, headquartered at Gaborone. Okavango Air was originally part of Aer Kavango, with a main branch in the north and a small branch in Gaborone. "The fellow who was running the branch in the capital bought it from the main company, and he asked me to come and work for him."

His passengers were government and construction company officials, as well as tourists heading for the bigger tourist camps in South Africa. Langemann's business card shows his address as Zebra Way, Gaborone, Botswana.

Langemann returned to Botswana in 1993, flying for Okavango from early May to early August. He found the tourism business was down about 40 percent because European tourists were concerned about political unrest.

Langemann was again doing charter work, flying a Cessna 402. On one trip he took some people to a scuba-diving camp on the Indian Ocean close to South Africa, just south of the Mozambique border. "So I had four days of sitting on the beach, drinking beer at their expense, and then we came back! They were just working people, willing to spend their money on having a good time. People generally don't understand how cheap chartering an airplane is compared to driving; it would have taken them 18 hours as opposed to 50 minutes by air. If you get enough people to spread the costs among, it's quite cheap."

But Langemann says, rather sadly, that there were no exciting flights this summer—no crocodile eggs, no bushmen—strictly moving people and supplies to scuba-diving camps, safari camps, engineers going out to mining sites.

He won't be able to go back in 1994 because of job commitments at the college. "But the summer after, I'm gone!"

While Langemann has had forced landings due to engine trouble, he has never crashed an aircraft. "I've been really lucky. When I've had engine trouble, I've always been at an airport. Well, a lot of it was planning in the sense that a number of these occurred when I was doing test flying. If I thought the engine was shaky at all, or I was just trying to figure out what was wrong, I'd circle up over top of the airport; then if anything went wrong I could just circle back down and land."

Good pilots, Langemann says, think in a certain way; they are careful, systematic, and analytic. "Flying is that way. Just a myriad of details, and you can't miss any of them."

He believes this thought process can be learned, "but if you're an abstract thinker, not given to linear thinking, it's probably hard to learn it."

He talks of legends such as Weldy Phipps to illustrate the kind of scientific, analytic mind, that adapts modern technology to harsh environments. "He's the type who'll look at the Super Cub and say, 'If we put big tires on that sucker, at low pressure, I can land on the tundra without having to have an airport.'

"A pilot flying for a Calgary company doing geological survey work in the Arctic said they could total two or three of those a year, and it would still be cheaper than a helicopter."

Langemann thinks that his years as a test pilot in the air force taught him a lot about airplanes—how they're built and what to look for before you go flying. He emphasizes that a strong sense of navigation is another "must" for pilots. "If they rely totally on their instruments, and their instruments fail, they're in difficulty." During the spraying operation, they would send out teams of three, with the lead doing the navigating and the two wing men following. "We had so many pilots who had no sense of navigation or space, that we had trouble getting one guy to lead the team."

Mechanical savvy is another very important feature of a good pilot. "You've got to be able to tell the mechanic what's wrong with it, and describe it accurately, because he can't go up there and fly it—especially in a single-seat airplane. Also, if you understand mechanical things, you can frequently tell that something is going to go wrong long before it does. Which means, if you've got enough warning, you can usually be at an airport before things go all to hell.

"If you have to go down in a remote area, a pilot with mechanical ability can often fix it, if it's fixable, although I tend to leave that kind of work to the engineers."

Flying has changed with modern technology, Langemann says, and now airline pilots go by lists rather than by feel. "'Seat of the pants' flying with modern airplanes will kill you. You have to go by the numbers. With hydraulic controls, and critically designed wings, you can no longer *feel* when the air is starting to break loose from the wing; it's just not there. They're designed differently to get the speed out of them.

"Engines now are very different. A jet turbine doesn't have the physical symptoms of what's happening that the old piston engines did; they're so smooth, they're trav-

Ralph Langemann, 1993. *Author Photo*

elling at such a high rpm, and things are very critical. In the old airplanes, you roar down the runway, and pull back, and you can feel when the air is starting to bite on the controls and when it's ready to lift off. You have to feel when the air is starting to nibble. You're slowing down and you're turning, and you start feeling the air break loose from the wing and you know if you turn it any tighter it's gonna stall. You can lose it.

"The latest airliners are totally computerized. Your control column is no different from the joy stick on your computer games. But small planes are still 1930s technology. You still have to feel them. I prefer that. I'm a relic from another era.

"I'm not a 'by the numbers' pilot—I'm a 'by the seat of the pants' pilot."

His advice to people who want to get into flying for airlines is to get a degree in engineering. Learn math, physics, and computers. "It's that kind of a field now."

Should someone ask him about bush flying, maybe buying into a little northern airline, his answer would be blunt. "Little airlines tend to go bankrupt with disgusting regularity. And even the bush airplanes are becoming much more sophisticated, such as the Twin Otter."

Langemann has enjoyed the balance between the academic and aviation fields. "Flying has been a key for me to explore many different worlds." But Langemann does not belong to any aviation organization, where members gather to talk about the flying business or to work toward restoration of aircraft or preservation of aviation history, nor does he want to. "No, not at all. I don't have any feelings about airplanes at all. They were fun, but they were a means to an end. Flying got me out of Coaldale!"

Awards for his work in the aviation field likewise hold no interest for him.

"Line bush pilots, we don't get awards! We just work on the line," he says, and closes the log book.

Notes

1. Lynn Garrison, in 1993, gained a certain notoriety as Haiti's "Le Blanc," or "White Shadow," purportedly associated with Haitian dictator Lieutenant-General Raoul Cedras. *Alberta Report*, 8 November 1993, article titled, "In the Slipstream of the White Shadow"; and *Maclean's*, 1 November 1993, article titled "Haiti Braces for Violence after U.N. Peacekeepers Withdraw" and sub-article "A Shadowy Canadian Connection."
2. "When our museum folded, that particular Lancaster (KB-976) ended up being sold to Terry Harold from Edmonton, who equipped it for fire-bombing. From there it went to Scotland to an aviation museum; that's the last I heard of it, that it was in flying condition at a museum," Langemann says.
3. Excerpted in the Smithers, BC, newspaper from a Special to the Vancouver *Sun*, June 1967.

Picking Up the Pieces

*T*HROUGHOUT HIS CAREER, Chris Templeton has flown in more than 80 different types of aircraft on missions including NATO Sabre Squadron leapfrogging, air force search and rescues and medevacs, and aircraft salvage operations. But Templeton is not a pilot—his career in aviation has involved everything except flying airplanes.

Templeton, born in Montreal in 1933, joined the air force as a young man, and learned the trade of aircraft electrical technician. He was then transferred to an F-86 Sabre Squadron in Uplands, Ottawa, where he stayed until the end of August 1953. At that point, his career took off. "I was one of 25 guys taken from the squadron to service the Sabres on their ferry flight to open Number Four Fighter Wing in Baden Soellingen, Germany. The operation, called Leapfrog Four, ferried 63 Sabre aircraft from three different squadrons, and we travelled by North Star aircraft to their stopping points enroute."

The mandate of Number Four Fighter Wing was to complete Canada's NATO contribution by providing four wings, each comprising three squadrons of F-86 Sabres, to the RCAF's Number One Air Division.

"They called the operation 'leapfrogging' because each of

Chris Templeton just prior to departure on Leapfrog Four operation from Ottawa to Germany, with 422 Fighter Squadron, 24 August 1953. Note markings on fuselage (partly obscured by Chris) on Mark IV F-86 Sabre: Indian man's arm with war paint, holding a tomahawk, with motto: "This arm shall do it." *Chris Templeton Collection*

the squadrons used its own North Star aircraft for transportation of the ground crew," Templeton says. "My job as an aircraft electrician was to look after all the electrical systems on the aircraft."

Templeton's crew flew their North Star from Uplands to Goose Bay, Labrador. The other squadrons met them as soon as they landed, to refuel and do the daily inspections on the 63 aircraft as they came in.

If the weather was good, the mission could theoretically have been completed in two days. At Goose Bay, however, they were forced to wait three days for the weather to clear. "The Sabres had a very limited range. They had large drop tanks, and with full fuel tanks they could fly a total time of two hours and 20 minutes. The flying time from Goose Bay to the next stop at Bluie West One, an American Search and Rescue base on the southern tip of Greenland, was two hours and 10 minutes. It was definitely a case of 'get there and land' under good weather conditions, or bail out somewhere over the North Atlantic.

"It took us eight days altogether. The group before us, Three Wing, took 27 days to make the same trek."

Out of the 63 aircraft, only one met with mishap when it ran off the runway at Bluie West One (also known by its traditional Eskimo name of Narssarssuaq). "You have to come in over the water, up a fjord, make a 90-degree turn to line up with the runway, and land. The mountains at the end of the runway are in the 9,000-foot range, so it's quite interesting if you overshoot. When you take off,

Chris Templeton chatting with a German farmer near the Baden Soellingen base, 1956. *Chris Templeton Collection*

you have to go back over the water, regardless of what wind is blowing."

Because of bad weather, the squadron again was held over for two days at Keflavik, Iceland, leaving their aircraft parked on an unused runway. Enroute to Prestwick, the weather turned again, forcing them to divert and overnight at the Royal Naval Air Station Lossiemouth in northern Scotland. They finally arrived in Baden Soellingen at 7:00 P.M, 5 September 1953, to numerous celebrations.

Templeton cannot overemphasize the importance of proper electrical maintenance of aircraft. "The electrical systems control almost everything on the aircraft: they provide power to the engine, instruments, radios, and to the generator system to enable it to charge the battery. We had to ensure the batteries were providing power for ignition purposes, and also for emergency power if a generator was lost in the air. The trim-tabs and the undercarriage are also electrically controlled, as are the hydraulically operated systems such as wing flaps and ailerons. If one thing goes, if that electrical system fails, the pilot generally looks for a place to land."

After three years in Germany, Templeton was transferred to a search and rescue squadron in Edmonton, then to Sea Island, Vancouver, where he spent the next six years servicing Cansos, Dakotas, and Single Otters. The squadron also had two H-21 Piasecki helicopters (called "flying bananas" because of their two huge rotors, one at the front and one at the back, that made the fuselage look bent in the middle).

The small squadron of about 100 men was heavily involved in medevacs. "The search and rescue medevac part kept the aircraft really busy, flying out

Piasecki "Flying Banana" helicopter, used mainly for search and rescue operations by the RCAF. *Royal Canadian Air Force Photo*

many people from remote locations around the province in to Vancouver for treatment, especially in 1957-58 when there was a polio epidemic in BC."

Templeton's duties combined ground maintenance work as well as accompanying the crew on flights. "There were 15 electricians in the section I worked in, and theoretically everybody took a turn at being on stand-by seven days at a time. They always took an aircraft electrician on medevac flights in case of electrical power failure in the air. Some of the patients were flown out in iron lungs, big cumbersome things that could only fit into some of the larger aircraft such as the Cansos and Dakotas. The iron lungs were operated electrically, so our job was to ensure that electrical power was uninterrupted.

"Some medevacs involved bringing out premature babies in incubators. On New Year's Day of 1960, we went over in the Dakota to Tofino, on the west coast of Vancouver Island, and flew out a baby girl. She weighed only a couple of pounds at birth and since then she'd lost some weight. I could have put her in the palm of my hand, she was so tiny. We flew her back in an incubator and she survived. She'd be in her thirties now. That was one of the positive things about the job."

An experience that wasn't so positive occurred in June 1959. The squadron was involved in a search for an American flyer who had gone missing between Port Hardy, BC, and Ketchikan, Alaska. He had been flying a Super Cub on wheels, ferrying it to Alaska, when he'd disappeared, never to be found to this day. The search for this aircraft had been going on for four days when the base received a call for the medevac unit to come to Prince Rupert to pick up a 14-year old boy. He had found a dynamite cap, brought it home, and put it into a wood-burning stove just to see what would happen. The stove had blown sky-high, sending its heavy door flying, hitting the boy and taking a chunk out of his neck. The injury was considered too serious for the hospital in Prince Rupert, and they asked that he be transported to Vancouver.

Most of the squadron, however, was on the search for the American pilot, so the air force had to scramble to find a medevac crew. Without bothering to tell the personnel their destination, they managed to recruit a few willing bodies to go on this second call.

"We assumed we were going up into the interior—to Kelowna or Kamloops. I went home and told my wife I was going on a medevac, leaving at noon. My neighbour, who was also in the air force, caught a ride back to the base with me.

"We loaded up the two pilots, the flight engineer, radio operator, navigator, a medical assistant, a nursing sister, myself, and George Smith, the other electrical technician. Normally we carried a crewman but all the crewmen were on the other search as well.

"There were no seats or seat belts in the Canso freighter so the three men—the medical assistant and the two electricians—half-inflated their Mae Wests [inflatable military life jackets, named for the buxom Hollywood film star, Mae West] with mouth pieces, and used them as cushions, sitting casually as loose cargo."

The flight to Prince Rupert was uneventful. Flying low in the clear weather afforded them spectacular views of the coastline.

On reaching Prince Rupert, they circled the island in the bay and made a perfect let-down. But as soon as they touched down, all hell broke loose.

They thought at first they'd hit a log. When they landed on the water, the left propeller, along with the reduction-gear housing, tore off. Because of the rotation of the prop, it flew across through the top of the fuselage, ripping it open.

The pilot, still strapped in his seat, was thrown from the aircraft and knocked unconscious. He landed, tipped back in his chair in the water 15 feet from the aircraft.

When the copilot came to, he found himself under 12 feet of water seated in his broken chair. He managed to squeeze out from under the control yoke where the chair had lodged, come to the surface, and crawl up onto a wing.

The wing of the Canso is mounted on a pylon about three feet above the fuselage. The flight engineer's position was on a suspended seat reached by climbing a ladder inside the pylon, between the wing and the fuselage section. There were two small side windows but no front window, so he could only see to the sides. He had managed to escape the wreck by crawling through one of the tiny side windows.

Canso at Edmonton Airport, 1946, similar to the one involved in the medevac crash. *Canadian Pacific Limited Photo 26264*

The navigator had been looking out through the cockpit windows while standing in a little rounded bulkhead doorway that separated compartments. When rescued, his head bore a strange-looking cut that ran from the tip of his nose, over the top of his head, and down the back of his skull to his neck, the result of being "rolled around" in the rounded metal doorsill.

The radio officer had been standing behind the navigator watching the landing, holding onto a rack that supported the aircraft's large radio system. When the aircraft came to a stop, he was still holding onto the angle-iron rack, which had torn right off its moorings.

The three men in the back, the medical assistant and two electricians, were thrown, along with portable oxygen bottles and bags of medical supplies, against one of the bulkheads.

The nursing sister had been sitting just ahead of where the props were located. She had now completely disappeared.

Once the aircraft came to rest, it started sinking to its wings. Cansos have a 110-foot wing span and the wings carry about 600 gallons of fuel. Four hours flying time had reduced the amount of fuel, leaving mostly air in the wing tanks; the wings were the only things keeping the aircraft afloat. The cockpit was totally submerged, and was connected to the rest of the aircraft only by hydraulic lines running through the bottom of the keel.

As soon as the aircraft stopped flipping about in the water, the three men in the back hurriedly got out one of the dinghies located inside the rear "blisters"—big observation bubbles that had been used during wartime for machine-gun installations—and inflated it.

They got into the dinghy, and picked up the flight engineer, who came swimming out from beneath the wing. They frantically paddled around the front of the airplane and rescued the pilot, still strapped into his seat. Flames flickered from the left engine. They paddled as close as they dared toward the engine, splashing water until they had drowned the flames. Then they spotted the navigator, the radio officer, and the copilot clinging to the top of the wing. "Where's the nurse?" someone asked.

"She was sitting right in front of me!" the radio officer said. "I'm going to find her!" and he dived into the sea. He surfaced, caught his breath and dived again. There was no sign of her, and by now the cockpit was dipping down 20 feet into the water, a mess of jagged tin, poised to plunge, held aloft only by the wings and the water, slap, slapping against them.

Although the area was later dragged, no sign of Muriel Kerr, the nursing sister, has ever been found. Investigation concluded that when the aircraft crashed and flew apart, the fragmented left propeller had ripped through the fuselage, killing her instantly and hurling her body into the sea.

The accident was blamed on a freak occurrence: when the Canso had hit the water, the right nose door had torn loose, breaking the front hinge. The heavy door, three feet high and six feet long, had pivoted on the back hinge and flown around through the side of the fuselage.

"On a water landing," Templeton says, "that isn't exactly a good way to keep afloat."

An ambulance took the crew to the hospital, where doctors had to "pull little pieces of plexiglas out of the heads of the pilot, copilot, navigator, and radio operator, who were all up front."

The one fatality notwithstanding, Templeton admits that it could have been a lot worse. "We felt lucky we'd come out of it with nothing but bruises and bad memories."

Their intended patient was picked up later that night by another medevac team, and survived the incident better than his would-be rescuers.

When asked if the crew received any kind of psychological counselling after such an experience, Templeton said, "No. We're talking the 1950s, not the '90s. It was a different world in those days."

After six years in Vancouver, Templeton spent a year, 1963–64, based in El Arish, Egypt—the only base where the RCAF was operating at that time as part of the United Nations program.

Ground crew and pilots, says Templeton, make necessary teams for successful flying, and generally they get along. In some cases, however, there can be an "attitude" problem, with pilots and crew each assuming the upper rung of the hierarchy. Team spirit—or lack of it—"depends on the pilots themselves. A lot of them are just super guys, who treat everyone on the crew as equals, each person as important as the next. But some do have an attitude of superiority: 'I'm a pilot, a flying officer, a flight lieutenant,'—which the majority were in those days—'and those guys back there are just LACs (leading aircraftsmen), therefore they are at a lower level.' That wasn't the case with all of them, but there certainly were some.

"I ran into a few who had the 'I-am-God' attitude, and who thought we were nothing. But, if it wasn't for the aero-engineer, the airframe, electrician, and instrument guys, there wouldn't have been an airplane to fly."

Although he rose through the ranks from LAC to corporal, aircraft electrician, after 15 years in the service Templeton decided "there had to be more to life than going through that routine." He left the air force in 1967.

In February 1969 the Templetons moved to Calgary, where Chris joined Field Aviation as an aircraft electrician.

Field Aviation were—and still are—in the business of operating a major maintenance-and-overhaul facility, and for a time were Beechcraft dealers. They overhauled, maintained, and rebuilt aircraft from small single-engine Cessnas and Pipers up to DC-3s and Cansos as well as helicopters. One interesting job they undertook was converting a number of Cansos into water bombers.

When Templeton started at Field Aviation, his supervisor was George Simpson, head of the electrical department.

"Have you ever seen a Canso?" Simpson asked Templeton on his first day on the job.

"As a matter of fact I worked on them for six years in Vancouver," Templeton replied.

"Good. Come with me."

Simpson took him downstairs to see the Canso (CF-HHR) of 1940 vintage that they had sitting in the back hangar. Field Aviation had bought it in the hope of converting it into a water bomber and then selling it. They had torn the wiring out from one end to the other as part of the rebuild. They wanted to start from scratch and build virtually a new airplane, and Chris spent the first three months on his new job rewiring the aircraft.

Salvage work was also a major part of Field Aviation's operation. "I thought that it would be interesting to go out and fix the aircraft on site, so it could be flown back for major repairs in the hangar in Calgary. So after 18 months in the electrical department I asked if I could go out on one of the salvage trips."

At that time, Twin Otters were becoming popular for work in the Arctic. They could get into and out of short strips inaccessible to other aircraft that required longer areas for take-off and landing, and they could haul good payloads. "As a consequence, when you've got 40 or 50 Twin Otters up there, some of them are bound to get bent from time to time. Field sent bids to the insurance companies to do the salvage; if their bid was accepted, they'd select a crew to go and pick up the Twin Otter, wherever it might be. We'd either try to fix it on site and have someone ferry it out, or take off the props, engines, wings, and wheels. If there was a strip good enough to get in a Hercules or some such aircraft, we'd package everything up, load it on the Herc, ferry it back to Calgary, unload it at the hangar, and then rebuild."

These aircraft were well worth salvaging. "In those days you could buy a used Twin Otter for about $200,000. Now that probably wouldn't buy one engine for one."

Most of Templeton's salvage and repair work took him to the Far North, the territories and the Arctic, to places like Eureka, Brock Island, Resolute, and Banks Island.

One of the salvage trips that Templeton vividly recalls was an order to pick up what was left of Weldy Phipps's old Twin Otter, Whiskey Whiskey Papa. Although it still wore the Atlas Aviation Limited colours, the company and its aircraft had been recently purchased by Kenting Aviation Limited of Toronto.

"Like so many aircraft accidents, it wasn't one single thing, but rather a series of events that caused something unexpected to happen," Templeton explains.

It was late evening in the middle of August, when darkness was returning to the North. The aircraft had been at Eureka, a weather station on Ellesmere Island in the Arctic. Whiskey Whiskey Papa, along with a helicopter, was based at Eureka for a few days, flying supplies and personnel out to different locations for oil exploration companies that had started drilling in the area.

"The pilot of the Twin Otter had to take a 400-gallon bladder of fuel—a rubber tank installed in the back for holding fuel—over to Irene Bay, about 100 miles east. It was normally an uneventful trip over the mountains, down the other side, land, cache the fuel, and come back again."

A new navigation system had recently been installed in the Twin Otter. Because the instrument panel was already full of instruments, they'd had to locate the control head—a little box two inches deep and 10 or 12 inches long—underneath the sub-instrument panel right in front of the pilot's shins.

It was lower than the normal location for mounting an instrument, and it left the pilot with barely enough room to operate the rudder pedals.

The helicopter pilot stationed in Eureka didn't have a lot to do, and was bored, so he talked the Twin Otter pilot into inviting him along. He was sitting in the right seat, the copilot's seat (although many Twin Otters didn't fly with copilots; it wasn't really necessary for the sort of flying they were doing), with a 35 mm camera on his lap.

They took off for Irene Bay, crossing the Sawtooth Mountains. "As they flew along, the pilot apparently was trying to set up the nav system," Templeton says. "You can 'trim' the aircraft [adjust the flight controls, i.e., ailerons, elevators and rudder] to fly itself—although it doesn't have an auto-pilot—by putting in the appropriate headings and then hoping the aircraft is going to end up where you want it to. Because of the location of this control panel, the pilot had to lean forward to see the panel beside his right shin; he didn't realize that he was also pressing on the control column. The airplane gradually started to descend.

"The guy in the right seat was watching him, but didn't think anything of it. He looked up to see a mountain right in front of them. 'Rocks ahead!' he yelled. The pilot jumped back in his seat and pulled back on the control column.

"They hit the edge of a rock face with the nose wheel and the left wheel, bounced 200 yards into the air, and thumped onto a plateau. Because the nose gear and left wheel were gone, the right wheel then swung around and the aircraft actually ended up pointing in the direction from which it had come. Then it ground to a halt.

"The helicopter pilot's camera flew out the window and hit the right propeller. The prop tore the camera apart, and drove a piece of the camera casing into the side of the fuselage right beside where he was sitting. We dug the piece out later.

"Ironically," Templeton adds, "another company had a fairly new pilot up there flying another Twin Otter to drilling sites such as Hoodoo Dome and Malec Dome. This pilot had missed his location and ended up flying up over the Arctic Ocean. He had turned around to try to find it on the way back when he noticed he was nearly out of fuel, so he landed on the shore of the Arctic Ocean. A search and rescue operation was searching for that Twin Otter when WWP went missing. The two situations happened within a couple of hours— both these aircraft had kind of disappeared.

"The two men sat on the mountain for a day and a half, until they were rescued by helicopter. The copilot had received a cut on his forehead that was not very serious, and the pilot suffered strained back muscles. They'd both had seat belts on, and that's all that happened to them."

Field Aviation's five-man salvage crew arrived in Resolute three weeks later, following the insurance company's estimate of the damage. Field's proposal was to disassemble the aircraft on site and fly the pieces back by helicopter to the airstrip in Eureka, which was about 40 miles west of where they'd crashed.

"We flew in to Resolute with PWA (Pacific Western Airlines), and from there to Eureka in one of Weldy Phipps's DC-3s, along with a helicopter. We knew that the aircraft we'd come to salvage was perched on the top of the Sawtooth Range, and could see that the clouds were down to 500 feet above the valley. So we sat there and looked to the east, and watched these stupid clouds just hanging there. Finally about eleven o'clock on the second night the clouds started to dissipate. Jim Lewis, the helicopter pilot, and Paul Lawrence, his engineer, said, 'Let's go and have a look at what's facing us.'"

The crew loaded all the tools needed to take the aircraft apart because they were sure it couldn't be flown out, and followed the latitude and longitude coordinates they had been given by the base manager in Resolute. But there was no Twin Otter to be found. They started sweep searches to the south, back and forth across the mountain range, which was only a few miles wide at the elevation they were at, but could see no sign of Whiskey Whiskey Papa. No one could possibly have flown it out because it didn't have any wheels and it was badly banged up.

Then they started searching to the north, but still no sign, so they flew back to Eureka for further instructions. By this time it was two o'clock in the morning. They called the Resolute base manager, waking him. He got out a map and discovered he'd given them the wrong coordinates. The crew got back into the helicopter and flew until they came upon a glacier a mile-and-a-half wide and a few miles long. Although they couldn't see anything because of ground fog, Jim Lewis decided to set the machine down and walk across the glacier to see if they could find the aircraft hidden in the fog.

"We five crew members, and the pilot and engineer of the helicopter, seven abreast, walked a good mile across the glacier through the fog," Templeton recalls. "Still no sign of the Twin Otter. We turned around and swung over to the other side, came back. No sign. Then we did a grid search with the helicopter, and just kept going north.

"Finally we found it 12 miles north of where they said it was."

These things happen up North, sometimes, Templeton says. "People just don't bother doing their homework. Perhaps they didn't mark the map when they were actually at the site, but flew back to Eureka or Resolute, got a map out and said, 'Oh yeah, this should be it, about here.' With the mountains resembling a fairly even row of teeth, it was easy to confuse one mountain with another."

They found the Otter perched on the rock ledge, its damaged nose pointing back towards Eureka, with the nose wheel, oleo, and left main wheel lying on the plateau beside it. At three o'clock in the morning they started dismantling Whiskey Whiskey Papa.

Templeton's work primarily concerned the electrical salvage, removing parts as completely as possible, disconnecting at the junction boxes where they were designed to be disconnected, rather than going in with a pair of wire cutters.

Salvage of Whiskey Whiskey Papa, August 1972, fuselage ready for slinging. Although WWP still sported the Atlas Aviation colours, Weldy Phipps had just sold the company to Kenting Aviation of Toronto the previous year. *Chris Templeton Collection*

They removed the propellers, and then the engines. A 110-volt unit provided power for lights, electric drills, and other tools. Two air bags, of a type used extensively in salvage work, enabled them to lift up the huge aircraft with very low air pressure. They removed the remaining gear leg and wheel, skirting panels (fairings), then the wings. An S58T helicopter took each wing down from the mountain and left them at the bottom of the valley, but it was about all the helicopter could do to move the fuselage.

"Often, when working in mountains, a good helicopter pilot will drag the load off to the edge of the mountain, as Jim Lewis did here. The helicopter was dropping altitude, which gave it a little more power and allowed it to build up air speed. The fuselage swung away underneath. He couldn't quite lift it, but he could stay airborne as long as he had some forward motion."

By the time Lewis had transported the fuselage to Eureka, set it down, and returned to the mountain, it was becoming foggy and the crew was concerned. They hadn't brought sleeping bags or food. When the helicopter returned on schedule, they quickly loaded the engines, propellers, and everything else.

"We didn't leave a thing. It was always part of our salvage job to clean up after we were done. We picked up all the scraps and left it so that other than a few skid marks, you'd never know an aircraft had been there," Templeton says. "We tried to never leave a mess. We normally took just what we'd need."

The ultimate fate of Whiskey Whiskey Papa was rather ignoble for an aircraft with such an auspicious career. "We brought everything back to the airport in Eureka, and the aircraft later was flown to Calgary by a Hercules.

Then, sadly, it sat for years on the north end of the Field Aviation hangar in a kind of storage area. I think eventually it was cut up and put in the dump. It never flew again."

Templeton feels that the salvage of Whiskey Whiskey Papa was significant. "It was the first commercially operated Twin Otter in Canada, and we were there when it made its last flight. I guess you could say it was the end of an era."

A peculiarity that Templeton noticed on 10 different salvage jobs in which he took part involving Twin Otter aircraft was that there was not one loss of life. "To my way of thinking, given the Arctic flying conditions in which they operated, that certainly speaks well of Canadian-built aircraft. The Twin Otter did a heck of a job for years up in the Arctic, and there are still a bunch of them up there. It's nice to recall that safety record."

Although many aircraft accidents do result in loss of life, Templeton, fortunately, wasn't involved in cleaning up any of them. "It wasn't by choice; it just happened. I was very thankful."

Templeton says that salvage crews often decipher clues to detect what went wrong, whether the crash resulted from mechanical or human error.

Most crashes were due to terrible weather conditions, or to "silly little things," such as the situation that brought down one of the first Twin Otters, Serial Number Two. "Its registration was PAT, one of Pan Arctic's aircraft that we'd salvaged years ago up on Brock Island when Pan Arctic had a drilling rig there. The pilot flying the aircraft on this occasion was filling in for one of their regular pilots who was on holidays. He came in looking for the rig in really bad weather conditions—snow, ice crystals, and things like that—in the middle of winter so it was black 24 hours a day. The pilot saw the lights on the drilling rig and had to take evasive action so he wouldn't fly into it, because in ice crystals and fog you can't see these things until you're a couple of hundred yards away. He made an abrupt right turn to miss the tower, then levelled out and did an immediate left turn to come back to line up with the runway. Unfortunately, when he did the left turn, the left wing-tip hit the ground and pulled the aircraft out of the air. One of the six passengers suffered a broken leg, and that was the only injury, which is a miracle!

"They had a radar altimeter on the aircraft, but the sensing antenna was underneath the right wing-tip. It was reading 40 or 50 feet when he made the left turn, but the wing-tip on the other side was down at ground level. So it's one of those fluky things—a few feet higher everything would have been fine."

Templeton says it was always a challenge to view photos of the crash site they were going to, and try to figure out just what equipment they'd need, and estimate whether they could fix the aircraft on site and have it ferried back, or if it would have to be taken apart and ferried back in pieces.

He estimates he has serviced 25 or 30 different types of aircraft. "They're all the same, yet they're all different. Like cars, they'll all get you from A to B, but in different ways, with different levels of comfort."

After four years at Field Aviation, working first in the electrical department then in maintenance, Templeton applied for the job of flight services manager. This involved looking after all the visiting aircraft, and the tenant aircraft owned by oil companies such as Shell, Imperial, and Mobile Oil.

Through this job, Templeton was privileged to meet many interesting people in the aviation business. One was the late Molly Reilly, who at that time was flying a twin engine Beechcraft Duke propeller-driven airplane for Canadian Utilities. Field were Beechcraft dealers, so did the maintenance work on this airplane.

"Molly was extremely particular about how her aircraft was maintained, and how it was cleaned and polished," Templeton recalls. "You had to use particular products on her aircraft— never Varsol!

"One day we were sitting in the flight lounge talking to an old-time pilot from the United States. He and Molly had started flying during the war, and they each had 12,000 or 15,000 hours experience. Another American pilot came in and joined in the conversation. He'd had a fairly extensive aviation career, not going back as far as the other two, but he proceeded to tell us about all the huge projects that he'd been involved with; he'd flown this and he'd flown that. He didn't give Molly and the other chap a chance to say a thing. When he finally stopped for breath, the old fellow said, 'Gosh, I haven't flown some of those airplanes you've mentioned, but I've got a couple here that maybe you haven't flown.' He pulled his licence out, and it showed he was qualified for about 50 different aircraft—more than this other guy had ever even seen.

"Without another word he put his coffee cup down and left. And I thought, boy, that was such a calm putdown. Working for Field Aviation, I got to know the best—and some of the others. And to hear all their stories."

After working for eight years with Field Aviation, Templeton and his wife started their own business. On 1 June 1977, they opened a pilots' supply store, called Air Flair Limited, which they ran for 14 years.

The store sold basically everything that a pilot or an aircraft engineer would need for their job: maps, training manuals, kits, computers, and books on rules and regulations for flying school students, instructions on how to fly a particular airplane, aerobatic training manuals, requirements for commercial and airline transport licences, sunglasses, flight suits, and white shirts with shoulder epaulets and big pockets. Books—"just about every Canadian aviation book that's in print, and a lot of American books as well, on how to fly, mountain flying, different ratings in the States, the various licences that are available, and flyers' biographies. We built up a very good clientele of people who loved reading about aviation. It was a very interesting business."

In 1979, Templeton started taking flying lessons, but he found it was "taking three hours to do an hour's flying training." Because the flight training was held at Springbank airport just west of Calgary and his business was located at the Calgary International Airport, one hour was taken up in transit; then before flying he had to do a walk-around and ground-checks; following the flight there was a debriefing session between student and instructor. The Templetons' business was thriving, so he decided to forego the flying lessons for the time being.

Unfortunately, their business, newly located in Number Three Hangar, was destroyed by fire in February of 1980, making it necessary to rebuild, "so I couldn't afford to go back flying. It was just for pleasure anyway."

Templeton has a fine collection of books, dealing with the Royal Canadian Air Force, Canadian aviation, pilots' adventures, and subjects of general interest— and believes that he owns at least 90 percent of the books written in Canada about aviation dating back to 1917.

In addition to his library, Templeton's archives house a complete collection of RCAF wings worn by air crew members during World War II—11 different wings for pilots, flight engineers, navigators, air gunners, wags and observers.

He has wings worn by members of the Pathfinder Squadron, which marked out and led bombing raids; he also has Tour of Operations wings, which all members of the air crew were entitled to wear once they had completed a tour of operations.

He has King's crown and Queen's crown (1953-1968) wings, and the wing given by the RCAF to all graduates of NATO member countries that sent flying

Chris Templeton at 10th anniversary of Air-Flair Limited, by RCAF memorabilia display, 1987. *Chris Templeton Collection*

students to Canada. Graduates wore the Canadian wing on the right side of their tunic, and their own country's wing on the left side.

His collection includes 71 different "sweetheart" pins, which the men gave to their wives, girlfriends, or mothers to show their position in the RCAF.

He has pieces of plexiglas that have been taken from gun turrets or windshields of aircraft and cut into heart-shapes, fronted by RCAF crests, to be worn as pendants.

His badge collection includes one from the High River, Alberta, Number Five Elementary Training School, which displays a propeller hub with five nuts around the outside. This cloth badge was worn by qualified civilian mechanics who were working for the RCAF, because of the shortage of military mechanics.

His RCAF cabinet contains memorabilia such as a World War II airwoman's cap, an original World War II flying helmet and goggles, a throat mike used during the war; mugs from different messes, writing tablets in blue leather cases; writing pads and envelopes displaying the RCAF insignia, and a World War II pilot's survival kit.

He has a memorial Order of Service for Buzz Beerling, killed in 1948. "He was one of the most famous World War II pilots, although he was a bit of a rebel," Templeton says. "He was often referred to as the Hero of Malta because he was extremely successful in shooting down enemy aircraft. He ended up as the leading ace in the Canadian forces. He was killed in a crash of a Norseman, just outside Rome when he was on his way to Israel to join the Israeli air force in 1948. Some people to this day still think there was sabotage involved, that he was deliberately killed by somebody loosening the fuel line."

He has 12 pictures of the Snowbirds, signed by all the pilots. And a photo of a replica of the Spirit of St. Louis aircraft that Lindberg flew across the Atlantic.

He has periscopic sextants and nearly every kind of navigation computer. A special treasure is an old Mark Nine Course Setting Bomb Site used to train pilots in the Calgary area during the war, along with the original log book.

A cabinet is full of old TCA (Trans Canada Airlines) and Canadian Pacific Airlines items—ashtrays, glasses, lighters, penny matches, plastic baggage tags, flight bags—one that has TCA on one side and Air Canada on the other from a changeover period. He's got "a ton of stuff" from Pacific Western, Nordair, and Eastern Airlines.

"But this is only a part of the collection," he says with a grin. "I have a bunch more in a storage unit! People have told me it's the best private collection in Canada."

Since moving to Penticton, BC, Templeton has given up his membership in most organizations except for the Quarter Century Aviation Club and the Western Warbirds (he is their newsletter editor).

His love of flying prompted Templeton to record each flight he has been on. He has so far flown on 81 different types of aircraft, 10 helicopters, and a hot air balloon. "For a nonpilot, I think that's a pretty good record," he says with a laugh.

Templeton notes, with regret, the changes that have occurred in the aviation world. "It used to be a pretty close-knit community; everybody knew everybody else, what aircraft they flew. We referred to aircraft by their registration numbers, like PAT and WWP. All you had to do was mention those call letters, and people knew what and whose it was, and where it was flying. Now, that sort of closeness in the industry doesn't exist. Because of the economic times we're in, people have had to sell aircraft. There used to be many corporate aircraft in Calgary; I doubt if there are 15 left out of the 90 that we had 10 years ago.

"In the North, you used to know all the pilots. Now the pilots who fly into communities on daily skeds in 737s and that sort of thing are based in Calgary, Edmonton, or Vancouver. That whole aspect of aviation has changed a lot. But there are still some small operators out there, and they do a fine job."

Chris Templeton, a flyer without wings, has flown over a vast part of the world, maintaining and servicing—sometimes salvaging—aircraft, as an airman and as a civilian. He revels in memorabilia from the past—old airplanes, old badges of valour and distinction earned during old wars, things that tell stories of the wonders human beings have performed since they invented flying machines.

Olden Bawld

*C*HARLES *"CHARLIE"* REDMOND ROBINSON, (a.k.a. Olden Bawld, the Pilots' Poet Laureate), had a flying career of the headline-making variety. Born in 1907 in Fort William, Ontario (now part of Thunder Bay), in 1930 he became the first graduate to earn a commercial pilots' licence with the Fort William Aero Club, training in a Gypsy Moth (CF-CAT).

It was as a bush pilot that Robinson excelled. He first flew out of Sioux Lookout for Patricia Airways, then for legendary mining mogul and pilot H.A.

Charles R. Robinson became the first graduate to earn a commercial pilot's licence with the Fort William Aero Club. *Larry Robinson Collection*

"Doc" Oaks's company, Oaks Airways Limited, flying such aircraft as a Junkers W-34 (CF-AQV) and a Fairchild KR-34.

His long-time employer was Starratt Airways & Transportation Limited, based at Hudson near Sioux Lookout.

"Pilot Brings Burning Plane Down to Earth" stated a Kenora, Ontario, newspaper on 24 December 1935, accompanied by a cartoon depicting a confident-looking pilot with an decidedly uncomfortable-looking passenger in an aircraft held together by baling wire. The caption read, "Kenora Pilot safely sideslips blazin' plane, with terrified passenger, to frozen lake."

The incident occurred when Robinson was flying for Starratt in northern Ontario. Robinson and his passenger, miner Gus Johnson, were flying over the Red Lake region at 1,500 feet when their Fox Moth caught fire—a pilot's worst nightmare. A Fox Moth has a cabin under the cockpit, and when a panic-stricken Johnson tried to open the cabin door to jump out, Robinson had to side-slip the airplane to keep his passenger inside. The pilot made a forced landing on a small frozen lake, and pulled Johnson out just as flames enveloped the aircraft.

On another trip, this time in a Fairchild 82 (CF-AXG) between Gold Pines and the Jackson-Manion Gold Mine, Robinson was coming up on the shoreline when the aircraft suddenly grew quiet—the fan had quit. As Robinson glided the silent "82" to its inevitable descent, he passed over the mine manager's house and noticed a woman standing on her back porch shaking a rug. She looked up at the silent orange and yellow Fairchild, then went inside. The crash came moments later, into a stand of poplar and jackpine trees. Robinson fortunately was unhurt. He clambered out of the airplane, and, not knowing quite where to go or what to do, sat down on a stump to think things over. He heard a crackle from the brush, and through the trees came the woman he had observed shaking the rug. She obviously hadn't spotted him. "Hello!" he said, and the woman fainted. Soon, two rescue officers appeared from the nearby mine. But when they saw the woman lying prone on the ground, they loaded her onto a stretcher and took off—leaving the pilot, who had barely escaped death, sitting on his tree stump.[1]

In 1942, Starratt Airways was bought out by Canadian Pacific Airlines, and Robinson went with the new parent company, flying a Curtiss T-32 Condor (CF-BQN)—the only such airplane operated in Canada—out of Whitehorse, Yukon, and a Boeing 247D out of Edmonton into northern territories. He was the first to land with a Boeing on wheels on the new landing strip at Yellowknife.

He later flew Lockheeds, DC-3s, North Stars, and Vickers Viscounts for Trans Canada Airlines. Although he retired in 1961, he continued to fly until 1990, amassing 30,000 hours in the air, including 8,000 on floats.

Charlie and Rae Robinson's three sons (Larry, Errol, and Phillip) all became pilots, and their three daughters (Lois, who earned a private pilots' licence, Susan, and Margaret) helped rebuild a Stinson SR-8 (CF-AZV), which is now in Winnipeg's Western Canada Aviation Museum.

Robinson's penchant for poetry manifested itself during the long hours he spent in the air, especially after he started flying the larger aircraft for Canadian Pacific Airlines out of Edmonton. On landing, Robinson would come into the base office and recite his verses for his fellow pilots, crew, and office staff.[2]

Charlie Robinson died on 28 May 1993, but the poems of a pilot who laughingly called himself "Olden Bawld" will forever reflect the fun, fear, and fortunes experienced by Canada's bush pilots.

Notes

1. Reworded from newspaper article in *The Times-News*, 6 November 1990 by Robert Grant, and reprinted in "Never Froze Our Eyeballs," by Robert S. Grant, *Air Progress* magazine August 1993.
2. Three of Robinson's poems are reprinted in this book in abridged form, by permission of his son, Captain Larry Robinson. In 1986 a collection of Robinson's poems were published under his pseudonym, Olden Bawld. *Poems for Pilots and Other People* is available through L.H. Robinson (Box 1904, Edmonton, AB T5J 2P3).

A Pilot's Soliloquy

Olden Bawld (a.k.a. Charles R. Robinson)

I'm an ordinary pilot of
a Fairchild 82.
But there's no limitation
to the things that I can do.

To be a pilot in the bush
is something really fine.
That is, if your mentality
is quite as low as mine.

I never bounce my landings,
I never bump the dock.
I've flown on floats eleven years
and never scraped a rock.

At 45-degrees below
and when I'm in a rush,
there's nothing I like better
than a pothole full of slush.

I'm really in my glory
loading double-decker beds
and diamond-drill equipment, too,
with greasy swivel-heads.

I like to see the grease ooze out
upon the cabin floor,
and mix with lime or flour, spilt
from loads I've had before.

There's fuel-oil, grub and dynamite
and baled hay by the ton.
I fly it all with joyous heart,
and work from sun to sun.

Three generations of Robinson pilots: Glenn, Larry, and Charles (1988). *Larry Robinson Collection*

I enter in the aircraft log
each trip in detail true,
and never make the blunders that
the other pilots do.

There's never any argument
'twixt engineers and me,
I never cause them any grief,
we're chummy as can be.

I never carry overloads
for that would be unjust,
and anyone that says I do
has got a lot of crust!

Neither do I fly at night,
I never break Air Regs.
If that I'm ever guilty of
I'll drink the bitter dregs.

So time draws on—and when I'm old,
I think 'tween me and you,
I'll miss the joy and comfort of
my Fairchild 82.

Although I'm just a pilot,
I think it's really swell.
And everything I've said is true,
Oh yes, it is—(like hell!).

(Composed in Fairchild [CF-AXG] while flying out of Hudson, Ontario, 12 August 1939)

Lucky Lucas

"NO MATTER HOW GOOD a pilot you are, you have to have luck," Phil Lucas often said, and he proved it on more than one occasion during his long and varied flying career.

Phil couldn't be sure of the exact number of flying hours he'd mustered over the years, but he figured it was somewhere in the neighbourhood of 7,800. He did remember every aircraft and most of their engines and registration letters, from the De Havilland 60X Cirrus Moth that he trained on, to the '29 Curtiss Robin, to his latest aircraft, a smart little Cherokee 180.

That's a lot of hours and a lot of years—when you start flying at 23 and don't quit until you're 83.

From the moment he obtained a pilot's licence in 1930, Philip Grainger Lucas became a hero in his home town of Vulcan, Alberta. He was a licensed flyer for nearly 60 consecutive years and, at the time of his death on 18 April 1993 at age 87, he was still seen as a "local boy who made good."

At Phil's funeral, stories were told of daring adventures where the element of risk was part of every flight plan. His family and friends, many of whom were also involved in flying, remembered, learned, laughed, or listened in silence as the stories emerged and history flew backwards.

But perhaps we should start at the beginning, and allow the legends of Lucky Lucas to unfold, once again . . .

Phil Lucas was born 1 April 1906 in Blackpool, England. In 1910, his family emigrated to the good wheat-growing country east of Nanton, Alberta. A quarter-section of land eight miles west and a mile-and-a-quarter south of Vulcan became the home place.

Phil, the eldest child in the family, attended school at Richmond Hill and Harvey country schools and worked with his father on the farm. During this time he met his lifelong friend, Joe Irwin, whose father farmed three miles away. The boys were one year and seven months apart in age, and shared common interests, including the flying bug.

"The old prairie air mail route of Western Canada Airways used to run directly over Vulcan," Joe Irwin recalls. "Prime sport for an evening was to drive out to the emergency airfield at Galbraith's place 10 miles west of Vulcan and watch the mail plane come over about eleven at night, Fokker F-14s and Boeing 40 B4s.

"Then I went for an airplane ride with Jock Palmer in the old Jenny, and that pretty well made my mind up. In the meantime, Phil, he's going to fly too."

Phil had his first flight in Calgary in April of 1929. He and his wife, Althea, and Joe Irwin drove Phil's 1928 Chev car from Vulcan to Calgary. For a very short time, before the Renfrew airport opened, there was an airport near the CFCN tower, on the east side of the hill. They drove there, and for $5 each, were taken for rides in Great Western Airway's 60X Moth. The pilot flew over to the Renfrew area and pointed out the location of the future Calgary Municipal Airport.

Joe Irwin describes the next stage: "Three months later, in July 1929, we came to the Calgary Stampede. Great Western Airways and the Aero Club had displays at the grounds. GWA told us if we could get five or six guys together they would come down to Vulcan and start a satellite school. So we rounded up six guys.

"An Alberta pilot, Louise Burka, brought down Baron Josef Csavossy's Gypsy Moth, and other local pilots, Gil McLaren and Archie McMullen, each brought a Cirrus Moth. Phil and I took one-half hour dual instruction, along with the other guys that we'd lined up, but that's as far as the others went with flying.

"That fall, Phil and I started coming to Calgary on weekends to take lessons."

Raising the money for the lessons demanded certain sacrifices.

"I had a 1928 Chevrolet," said Phil. "I traded it in for 50 hours of lessons, mostly on an open cockpit 60X Moth.

"Those airplanes were open, all right. That's how pilots could tell if they were side-slipping around—by the slipstream on their faces!"

Phil started taking flying lessons from a grass strip out on the Old Banff Coach Road. His instructors were Fred McCall and Jock Palmer. In September of that year the Calgary Municipal Airport (often called the Stanley Jones field) opened.

Joe Irwin also came to Calgary that winter, working two jobs to pay for lessons. It cost a flat rate of $300 for a private licence, which was issued as soon as the student could pass the test. A commercial licence cost $1,000, and at the time took 50 hours. "I had four hours and 55 minutes dual, and three hours and 10 minutes solo on the Cirrus Moth when I got my private pilot's licence," Joe Irwin recalls. "So now my 300 bucks is gone, see, and I've got to borrow some dough, another $700 to get my commercial."

Irwin laughs when he recalls the instruction they got for their money: "When Phil and I started flying, Archie McMullen was the head instructor at Great Western Airways, and he had 74 hours! Gil McLaren was the 2-I-C [second-in-command], and Gil had 60-some total hours flying! Fifty hours was a commercial licence in those days. The blind leading the blind."

Phil Lucas described the test he took for his licence:

"Howard Ingram and Jock Currie were the Department of Transport

Phil Lucas taking lessons in 1929 on a DH 60 Cirrus Moth. *Phil Lucas Collection*

inspectors. They were based in Regina at the time, but they came here to check me out.

"I had to do a cross-country trip for the commercial test, and Freddy McCall, one of the senior instructors, told me, 'Just go straight east to Bassano, and the RCMP will check your time. Then go from Bassano to the RCAF station at High River and fly around High River. Then come back to Calgary.'

"The wind was from the southeast about 10 miles per hour. I flew out to Bassano, then rode the wind all the way back. When I got back, they said, 'Where's your flight plan?' I hadn't known I was supposed to have filed a navigation log prior to making the trip! I said, 'How do I do that?' Fred McCall said, 'Oh, don't worry. I'll fix that up for you.' And he did—so I got my licence. Joe Irwin received his a couple of months later."[1]

As Phil's flying hours increased, however, so did the time conflicts. Phil's son Jack says, "When he first got his licences, it was quite a novelty. It seemed as if Phil wanted to fly more than he wanted to farm or anything else."

Phil's father insisted that he farm, and it did seem the more practical option. He had a family to support, and no one could survive by eating an airplane. The conflict between flying and farming, however, would continue for many years.

In March 1932, Phil Lucas and Jock Palmer, a World War I pilot who had lately been flying and instructing with Great Western Airways, formed a little company called Western Flying Services.

"Rutledge Air Service had shut down, Great Western Airways had gone into receivership, and the Calgary Flying Club had also temporarily ceased operation," Joe Irwin explains. "So Jock bought an Avro Avian (G-CAVB) that had previously belonged to Rutledge, and Phil and Jock together bought the

The A-129 American Eagle (CF-AHZ), a three-place biplane powered by a Kinner K-5 engine, that Phil Lucas and Jock Palmer purchased and rebuilt in 1931–32, shown here with Goodyear air tires (4" hubs with 24" tires). *Phil Lucas Collection*

remains of an A-129 Eagle (CF-AHZ), a three-place biplane, also off Rutledge Air Service. During the winter of 1931 and '32 they rebuilt the Eagle at the airport in northeast Calgary, and by the summer of 1932 they had it flying."

Western Flying Services advertised for flying students but, according to an article in the Vulcan *Advocate* on 29 June 1988, "Lucas and his partner never taught a Caucasian student." Phil explained this unusual circumstance: "Very few people could afford to fly in those days, but as the Chinese-Japanese War was taking place there was no lack of Chinese-Canadian youngsters wanting to learn how to fly." Most of their students held full-time day jobs, so hours of instruction were often from 4:00 A.M. to 8:30 A.M.

Jack Lucas remembers this period as one of the good times. "I was about four years old when all this was taking place. We didn't get much money but we did get a lot of vegetables from the Chinese people to pay for their lessons. So, we ate pretty good."

Phil told friend Chris Templeton about some of the situations he encountered because of the language barrier. "A lot of the instruction was by pointing, motioning, and gesturing," Templeton says. "He told about having one of the Chinese students in the rear cockpit while Phil was in the front of the training aircraft, flying east along the Bow River toward Forest Lawn. Apparently there were a lot of market gardens there, operated by other Chinese people. This student became so absorbed looking at the market gardens that he forgot to fly. The airplane wasn't in the proper attitude at all, and Phil had to go through amazing contortions to get him to wake up and get his head back in the cockpit and fly. There were dual controls, but Phil wanted him to recover rather than do the recovery for him."

By the fall of 1932 the Chinese-Japanese war had temporarily died down and with it went Lucas's students.

"By that fall we were broke, like everyone else," Phil recalled, "so then I went barnstorming, charging people a cent a pound. And everybody said they weighed 140 pounds, it didn't matter how big they were. I could carry two in my airplane (the Eagle CF-AHZ), so I didn't do too bad. A fellow named Charlie Tweed, who was running the airport at Lethbridge, joined us with a little Monocoupe (CF-AKO) but he could only carry one passenger.

"We were at Arrowwood on a kind of gloomy day—we could get up about as high as the grain elevators and fly around, come in and land, $1.40 worth—when a great big guy came walking up and said to Charlie, 'I'd like to go for a ride.' 'How much do you weigh?' 'Two hundred ten pounds!' Charlie reached over and said, 'Shake hands. You're the first honest man I've seen today.'"

Joe Irwin picks up the barnstorming escapades:

"In the fall of 1932, Phil had the Eagle down at Vulcan and we made three or four barnstorming trips. I had Scotty Love's Waco 10 CF-AOI, Phil had AHZ, and Charlie Tweed had AKO, his little Monocoupe. As I recall, we went to Nanton and Arrowwood that fall, until a horse ate us up!"

It was in the late fall and the pilots had stayed overnight at Arrowwood. Before they settled their airplanes down for the night in a field, they asked the farmer if there was any livestock in the field. He said no. What he didn't know was that the local druggist's boy had borrowed a saddle horse from a farmer and was using the field for pasture. During the night a freezing rain formed ice crystals on the wings and tail sections of the airplanes. When the three pilots came out to start their planes in the morning, they found that the horse, in trying to quench his thirst, had gouged holes in the fabric between every rib on the lower wings on both AHZ and AOI. They managed to repair the airplanes and fly them home—but that ended the season's barnstorming enterprise.

The following summer, Phil sold AHZ to the Koenen brothers in Edmonton. Western Flying Service folded at that point, and Phil went back to the family farm at Vulcan.

Phil took turns with the seasons, working on the farm in the spring and fall during the years 1933-36, and barnstorming during the summers using Scotty Love's Waco CF-AOI.

"Nobody had any aviation gasoline," Phil recalled. "We used to buy four-gallon cans of naphtha that cost 30 or 40 cents a gallon. People used it in their gas lanterns. It was a lead-free gasoline and worked good in the plane, at least we thought it did, and we always got there and got back." He adds with a grin, "I must have always got back—because here I am!"

Phil's son Jack, old enough by then to admire his fearless father, recalls the sometimes unsettled schedule. "He did some barnstorming, went to the fairs in the little towns around southern Alberta and into Saskatchewan. He wasn't much for doing stunts, some people did but he didn't, but he took people for rides, things like that. It brought in a little money—barely enough for gas. It was a very difficult situation."

Phil's first paying job in the aviation industry came about because of his engineers' rather than his pilots' licence. In 1938 he went to work for Peace River Airways, flying for them until 1939, and again in 1941.

"I had three airplanes to look after: one of the first Fairchilds, an FC2-W2 powered by a 225-horse Wright Cyclone. I also had a Waco Custom AQC-6 (CF-BJS) with a Jacobs L-6 engine, and a Waco Custom ZQC-6 (CF-BDJ) with a Jacobs L-5."

Luck was with Phil right from the start of his flying career, never more significantly than at Outpost Island

"I was flying [Waco] BJS from Hay River to Yellowknife, taking the [Peace River Airways] company president [Jack McNeil], the book keeper, and there was a girl along—I don't know what she was along for but she was there anyway," said Phil. "I knew I shouldn't have left Hay River. It was winter and we were on skis, but Great Slave Lake still had open water. So it wasn't what you'd call a good deal.

"When I got to where I thought Yellowknife should be, I couldn't get down. I couldn't see a damned thing for fog. I was about 3,000 feet and there was no way of looking down through that fog. I'd have to go back to Hay River. So I turned around and started back.

"I was going along trying to keep the Shaky Jake in the sunshine and also in the shade at the same time, which is pretty hard to do. In the meantime, the fog had closed in over the lake.

"I flew around for 20 minutes, getting lower and lower beneath the fog, trying to keep the skis out of the water. I didn't need any coat to keep warm, I'll tell you that."

Joe Irwin picks up the narrative: "He was on skis, and they had flown to Yellowknife, first trip after freeze-up, first airplane in, and they shouldn't have been there. No one else was getting in for that very same reason.

"So he was on skis, and by the time it dawned on him that he was in trouble, he was in so far that he didn't have room to turn around and go back. He kept getting lower and lower as he got out over the cooler water. The fog finally lifted a bit until there was maybe 30 or 50 feet of clearance, but the bottom of the fog was, of course, wringing wet. If you got in it you were dead, that's all. You were building ice."

Luckily there was a little breeze making a ripple on the water, so Phil could see where it was. He didn't dare take his eyes off the water because if he did he was into it; if he went any higher he'd be into the bottom of the fog.

"I kept my passengers calm by telling them some kind of a story," Phil said, "but, yeah, they knew there was a problem all right. But you can never panic. You don't have time. You can't give up—never, never, *never!* You just keep looking for that one place to land."

All at once a vision swept past one side-window—the draw works of a mine head-frame! Then he saw ice and a high rock pile. He flew around and looked it over.

What he'd come upon were two strips of rock a couple of miles long, with a mine operating on one side. The heat from the plant had pushed the ceiling high enough to enable him to turn around. He came in for a landing on the narrow strip of ice between the two rock islands.

"I landed on the ice and was heading for open water. There were guys on shore waving, 'Get in here! Get in here!' We got down, and they pulled me up on shore," Phil said.

"When I got out, they told me there wasn't enough ice out there to hold an airplane. 'Well,' I said, 'It didn't sink under us, so I guess we're all right.' Pure good luck."

The place, which Phil Lucas had never heard of before because he'd never flown over that particular area, was called Outpost Island, located southeast of Yellowknife.

They stayed overnight on the island, and the next morning he started up the airplane, got it up near the edge of the rocks and took off on the ice between the two islands.

"I've always said that it didn't matter how good you were at a job, you had to have a certain amount of luck," Phil concluded. "And I've proved that quite a few times."

Peace River Airways had also acquired a Fokker Standard Universal (G-CAHE), an airplane Phil had no use for.

Although Phil flew many types of aircraft throughout his career—Bellanca, Beechcraft, Norseman, Fairchild, Stinson, and Waco—he says the worst airplane he ever flew was that old Fokker, one of five built by Anthony Fokker near New York City in 1927 for the RCAF Hudson Straits Expedition.

"God, that was a clunker, that one. I didn't like anything about it. You sat up in the front end alone, with just the bare windscreen in front of you, although later Stan Green, an air engineer and aeronautics instructor, built an enclosure for it. It had a 47-foot wingspan, which wasn't bad, but the wings were covered with 3/32-inch three-ply mahogany that absorbed moisture, which weighted down the airplane and cut into your payload. Also, the plywood would buckle from absorbing moisture, distorting the airfoil. It was powered by a Wright J-4, with only 200 horsepower.

"I picked it up at McLennan, about 50 miles south of Peace River, one day in 1938. When I got into the air, I noticed that the airplane wanted to fly crooked," Phil said, sounding indignant about even having to fly the thing. "I thought there was something wrong with it but I didn't know what.

"Finally I got to the town of Peace River and flew around over our office. Some of the guys came running out, waving at me and pointing at this one ski. I looked out the glass on one side and I couldn't see the ski. On the other side

I could see the point of it, so I knew there was some damned thing wrong down there . . . but what?

"The guys jumped in the car and headed for the airport, which was up on the hill about seven miles. I thought, 'Well, I'll come in real low and slow.' The old Fokkers landed at about 40 miles an hour. I came in real slow, and real low. Too low."

That's when Phil discovered the problem. The ski, which normally had about three degrees of incidence in flight, was held in position by tension cords, but the rear check cable fitting on the ski rigging had broken and the cable was hanging down below the ski. The telephone line was about eight feet off the ground and situated right at the end of the runway. Phil snagged the lines with the dangling cable.

"I wrapped that damned broken cable around the telephone line," Phil says. "I got down to the airport all right, I made it okay—lucky—but it didn't do the telephone line any good.

"I didn't like anything about that airplane."

Although Phil says he does not remember having any "close calls" flying for Peace River Airways, his forced landing in June 1940, with the float-equipped Waco CF-BJS, nicknamed "Bejeesus," could very well have been his last.

Phil Lucas, 1938, with Waco CF-BJS at Yellowknife. *Phil Lucas Collection*

"I had taken a bunch across Great Slave Lake to Yellowknife, which is about 130 miles across the lake from Lower Hay River. When I was leaving to come back that morning, a contracting company named Bennett & White asked if we could move an engine and a compressor up to Blue Fish Lake on the north side of Yellowknife. They were starting a hydro project up there and they needed the pump.

"I took the pump and the engine and all that stuff, and I overdid it a little bit, I guess. The Waco was powered by a 330-horse Jacobs engine we called the Shaky Jake. They weren't a bad engine, but they weren't the best, either.

"They couldn't stand any heat. If you got them too hot by taking off on water, it took a while to get off. You had to fight to get up on the float step if you were heavy-loaded. You're full throttle on the engine all this time, and as the heat builds up, your power goes down because the engine overheats, which means you need a little longer run, and by the time you get off, everything's smoking!"

Phil got up there all right, delivered the engine and compressor, turned around and headed south to Hay River. Then he noticed that it was getting pretty warm and the cylinder-head temperature was quite high. "I thought at the time that wasn't a good thing, but oh well. I was over halfway across the lake, at about 3,500 feet, when the engine started to shake. I reached up and pulled the throttle back a little bit and it started to shake some more.

"I was looking at Hay River down there about 20 miles across the lake, and I was thinking, 'Boy, I've got to get there.'

"Suddenly, bang! that was it. It quit.

"I glided as far as I could—and there again was luck. I've seen all kinds of waves on Great Slave Lake, 15- or 20-feet high, because it's a shallow lake and the wind really whips it up. On this particular day it was absolutely calm, and I was able to glide a long way. I finally got down on the water. But I still had the problem of getting the few miles to shore. I was by myself and I thought, how am I going to paddle this damned thing?

"We carried a short paddle on the float for docking, for pushing away from the docks, so I got that out. I was standing on the float holding the paddle and looking down at the water, thinking how I'd have to paddle this side for a while, then the airplane would go around and I'd have to run across the spreader bar between the floats and paddle on the other side."

As Phil was considering his dilemma, compounded by the fact that he'd never learned to swim, some Indian men who had seen him go down ran into the Hudson's Bay and told Bob Dodman, the Hudson's Bay factor, "An airplane's down on the lake!"

Dodman got out his glasses, and saw Phil standing there on the float. He knew the pilot was in trouble. Bob rigged two nine-horse Johnson outboard engines onto canoes, and two Indian fellows came out to the rescue. They towed the airplane to shore.

"I was there for 10 days. Something had definitely gone wrong with the Shaky Jake—aluminum was spread all through the dang engine."

At that time the only buildings at Hay River were an Anglican mission and the Hudson's Bay store. There were no radios. The Hudson's Bay steamboat arrived in June and went from there down the Mackenzie River to Aklavik. As luck would have it, the boat, piloted by Captain Naylor, arrived shortly after Phil did. ("I'll never forget his name because if it hadn't been for him, I'd still be there.")

"I've got to get word out—I have to have a new engine!" Phil pleaded.

"We'll fix that up," the captain assured him. The boat had its own 12-volt radio system. Captain Naylor got on the radio, contacted Fort Resolution, gave them the information, they in turn relayed it to Fort Smith, and then to Fort McMurray, and finally to Edmonton.

Ten days later, pilot Hank Koenen arrived in the infamous Fokker (G-CAHE), bringing a new engine with him.

As the pilot prepared to leave, Phil stook on the dock, looking at the engine, then at his airplane. "Well, aren't you going to help me change it?" he asked.

"Sorry, I can't. I've got perishables on here for the hotel in Yellowknife, and I've got to keep going." With a roar, the Fokker was off, leaving Phil to contemplate the job before him.

The pilot had also brought a chain, block, and a set of tools, so Phil "rigged up a three-leg," and asked for some help. His assistant was "a one-eyed Indian fellow who was an interpreter at the Hudson's Bay." In the north country, in June, there is daylight 24 hours a day, and Phil and his helper took advantage of it. Together they worked nonstop.

"I hooked it all up and test flew it that night, about midnight. I came back in, put the cowlings on, and was on my way back to Peace River within 24 hours."

It was a hard way to make a living but Phil loved flying in the North. "I was young and full of pep, it didn't bother me then."

His uniform was simple but practical. "I had an old parka that I wore in the wintertime, with a hood on it. Felt boots mostly, and overshoes—we found they were the best. Long underwear."

When asked if he wore the same suit from fall to spring, like some of the old miners did, he laughed and said, "Yeah!"

Phil particularly liked meeting the people in the outlying areas that he served. "I met a lot of good people! And I was always welcomed."

He stayed where he had to, sharing food and shelter with people who lived year-round in the remote bush country. "I didn't get very good meals. Dried fish, gone a little bit bad, been hanging up for the dogs and they decided they were short on grub so they borrowed it back," he said, with a twinkle in his eye.

Although Phil's almost-accident-free flying career attests to his skill and luck, evidenced by the experiences at Outpost Island and Hay River, northern pilots shrugged off such down-time as natural when flying in tough conditions in the 1930s and early 1940s.

From 1940 to 1942, due to changes in the aviation business, the Mackenzie district operated under the name of United Air Service, run by Lee Brintnell's Mackenzie Air Service. Phil's employer thus became United, and a Peace River newspaper of December 1942 recounts one of his forced landings in a United airplane:

NORTHERN AIRMEN IN FORCED LANDING

Pilot Phil Lucas, United Air Service, made a forced landing in a field 25 miles north of Peace River on Monday. Engine trouble caused the forced landing, Lucas reported by radio. The landing was made in a settled area, and any assistance needed to make repairs can be taken in by road. Lucas had been unreported since Monday morning when he took off for Keg River because radio signals were out on account of atmospheric conditions. He made contact Tuesday with Peace River. Lucas reported that he had not walked out to a telephone because of deep snow.

The Stagger-Wing Beech C-17R, (CF-BBB) commonly called "Brintnell's Bastard Beechcraft," was a Mackenzie Air Service airplane used on the mail charter to Carcajou, Keg River, and Fort Vermilion. On 20 December 1942, Phil and his mechanic, Walter Lawrence, were hauling mail and supplies from Peace River to Fort Vermilion. About 50 miles out of Peace River the crankshaft broke without warning, and everything came to a shuddering halt.

Phil noticed they'd just passed over a little lake so he immediately banked the airplane, but the lake was very short. The stagger-wing Beech is a high-performance aircraft requiring more room to operate than some of the other old bush-type airplanes they'd been using. Because of his position and the emergency situation, they had to come in the short way on the lake, flying through four feet of powdery snow.

"If we hadn't had deep snow," Phil said, "we'd never have been able to stop. Even so, we taxied to within 50 feet of the trees."

Phil told the story at a conference celebrating the tenth anniversary of the AeroSpace Museum in Calgary on 11 November 1987. It was one of Phil's favourite tales, often repeated over the years.

"When the engine quit, another minute and a half at the speed we were going, we couldn't have made the lake. There were 40-foot spruce trees around that lake, so the chances of us coming out of it wouldn't have been very good."

"But we made it over the edge of the trees and onto the lake, and we were there for three days and three nights."

He and Walter weren't hurt because the snow cushioned their landing and the aircraft wasn't damaged. They decided to walk to the Indian settlement of Deadwood, as they remembered seeing smoke a few miles back.

But when they tried to walk, Phil, who was just over five feet tall, found himself in snow up to his armpits. Walt, who was taller, found it easier, but after a short time the temperature dropped to near 40 below zero and by then their clothing, made of canvas material and wool, was completely soaked. They decided to return to the airplane. They had bedrolls and food supplies, so they pulled out the seats, rolled the sleeping bags out in the aircraft, stripped off all their clothing and got inside their bags. Hopefully the next day someone would come looking for them.

They had a good night's sleep, but the next morning their clothes were frozen, and they had no heat inside the airplane. Luckily, they always carried a blowpot, a little heater used to warm up the engine oil before starting the aircraft. The only problem with the blowpot is that when you first light it, a flame about five feet high shoots out until it stabilizes. The aircraft fuselage was fabric and only a few feet high. Obviously, lighting the blowpot inside the airplane was out, so they came up with a plan.

Phil's rendition of the tale at the 1987 conference was elaborated by years of telling:

"Walter says, 'You get the blowpot all ready to go, and I'll get out in the snow and light it.' Walter jumped out and lit the pot. The flame shot up high, then when it got hot, it burned down, like a blowtorch. Walter stood out there in four-and-a-half feet of snow, with no clothes on, just his socks, waiting for the flame to go down. Then he handed it to me.

"We set it up in the cockpit, and in nothing flat it was about 80 or 90 degrees in that small cabin."

It was the funniest thing Phil could remember seeing, Walter Lawrence jumping out stark naked into the snow to light the blowpot, then jumping back into the airplane.

The next day, Walter said he knew of an old trapper's shack close by, but when he checked, it wasn't in good enough shape to provide shelter.

"We didn't keep very warm," Phil admitted. "At nighttime we slept in the plane, and in the daytime we'd cut down a tree and burn it. Make a campfire."

They had a radio but it wasn't working. "I'm not a radio guy at all so I said forget it. It was frozen, it just wouldn't run. But we finally got it inside the cabin and warmed it up. The next afternoon I started pressing the mike button and a radio operator in Peace River, Johnny McNamee, came in: 'Okay, Phil, we've got you.' I hadn't even said anything yet! 'I heard that carrier come on,' the operator laughed. 'Fort Vermilion wired, saying you hadn't arrived. I've been sitting here since two o'clock yesterday afternoon, all afternoon and all night, waiting to hear from you.'"

Phil asked the company to bring in the Fairchild 71, the only aircraft he thought could get in and get off the lake. Alf Caywood, who was flying for United Air Service, came in with the Fairchild from Prince Albert, Saskatchewan, and brought them out.

"We did all right," Phil said philosophically, "A little cold at night."

The Beech sat "beached" for a few months, until a crew was hired to cut a road into the site and bring in an engine. Joe Irwin became involved in his friend's dilemma at this point:

"When BBB blew a crankshaft—it had a hell of a poor engine to start with, an E-Series Wright—they couldn't get parts so it sat there until March 1943. I took Phil in after they'd put a new engine in it, and then Phil flew it out."

The deep snow had gone, leaving glare ice. Although stories abound about tying the tail of the airplane to a tree, then releasing it for an accelerated take-off, leaving wasn't as much a problem as landing had been. When the engine had blown and Phil suddenly had to land, he'd had to come in crossways on the lake. For take-off they had the advantage of the ice and the length of the lake (later named Beechcraft Lake in honour of the event).

Phil flew BBB in to Peace River that day, and Joe then took it in to Edmonton. Phil kept a Fairchild 82, a Mackenzie Air Service Airplane, at Peace River, and operated with that for the rest of the summer. He then came to Edmonton to go on the 247 Boeing for Canadian Airways.

During his tenure with Canadian Airways, Phil's run was from Edmonton to Fort McMurray, Athabasca River, Fort Chipewyan, Slave River to Fort Smith, Fort Resolution, Hay River, and Fort Providence. Then he went on to Fort Simpson, Liard River, Fort Wrigley, Norman Wells, Fort Norman, Fort Good Hope, Thunder River, Arctic Red River, Fort McPherson to the Delta and Aklavik, and to Tuktoyaktuk on the Beaufort Sea.

The pay was $130 a month to start, and the airplanes were equipped with "an oil gauge, a tachometer, and a turn-and-bank indicator that floated in a solution, but you never knew for sure," said Phil. "The compasses weren't much good up near Yellowknife because of the mineral pull and proximity to the magnetic pole. Maps were not the greatest, and much of our flying was done from lake to lake."

Joe Irwin explains the changes going on in the aviation business at the time. "Canadian Airways, in 1940, became the nucleus of Canadian Pacific. Mackenzie Air Service and Yukon Southern were two holdouts who would not sell out complete, bickering for a better deal. Harry McConachie, Grant's uncle, who was the capital behind Yukon Southern, had held back 10 percent, and Lee Brintnell of Mackenzie Air Service did likewise, so they did not get this deal ironed out until 1942."

Jack Lucas reviews how his father's career was affected by these changes: "He flew for Peace River Airways for two or three years. Then they folded up—so many of the aviation businesses folded in those days—so in November of 1941 he joined his old friend, Joe Irwin, at Canadian Airways, which eventually became Canadian Pacific Airlines. At that time, our family moved to Edmonton."

When Canadian Pacific Air Lines absorbed 10 smaller airways, including Canadian Airways, Ginger Coote Airways, Mackenzie Air Services, Prairie Airways, Starratt Airways, and Yukon Southern Air Transport during the early 1940s, Phil Lucas continued to fly for this group, eventually coming onto the payroll of Canadian Pacific Air Lines.

With larger companies becoming the order of the day, the real bush flying with small outfits seemed a thing of the past. Phil recounted that his jump from flying Wacos, Beechcraft, and Fairchilds to flying Boeings for Canadian Airways occurred almost overnight. Stuck with routine runs to Fort McMurray twice a day, Phil lamented that he was nothing more than a high-altitude bus driver.

"I was a bush pilot. I wasn't an airline pilot!" he protested.

Canadian Pacific Air Lines system as illustrated in the Canadian Pacific Railway timetable issued on 28 November 1943. *Courtesy Canadian Pacific Limited*

"Phil was on the Boeing in the spring of 1942," Joe Irwin explains. "When the airport was finished in Fort McMurray on the route down the Mackenzie River, they ran between McMurray and Edmonton. Canadian Pacific Airlines had taken over the 247D Boeing from the Observer's School, after the school got some Ansons from England. They then ran one of these Boeings between McMurray and Edmonton. When the Fort Smith airport was completed, they flew as far as Fort Smith from Edmonton with the Boeing."

Joe himself was flying a big Bellanca (BKV), shuttling from Yellowknife and Fort Smith to Fort McMurray, and from Yellowknife to McMurray, to connect up with the Boeing. When airstrip conditions improved on this run, Joe went off the Bellanca and went on the line with Beeches and Barkley-Grows.

The Airline Pilots' Association had entered the picture by this time, and Charlie Robinson, originally with Starratt Airways at Hudson, Ontario, had moved in to Whitehorse to fly a Boeing and an old Curtiss Condor. With his seniority in the amalgamated system, Charlie was able to "bump" in to Edmonton on the Boeing. This left Phil to go elsewhere.

In short order, however, he found a new flying job with the U.S. Engineers on the Canol (Canadian Oil) Project, building a 500-mile oil pipeline from Norman Wells on the east bank of the Mackenzie River south and west to Whitehorse, Yukon.

Captain Phil Lucas while flying for Canadian Airways Ltd. *Phil Lucas Collection*

Phil's first job was to ferry in a bargeload of ethyl lead, which had been frozen in at Fort Wrigley. Phil and fellow pilot Harry Marsh spent the bulk of the winter of 1942 and 1943 ferrying ethyl lead from Fort Wrigley to Norman Wells where it was needed for blending with aviation fuel to raise the octane rating to aviation requirements.

"I flew for the U.S. Army for quite a while," Phil said. "I moved personnel up and down the line, mostly along the Mackenzie River. That was a pretty good job. I got $5 an hour for daylight flying, and $7 for night flying, but you had to be going to a lighted airport at night, otherwise it wasn't allowed, according to law."

Ten airfields had been constructed between Edmonton, Alberta, and Norman Wells, NWT, to service the Canol project. By the time all road and pipeline construction was completed in 1944, the project had cost the U.S. Army a total of $135 million. On 30 June 1945, the U.S. War Department decided to suspend Canol operations.

"Well, the job was finished there, anyway," says Phil. "The war was over in 1945."

The North wasn't the only area where Phil had unusual experiences. In June 1945, he was asked to take a 1929 Curtiss Robin (CF-AHH) to Edmonton for Cy Becker, but he never got there.

Cy Becker was a bush pilot and one of the originators of Commercial Airways's mail run from Edmonton to Aklavik, with Becker flying one plane and Wop May the other. The operation was originally financed by brokers I.W.C. Solloway and Harvey Mills (who, in 1930, were found guilty of charges relating to improper business conduct, banned from trading in securities, and incarcerated in the Lethbridge jail).

Becker had asked Lucas if he'd bring the Curtiss Robin up to Edmonton.

Stan Green, who was head of the Southern Alberta Institute of Technology, aircraft division, had overhauled the engine. He told Phil before he left that he couldn't get Simplex three-piece piston rings for the old Challenger six-cylinder engine, so he'd put in a set of Pedricks. Although the substitution should have been all right, it didn't work.

"I had a forced landing at Olds to start with and went down in a ploughed field. I took off again, and got just past the Penhold air base, when it ran out of oil. So I had to land, and land quick.

"It was burning oil, using three to four gallons an hour, which is about all it held. If I'd stayed in the air for an hour, I'd have had to go down and put more oil in. But I didn't stay in the air an hour, so I didn't burn the engine out of it.

"I never did find out what caused that trouble. I landed and everything seemed okay. I started it up again and it ran good so I couldn't find anything wrong with it.

"Stan Green managed to get a set of Simplex rings out of Los Angeles and put them in, and he got the thing running okay."

Phil's next employer was Eldorado Aviation.

"Alf Caywood and Phil had flown a lot together with Canadian Airways," Jack Lucas relates. "Then Alf left and went to work for the air freight division of Eldorado, a crown corporation that produced uranium. Alf got Phil to come and fly for Eldorado, so every winter he went up and flew a Norseman, and a DC-3 and DC-4 for them. During the off-season, he was back on the farm at Vulcan with his brother, Bill."

Phil particularly enjoyed flying the Norseman. "Oh, they're a real airplane," he said. "We all chose them. A Norseman is the best plane I ever flew. They had a Pratt and Whitney engine—boy, they were a good engine, and reliable. They could take off and land in small places, really a good bush aircraft."

Eldorado Aviation's record for freight-hauling has seldom been equalled, and the company was certainly a leader in its time.

Phil also met interesting people on this job, particularly two old bachelors who lived on Black Bay on Lake Athabasca, about 50 miles west of Goldfields in northern Saskatchewan.

One guy, Ed, was a fisherman, who sold trout, pickerel, and whitefish to McInnes Fish Camp, which were then shipped out on freezer barges. The other guy, Joe, had a tunnel built back into a hill. "Right at the end of the tunnel he was convinced there was a gold streak. He never did find it, but he kept looking," Phil says. "So even though they had different work, as a fisherman and a miner, they lived together. For 16 years.

"The first night we were there, I heard Ed say to his partner, 'Stove's hot, Joe.' I wondered why he said that, but I found out that in the 16 years they'd lived together, they never ate each other's cooking. Each one cooked what he wanted, sat at the table by himself, ate, cleaned up, then the other one would cook and eat. Never had a fight."

Phil hauled up groceries for them, and one time Ed and Joe got the notion that they wanted some fresh lettuce.

"I was real careful because our airplanes weren't heated very good and it was hard to keep stuff from freezing. We got there that night and Ed took a bunch of that fresh lettuce and threw it into the frying pan. Joe says, 'What are you doing with that lettuce?' and old Ed says, 'Haven't you ever tasted wilted lettuce?' 'Yeah,' Joe said, 'but not because I wanted to!' The fight was on.

"That north country was full of people like that," Phil said, "Good people. Real good people."

"Phil flew for Eldorado every winter until 1960," Jack says, "until he had a machinery accident on the farm that pretty well destroyed his right hand. Of course that made him ineligible to do commercial flying. They took away his commercial licence—he couldn't pass the medical—but they automatically gave him a private licence to fly for his own pleasure."

When Phil's commercial flying career ended, he took up farming on a full-time basis. By this time, Phil and his wife had relocated in Vulcan. Their sons Jack and Lionel, and the children who followed—Leighton and Leslie, born a year apart, and then Leah—completed their schooling there.

But airplanes were still very much a part of his life.

"He pretty well was never without an airplane. He must have had a dozen different airplanes over the years, all kinds of them," Jack says. "We traded airplanes around, almost continuously."

Five members of the Lucas family at one time had flying licences: Phil and his children, Jack, Lionel, Leighton, and Leslie. "That was quite a novelty," Jack says. "In all of Canada at that time, we had the most licensed pilots in the immediate family."

Phil didn't teach his children to fly—they had to learn to fly somewhere else.

Jack "learned to fly starting with my father," in 1946 when Phil bought the Piper J-3(CF-DRZ), but he moved away from home at an early age and continued his lessons at the Victoria Flying Club. "Lionel stayed on the farm and helped out. But I wandered."

In 1962, Lionel helped organize the Vulcan Flying Club. They had several airplanes: an Aeronca Champion, a PA-12 Piper, a 170 Cessna, one De Havilland Chipmunk and another that Phil and Jack shared, which had been purchased from the government.

Five members of the Lucas family were licensed pilots at one time. (L-R): Phil, Jack, Lionel, Leighton, and Leslie. *Phil Lucas Collection*

On 7 July 1963, Lionel was flying over Vulcan, doing aerobatics. Jack Lucas describes him making a loop. "When you perform a loop you use a lot of power to the top of the loop, then cut your engine. When you come off the bottom of the loop you're in excessive air speed, so you just go out straight until you drop down to your normal air speed, then open up the engine, and you're flying.

"Lionel came off the bottom of this loop, and the airplane just went straight out, straight out, straight out. He never opened the engine again. It went straight out until it stalled. Then it went into a spin into the ground. The strip was lined with people watching.

"There were two of them in the airplane. Lionel's passenger was a pilot who was just learning to fly. The crash occurred about a mile-and-a-half west of Vulcan in a farmer's field.

"Nobody really knows what happened. Carbon monoxide poisoning was probably a factor, that's what they said, anyway," Jack says. "It was devastating for the family, but for Phil in particular."

It was the horse business that Phil turned to in his later years, one that gave him almost as much joy as flying.

The Vulcan *Advocate*'s 28 April 1993 issue summarized this stage of Phil's career:

With his retirement from farming, horses became the focus of father and daughter, and they developed an Arabian horse operation in the Red Deer Lake area where they showed and trained horses internationally until Phil retired in 1982. He moved to Okotoks and Leah continued on with quarter horses in competitive cutting. Leah was Phil's constant company during his last period of illness.

"Phil was the oldest licensed flyer in Alberta, but not in Canada," Jack says. "The Canadian Aviation Hall of Fame records Thomas Williams of Ontario holding a pilot's licence to the age of 87, after 56 years as an aviator. But one thing that Phil did do, though it isn't documented, was fly over 60 years, from his training commencing in July 1929, to November 1989. A lot of people who are older learned to fly in the war so they've flown for 50 years. But Phil had flown longer, continuously, than maybe anybody else in Canada."

Phil Lucas in original aviator's cap from 1929. Briefcase contains his original log books. *Phil Lucas Collection*

Phil was a licensed pilot from 30 January 1930, until November 1989.

"He went for his regular medical in 1989, they sent it in, and I don't know what was wrong, besides his age. The doctor had passed him in Alberta, but Ottawa never did renew the licence. That was disappointing for him."

"If they think I'm too damn old, then I won't be a licensed pilot," Phil told a Vulcan newspaper reporter. And that was the end of his flying career.

Was Phil Lucas really "lucky"? Or did he plan, and work for, his luck?

"I don't know how to answer that," says Jack. "He was a tremendously hardworking person. He earned everything. I don't call it lucky—he made his luck. He was observant. When you're flying in the category that we're discussing here, one of the rules is to always know where you can land the airplane if something goes wrong."

From all accounts, Phil Lucas was a well-liked, well-respected man.

"He was a perfect gentleman to begin with," says long-time friend Chris Templeton. "If a lady came into the room, he stood up; if he had a hat on, he always took it off. I think it's hard for anyone not to like someone who has manners like that."

He and Joe Irwin remained friends until Phil's death in 1993; they shared their childhoods, their flying careers, and even their sorrows, as Joe also lost a son in a flying accident.

Perhaps one of the reasons for Phil's popularity was that people felt comfortable being with him; he was just an ordinary human being, like themselves, who'd had his share of sorrows as well as joys.

At Phil's funeral, his family and friends retold the stories. And remembered the man behind them, Vulcan's famous flying farmer, "Lucky" Phil Lucas.

Phil Lucas and Joe Irwin, 1988, at the 75th anniversary of the town of Vulcan, in "Ercoupe" in parade (on float). *Joe Irwin Collection*

Notes

1. Phil Lucas held Private Licence #520 dated 30 January 1930. He obtained his Commercial Licence #A880, 13 July 1931, and an Air Engineers Licence #A834, 1 August 1932.

    Joe Irwin holds Private Licence #519, dated 8 March 1930, and Commercial Licence #A848, 13 May 1931. Other licences followed.